Intercultural Marketing

With companies actively marketing products and services beyond their borders, marketers must understand culturally ingrained consumer behavior throughout the world. Focusing on psychological and social dimensions of these behaviors, this textbook brings together academic research and contemporary case studies from marketing practice.

Built on a strong, cross-disciplinary theoretical foundation and extensive practice experience, this concisely written text is a practical guide to understanding the intricacies of cultural influence on consumption, and for the design and implementation of effective intercultural marketing strategies, focused on branding and promotion. The book uses representative, well-known corporate cases while also including dynamic examples from the sharing economy, blockchain, and emerging economy companies. Incorporating strategy, sociology, linguistics, cross-cultural communications, psychology, philosophy, religious studies, and economics, the book is particularly distinguished from the mainstream by introducing non-Western frameworks.

Upper-level undergraduate and postgraduate students of marketing and international business will benefit from the book's new concepts and novel methods, as well as clear objectives, examples, and discussion topics in each chapter. Instructors will appreciate the inclusion of a semester-long project for students, allowing them to wear the "practitioner's hat" and including practice in a netnographic research method.

Ivana Beveridge is Lecturer in Marketing at the University of Houston, U.S. She has extensive international marketing experience with global marketing agencies and corporations, including award-winning campaigns and a client portfolio spanning Fortune 100 companies and various governments. Her PhD is from the Sorbonne University, France.

Intercultural Marketing

Theory and Practice

Ivana Beveridge

NEW YORK AND LONDON

First published 2021
by Routledge
52 Vanderbilt Avenue, New York, NY 10017

and by Routledge
2 Park Square, Milton Park, Abingdon, Oxon, OX14 4RN

Routledge is an imprint of the Taylor & Francis Group, an informa business

© 2021 Taylor & Francis

The right of Ivana Beveridge to be identified as author of this work has been asserted by her in accordance with sections 77 and 78 of the Copyright, Designs and Patents Act 1988.

All rights reserved. No part of this book may be reprinted or reproduced or utilized in any form or by any electronic, mechanical, or other means, now known or hereafter invented, including photocopying and recording, or in any information storage or retrieval system, without permission in writing from the publishers.

Trademark notice: Product or corporate names may be trademarks or registered trademarks, and are used only for identification and explanation without intent to infringe.

Library of Congress Cataloging-in-Publication Data
Names: Beveridge, Ivana, author.
Title: Intercultural marketing : theory and practice / Ivana Beveridge.
Description: New York, NY : Routledge, 2021. | Includes bibliographical references and index.
Identifiers: LCCN 2020024287 (print) | LCCN 2020024288 (ebook) | ISBN 9780367457914 (hardback) | ISBN 9780367902544 (paperback) | ISBN 9781003025344 (ebook)
Subjects: LCSH: Marketing—Cross-cultural studies. | Consumers—Cross-cultural studies. | International trade.
Classification: LCC HF5415 .B4448 2021 (print) | LCC HF5415 (ebook) | DDC 658.8—dc23
LC record available at https://lccn.loc.gov/2020024287
LC ebook record available at https://lccn.loc.gov/2020024288

ISBN: 978-0-367-45791-4 (hbk)
ISBN: 978-0-367-90254-4 (pbk)
ISBN: 978-1-003-02534-4 (ebk)

Typeset in Optima
by Apex CoVantage, LLC

Contents

Preface	vi
Acknowledgments	xiii

1	The Globalization Imperative	1
2	Decoding Culture: The Basics of Cultural Literacy	51
3	Universal Criteria for Understanding Cultures	81
4	Conceptual East–West Differences: Psychological Processes, Philosophical Traditions, Stimuli Processing, and Paradoxical Thinking	99
5	Conceptual East–West Differences: Intercultural Communication and Religious Beliefs	119
6	Frameworks for Interpreting Cultural Differences	140
7	Language Considerations in Intercultural Markets	162
8	Research Considerations in Intercultural Markets	182
9	Conclusion	219

Index	225

Preface

Introduction

With companies actively marketing products and services beyond their homeland borders, it is imperative for marketers to understand culturally ingrained consumer behavior throughout the world. Culture is an important antecedent, moderator, and mediator of consumer choice, and understanding culture is strategically important for marketers (Hofstede, 2015). Nonetheless, as one of the most "pervasive and thorny" influential factors in business (Cleveland, Laroche, & Hallab, 2013), cultural influence on consumers in international markets remains rather difficult to assess (Caprar, Devinney, Bradley, & Kirkman, 2015). Understanding the nuances of cultural influence on consumption remains one of the long-standing challenges for marketers.

Focusing on social dimensions of consumer behavior across cultures, this book brings together diverse academic fields from management and social sciences, and it incorporates case studies from the marketing practice. It offers a comprehensive synthesis of relevant topics in a concise, easy-to-comprehend manner. The book focuses on the rapidly developing issues surrounding the impact of cultural conditioning on consumer behavior, customer need identification, and purchasing decision making. Specifically, it sheds light on the important cultural factors influencing two marketing pillars inclusive of product (with the main focus on the brand) and promotion (with the main focus on advertising, message development, and personal selling).

With the rise of emerging markets, the applicability of traditional Western models in management and marketing research has been questioned

(Birkinshaw, Brannen, & Tung, 2011). In particular, much evidence suggests that the popular dimensional perspective on culture should be supplemented with new approaches (Gannon, 2011). This book provides a critical overview of the established traditional frameworks for analyzing culture, while also expanding the boundary of investigation to include the new concepts and methods for cultural analysis. By doing so, it answers calls for integration of novel theories and concepts to capture management puzzles or phenomena of the "East" (Barkema, Chen, George, Luo, & Tsui, 2015).

To that end, it introduces some more recent management topics such as the importance of paradoxical thinking and tolerance for ambiguity (Smith, Erez, Jarvenpaa, Lewis, & Tracey, 2017). Drawing on the rich body of research from both Western and Eastern research traditions suggesting that tensions between the opposing polarities could produce superior performance when managed in a complementary fashion, the book sheds light on the role of cultural conditioning in cultivating paradoxical mindsets (Gebert, Boerner, & Kearney, 2010).

Audience

This book is geared toward postgraduate or master's students as its primary audience. However, it could also be used for specialized undergraduate or bachelor's courses. It offers a comprehensive framework for understanding the intricacies of cultural influence on consumption, as well as practical guidance for the design and implementation of effective intercultural marketing strategies with the main focus on branding and promotion. As such, it also offers insights to practitioners looking to obtain additional frameworks that could help with marketing efforts across cultures.

Structure

Five different types of questions are used throughout the book, each with a different purpose. Each chapter starts with a warm-up question introducing the theme. Every section of the chapter also ends up with a question related to the relevant theoretical content, helping students to grasp it through inquiry. These section-ending questions also serve as in-class discussion topics that help to structure the class into instructional and brainstorming sections. Each case-in-point example includes a question which helps the students to understand applications of theoretical concepts in marketing practice. Each mini-case also contains questions that allow the students to critically assess the case example. Finally, the guiding questions at the end of each chapter focus on the group project, bridging theory and practice. Each set of questions addresses a different element of the project, helping the students to apply the course concepts in their promotional campaign more specifically.

The book includes relevant theoretical concepts from different disciplines as well as numerous examples from the practice. These examples are provided throughout the text to illustrate the main course concepts. Some are short, while others, such as the case-in-point examples and mini cases, are longer and offer various case studies that show how the theoretical concepts are applied in practice.

The main semester-long project consists of a cross-cultural campaign for launching a home market brand in another distinctly different host country or a region of choice. The deliverable of the project is two-fold. Each self-formed team should prepare a written report, as well as a group presentation illustrating key ideas and findings from the report. Each team should submit a one-page informal description of the project by a specified date mid-semester to ensure that the students are developing their plan in the right direction. Each chapter ends with a list of practical guiding questions to aid decision making in the process of project preparation.

Chapters

Chapter 1 discusses drivers and patterns of globalization as well as its consequences. It addresses the main globalization themes and variables affecting standardization/adaptation decisions, inclusive of "glocalization" and paradoxical tensions between globalization and ethnocentrism/xenocentrism. It discusses the allure of global brands and the responsibility they bear, as well as the important role of branding blunders for understanding cultural influence. The chapter also illustrates different levels of brand involvement in international markets including brand ignorance, brand tolerance, and brand engagement. It points at the importance of new middle classes in developing markets and their unique characteristics which drive

viii

consumption patterns. The chapter critically assesses the traditional idea of "modernization" that has been accepted in the Western research tradition. The case-in-point examples include China's Belt and Road Initiative (BRI), international education segment, yoga and K-pop, Paco Rabanne, Quorn in Asia, Coca Cola's Super Bowl ad, Uber in Asia, Club Med in China, Pepsi in China, and luxury industry. The mini-case included in this chapter is Sofitel Hotels & Resorts.

Chapter 2 introduces the basics of cultural literacy. It discusses various definitions of culture in the literature and it sheds light on different paradigms for understanding cultures, inclusive of etic vs. emic and essentialist vs. nonessentialist approaches. It critically assesses the commonly accepted concept of "national culture" based on the idea of culture of the nation-states defined by their geographical boundaries. It discusses the prevalent "onion" approach to understanding cultures, inclusive of material and immaterial elements of culture, as well as the concept of "cultural value orientations" which present empirically observable elements of culture that could be analyzed in large-scale surveys. The chapter also sheds light on the degrees of importance of cultural norms interpreted as cultural imperatives, cultural electives, and cultural exclusives. The case-in-point examples included in the chapter are "nazars" as the example of cultural symbols, "Bouba and Kiki effect" illustrating how semiotics could be used in branding, and an example of sensory approach to brand naming. The mini-case included with Chapter 2 is Barbie and Häagen-Dazs in China.

Chapter 3 focuses on the universal criteria for understanding culture. It first focuses on the main groups of basic human values and it discusses universal values used as a base for rhetoric and persuasion. It then focuses on the universal segmentation criteria across cultures from the perspective of usage and industry segmentation. It concludes by providing additional frameworks for understanding cultural universalities. The case-in-point examples included in this chapter include blockchain industry, Airbnb, and Oatly in the United States. The mini-case included in Chapter 3 is Fenty Beauty by Rihanna.

Chapters 4 and 5 discuss conceptual East–West differences. *Chapter 4* focuses on the mental models and thinking pattern differences between what is broadly understood as "Western" vs. "Eastern" cultures. This includes psychological processes, philosophical traditions, thinking styles, self-construal, perceptions of morality, and tolerance for ambiguity. It also discusses the influence of these differences on processing of stimuli and information framing patterns. A case-in-point example in this chapter is a Chinese etymological explanation of a paradox concept. The mini-case included in Chapter 4 is WeChat in China.

Chapter 5 further expands on these differences. It discusses the concept of communication competence across cultures from the perspective of Western communication theories as well as through the Asian theory lens. It then discusses the influence of religious beliefs and religious conditioning on consumer preferences, illustrating both the similarities and the differences among the five main world's religions. The case-in-point examples included in this chapter are Sulwhasoo branding, modest fashion, and Islamic art. The mini-case included in Chapter 5 is Islamic finance.

Chapter 6 focuses on the main traditional frameworks for understanding cultural differences. It provides an overview of Hall's (1976), Hofstede's (1991) and Trompenaars' and Hampden-Turners' (1997) frameworks which have traditionally been used to analyze the role of culture in international business and marketing. It offers easy-to-apply interpretations of these frameworks, as well as critical views. The case-in-point examples include IKEA's web design and processing of nutritional information. The mini-case included in Chapter 6 is Disney Land in Paris and Hong Kong.

Chapter 7 discusses language considerations in intercultural markets. It investigates the role of language in intercultural marketing, focusing on the interaction between language, communication, and culture. It sheds light on the influence of cultural conditioning on verbal and nonverbal communication preferences. It discusses the components of language, links between language and sensory experiences, and different layers of language which impact communication. It also reminds students of the classic communications model and sheds light on the cultural aspect of "noise." The chapter then discusses the notion of linguistic imperialism and ethnolinguistics, and it sheds light on some linguistic considerations for brand naming strategies. The case-in-point examples include unique characteristics of a language, brand naming in the car industry, K-pop, and universal principles for brand naming. The mini-case included in Chapter 7 illustrates brand naming considerations in China.

Chapter 8 focuses on research considerations in intercultural markets, encouraging the students to develop critical thinking in regard to cultural analysis. It discusses the choice of research methods and the ability of various frameworks to capture the intricacies of culture, such as large-scale surveys which have become the norm in culture study. It further expands on etic and emic research approaches, and points at the quantitative-qualitative research dichotomy in culture study. It also discusses the importance of choosing a suitable epistemological framework in culture research. The chapter sheds light on ethnography and netnography as the promising methods for cultural analysis. It also reminds of the importance of conducting cultural analysis against the backdrop of a broader political, economic, and legal context in a host country, as well as the links between economy and culture. The case-in-point examples in this chapter include use of ethnography by Best Buy, nethnographic research on the example of Listerine, and cultural metaphors. The mini-case included with Chapter 8 is Nike.

References

Barkema, H. G., Chen, X., George, G., Luo, Y., & Tsui, A. S. (2015). West meets East: New concepts and theories. *Academy of Management Journal, 58*(2), 460–479.

Birkinshaw, J., Brannen, M. Y., & Tung, R. L. (2011). From a distance and generalizable to up close and grounded: Reclaiming a place for qualitative methods in international business research. *Journal of International Business Studies, 42*(5), 573–581.

Caprar, D. V., Devinney, T. M., Bradley, L., & Kirkman, P. C. (2015). Conceptualizing and measuring culture in international business and management: From challenges to potential solutions. *Journal of International Business Studies, 46*(9), 1011–1027.

Cleveland, M., Laroche, J., & Hallab, R. (2013). Globalization, culture, religion, and values: Comparing consumption patterns of Lebanese Muslims and Christians. *Journal of Business Research, 66*(8), 958–967.

Gannon, M. J. (2011). Cultural metaphors: Their use in management practice as a method for understanding cultures. *Online Readings in Psychology and Culture, 7*(1). Retrieved from https://scholarworks.gvsu.edu/orpc/vol7/iss1/4

Gebert, D., Boerner, S., & Kearney, E. (2010). Fostering team innovation: Why is it important to combine opposing action strategies? *Organization Science, 21*(2), 593–608.

Hall, E. (1976). *Beyond culture*. New York: Anchor Books.

Hofstede, G. J. (1991). *Cultures and organizations: Software of the mind*. London: McGraw-Hill.

Hofstede, G. J. (2015). Culture's causes: The next challenge. *Cross Cultural Management: An International Journal, 22*(4), 545–569.

Schwartz, S. H. (1994). Are there universal aspects in the content and structure of values? *Journal of Social Issues, 50*(4), 19–45.

Smith, W. K., Erez, M. W., Jarvenpaa, S., Lewis, M. W., & Tracey, P. (2017). Adding complexity to theories of paradox, tensions, and dualities of innovation and change: Introduction to organization studies special issue on paradox, tensions, and dualities of innovation and change. *Organization Studies, 38*(3–4), 303–317.

Trompenaars, F., & Hampden-Turner, C. (1997). *Riding the waves of culture: Understanding cultural diversity in business.* London: Nicholas Brealey Publishing.

Acknowledgments

I would like to thank the reviewers for their valuable comments on the book proposal. I am also very grateful to Meredith Norwich at Routledge who has been instrumental in the process, and whose encouragement was invaluable. A big thanks goes to Emmie Shand at Routledge for her all help and enthusiasm and for her prompt and patient responses to my silly questions.

I would also like to thank my colleagues at Labbrand Brand Innovations in Shanghai and Paris Jacquelien Brussee and Nadège Depeux for their ongoing support and for sharing their resources and their invaluable insight from the practice.

I am thankful to Dr. Guo-Ming Chen at the University of Rhode Island, U.S., for his insight on the issues of intercultural communication and for endorsing the book, and to my colleague Dr. Betsy Gelb at the University of Houston, U.S., for her inexhaustible energy and ongoing inspiration for academic research. I would also like to thank Dr. Edward Blair at the University of Houston, U.S.; Dr. Catherine de La Robertie at the Aveyron Region Government and the Sorbonne University, France; and Milton Aldrete at EduExcellence, Finland, for reviewing the manuscript and providing endorsement.

The Globalization Imperative

Introduction

Chapter 1 focuses on the overarching drivers and expressions of globalization. It discusses the main variables affecting globalization of products and services. It also sheds light on ethnocentrism and xenocentrism as outcomes of globalization. It further discusses the allure of the global brands on one hand, and the responsibility and expectations placed on them in the somewhat uneven global branding playfield. The chapter also focuses on the importance of branding blunders for understanding cultural influence. It illustrates different levels of brand involvement in international markets, and points at the importance of new middle classes in the emerging markets and their unique characteristics.

The chapter critically assesses the traditional notion of "modernization" commonly accepted in the West as a concept of progress, implying that the non-Western countries should catch up with the West, which has set the standards for the "rest." Case-in-point examples include China's Belt and Road Initiative (BRI), international education segment, yoga and K-Pop, Paco Rabanne, Quorn in Asia, Coca Cola's Super Bowl ad, Uber in Asia, Club Med in China, Pepsi in China, and luxury industry. The mini-case included in the Chapter 1 is Sofitel Hotels & Resorts.

Chapter Objectives

- Understand the concept of globalization and its drivers.
- Learn the main variables affecting internationalization of brands.

- Become familiar with the concepts of ethnocentrism and xenocentrism.
- Critically assess the role and the importance of global brands.
- Understand the role of branding blunders in cultural analysis.
- Distinguish between different degrees of brand involvement in international markets.
- Understand the importance of new middle classes in developing markets.

Warmup question: *How can brands become globally recognizable* and *remain culturally relevant at the same time?*

Why Globalize?

Globalization is defined as a "growing interdependence of the world's economies, cultures, and populations, brought about by cross-border trade in goods and services, technology, and flows of investment, people, and information" (Peterson Institute for International Economics, 2020). The process of globalization is characterized by the growing interdependence between the world's economies, cultures, and consumers. The consequences of this process are in fact so profound and pervasive that some researchers even claim that globalization presents a new form of consciousness (Eriksen, 2007).

Globalization is reflected in an unparalleled interdependence of different spheres of economic, political, cultural, ideological, and ecological influence. Ecological globalization refers to global pollution, climate change, and resource degradation seen as a result of rapid globalization of trade (Steger, 2009).

The process of globalization is characterized by the unparalleled number of interactions happening in the increasingly fast and dense communication networks. Nonetheless, it is also characterized by the growing tensions between cultural groups due to their exposure to one another and cultural changes that happen in this process. The global flow of capital, technology, and information has led to the often profound changes in human behavior.

Because we share resources across the globe, our actions and consumption patterns in one location have a butterfly effect in another location. For example, the societal shift toward healthy eating in the West has contributed to the rapidly growing demand for quinoa, the traditional staple food in

Peru. This trend has brought about many benefits for the local farmers who saw a strong growth in the demand for their product. However, Peru's Ministry of Agriculture suggests that while quinoa production grew from 32,590 to 114,725 tons between 2005 and 2014, in the same period, the price of quinoa in Peru rose more than 500% (Livingstone, 2018). Consequently, it became less affordable for the local population than it used to be before the spike in global demand.

What are the main consequences of globalization?

Drivers of Globalization

Globalization of brands is no longer an alternative, but an imperative for most companies no matter where they are in the world. Globalization opportunities are brought about by cross-border trade in goods and services, technology, and flows of investment, people, and information. Some of the main drivers of globalization include the saturation of domestic markets, a more affordable production in international markets, emerging market companies expanding into developed markets, the emergence of new consumer groups across the world, and globalization of labor, to name some.

Due to the *saturation of domestic markets* and the intensifying competition, companies are actively seeking opportunities beyond their home boundaries. Manufacturing of products is often *more affordable* in developing markets, and this affordability is achieved through coordination of production across different countries and regions. Consequently, companies are either outsourcing specific product components or setting up manufacturing plants and service operations abroad to save costs.

At the same time, companies from emerging economies are making *inroads into the developed markets*. Some examples include companies like Korean Samsung, Chinese Huawei, or Mexico's Cemex. *New consumer groups from emerging markets* are also actively stepping onto the global scene, seeking products and services that were previously not affordable or not readily available in their home countries. Furthermore, emerging markets are increasingly investing in the developed, industrial markets through large infrastructure projects such as the Belt and Road Initiative (BRI).

Globalization also creates new power structures. In addition to the hard power such as military and political power affiliated with governments, or the economic power exercised through global corporations, we can talk about culture as a *soft power*. Soft power implies that the standards are introduced from one culture to another. Examples of soft power include lifestyle, body image, music, fashion, or parenting styles introduced, and at times imposed, from one culture to another. The influence of soft power moves in both directions – both Eastward and Westward, as seen in the example of K-pop discussed later in this chapter.

Are there examples of your home country's culture as soft power in another market?

Mega Infrastructure Projects

Recently, we saw the birth of mega infrastructure and transportation projects initiated in the Eastern hemisphere. These projects, aimed at connecting the Eastern and Western hemispheres, present new economic growth drivers. They have led to the unparalleled connectivity between nations and regions and opened many new business opportunities. These include, for example, China's Belt and Road Initiative (BRI), the China-Pakistan Economic Corridor (CPEC), the International North-South Transport Corridor (INSTC), or Dubai's Silk Road Strategy project, to name the main ones.

A Case in Point: Belt and Road Initiative (BRI)

Big global infrastructure projects initiated in non-Western countries have triggered a collision of cultural values between "East" and "West." In some cases, it is the value differences, rather than project-related reasons that have hindered progress of these projects. One such example is China's Belt and Road Initiative (BRI).

Launched in 2013, BRI is one of the most ambitious infrastructure investment projects in human history. Envisioned as a revival of the ancient Silk Road, it aims to enrich trades from the Atlantic to the Pacific. To date, countries representing nearly two-thirds of the world's population have either signed on or indicated interest in joining the project. In particular, many developing and emerging economies in need of an infrastructure boost have welcomed the project.

Nonetheless, the project has encountered a significant pushback, especially in the European Union (E.U.). Although building better connections between Europe and Asia is undoubtedly on everyone's agenda, ideas on how this should be executed diverge greatly between different parties.

The main areas of concern over the BRI project raised by the E.U. include issues such as a lack of transparency in the bidding processes, especially on projects required to use Chinese firms. There are also concerns over low interest loans as opposed to aid grants, and the alleged opaque and unaccountable approach to financing exposing already vulnerable economies to fiscal instability, to name some. The question inevitably arises: are most of these concerns really project-related, or is there a more underling crash of values in the face-off between the West and China?

Without a doubt, in order to utilize the emerging business opportunities that come with the similar large-scale projects, we must be willing to accept the differences in cultural values and norms. This also includes the differences between the systemic structures in different countries and regions. Understanding these differences will help to convert the apparent challenges into opportunities and marketing advantages (Stelling, 2020).

What are some possible expressions of value differences between China and the West on the example Belt and Road Initiative project?

Glocalization

The underlying decision that marketers need to make when internationalizing brands is how much to standardize and/or adapt their home country brands in the international markets. The debate over how much to standardize or adapt revolves around the idea of standardization for efficiency, or the economics of simplicity based on the assumption of the "least common denominator" across cultures, versus localization for effectiveness.

At the outset of globalization, many brands opted for the *economics of simplicity* and sold their standardized products with little or no adaptation in international markets. Such are the examples of Coca-Cola and Nestlé who applied uniform global marketing principles in the 1980s with success. If nothing else, standardization can certainly lower operating and marketing costs and help the companies achieve economies of scale and scope.

The ideal outcome of branding efforts is, however, neither a strict standardization nor full localization, but rather "glocalization." Glocalization is seen as a co-presence of both universal as well as particular tendencies in an effort to adapt global brands to local needs while also remaining true to the original brand identity. This effort is expressed in the "think global, but act local" slogan, the origin of which has been attributed to many.

However, achieving the ideal balance between global and local is in itself a goal ridden with paradoxical tensions between the two, and it requires continuous strategic adaptation. There are numerous examples of multinational companies that had to adjust their signature products and practices in international markets to fit the customs, laws, and preferences of a local market. Retaining universal brand values and remaining authentic to the home brand identity, all while also making the brands particular and tailoring campaigns toward the local tastes is particularly challenging for the marketers.

While many succeed, many also fail to adjust their efforts with a sufficient degree of success in order to remain relevant in the local markets. For example, Walmart's signature customer service aimed at enhancing customer experience in the U.S. was not well received in Europe. Walmart's greeters at the store door were met with dismay in countries like Germany where people are not used to someone addressing them as they walk into a store (Landler & Barbaro, 2006). Other brands, however, achieved great success with their adaptation attempts, such as Whirlpool, which customized their washing machines for washing the long Indian sarees without getting tangled in the washer (Marquardt, 2011).

What are the main challenges for brands in intercultural markets?

Variables Affecting Brand Globalization

One of the main decisions that brands need to make in international markets is how much to standardize vs. how much to adjust to local needs, and this depends on a number of factors. *Standardization/adaptation variables* include, for example, company's structure, company's country of origin, product category, product lifecycle, or the broader business environment of the host country, to name some.

To a great extent, global marketing strategy is influenced by *company's structure* and the culture of a company's country of origin. A country of origin and its business practices play an important role and they influence the vision of company's management, which in turn influence marketing decisions.

Standardization decisions are influenced by a *degree of standardization of company's business functions across the world*, which also drives the degree of independence of local or regional marketing managers. Tighter managerial control across different departments or global offices is most often found in the large bureaucratic structures. Consequently, in those companies, a higher degree of standardization is expected from the marketing managers, too.

For example, ExxonMobil, a U.S. energy company and the largest publicly traded energy company in the world, is characterized with a tight management control of all its functions and a rigorous appraisals process for all its new projects. Consequently, the company's marketing efforts are also rather uniform across different markets. In the 1970s, the original company, Standard Oil of New Jersey, changed its name to ExxonMobil. One of the main reasons for this change was because the use of the Esso trademark was restricted in the United States. However, the company was also looking for a brand name that was neutral, had no real meaning in any language and could not offend anyone either, and was thus universal and standard across different languages and cultures. Phonetically too, the double X helped them to get close to the Esso trademark. Allegedly, it was one of the most expensive branding exercises of all times!

Product category also plays an important role when deciding how much to standardize or adapt. Products that enjoy economies of scale and which are not very culture-bound are easier to market globally, such as some fast-moving consumer goods. Products consumed by younger and more cosmopolitan demographics may also be less culture-bound and thus they may need less adaptation.

The decision on how much to standardize and how much to adapt is also closely linked to the *product's country of origin*, or the "country brand." Some products are traditionally affiliated with certain countries. Examples include French wine, Swiss cheese or Italian ice-cream, to name some. Consumers hold positive or negative attitudes toward a particular country and may thus show favorable or unfavorable responses to products they relate to certain countries, or to country brands.

This perception is also affected by political and economic factors, and the geo-political context at any given point in time. Thus, political relations between countries, hostilities, economic sanctions, and trade wars can all influence these perceptions. Sometimes they are deeply engrained and remain rooted in long-standing historic reasons, such as wars, large-scale and long-term historic conflicts, or the colonial past, and at other times they are more fleeting and related to a specific context in time.

Another factor influencing the decision on how much to localize is the *phase in the product life cycle* across its five phases of R&D, introduction, growth, maturity, and decline. The phase in the lifecycle determines the possibility of standardization. For example, fresh brands at the introduction stage are easier to localize than mature products which have already gained popularity in the market.

The *business environment of a host country* is another important factor affecting standardization-adaptation decisions. In addition to the customer purchasing power and their cultural factors, important host country factors should be considered. These include political and legal systems, level of technology adoption, and patterns of information flow on the scale between censorship and complete freedom to exchange information. For example, due to the preferences given to incumbent telecommunications providers, certain countries do not allow the use of communication tools or apps which are otherwise popular in other countries. Equally, a ban on certain information sources or communication tools could be related to political reasons.

Differences in the infrastructure, competitive landscape, laws and regulations, and political landscape or media infrastructure all exert influence on the standardization and adaptation decisions. For example, advertising laws are different from country to country, as discussed later in the chapter.

It is also important to remember that the rules governing the international use of search engines vary from one country to another. Google as the main Web entry point for the majority of Internet users across the world varies in terms of ordering and ranking of websites in its search results. There are notable differences between the global Google (.com) and Google's national search engines in terms of websites rankings. In fact, Google is a series of national search engines, rather than a universal global search engine (Rogers, 2013).

In other words, what one can read on Google pages is also determined by the host country geo-political and legal factors. This affects search engine optimization (SEO) considerations in the global markets, which is based on the use of native words and global connections. However, these connections differ from one market to another, not only due to business factors, but also due to a range of technological and geo-political reasons.

Undoubtedly, fast-developing markets are setting new standards when compared to the traditional development path taken by the industrialized Western nations. We are reminded by expert practitioners that intercultural competence is perhaps more than ever crucial for continued global economic growth:

> Cities and entire regions across Asia are rapidly modernizing. Billions are being invested in roads, ports and railways, in energy, AI, healthcare, jobs and education. And it's not just replacing the old but upgrading to world standards. The investments are driving inclusive growth, regional integration and economic opportunity. And some are met with skepticism, especially when narratives collide because policies and communications are not aligned. . . .
>
> (Stelling, 2020)

What are the main factors that influence standardization or adaptation of branding efforts across cultures?

A Case in Point: International Education

International education has been a fairly globalized service segment. Therefore, marketing campaigns by the providers of private education have limited variation across cultures. This segment is developing rapidly at a global level and the statistics are staggering: in just the first decade of this century the number of students from non-English-speaking countries attending international schools that use English as instructional language grew by 140% globally. During this time the number of international schools also doubled and their fee income more than quadrupled (International School Consultancy Group, 2014).

This is not surprising considering the tertiary education statistics: the number of international students enrolled in higher education is forecast to more than double to 262 million by 2025, as compared to 150 million in 2012, and the number of students studying outside their borders is expected to triple to roughly 8 million by 2025 (University World News, 2012).

These statistics suggest that there is a greater standardization of study programs to meet the demands of the increasingly global and multicultural student body. This demand for international education is driven by the increased mobility, internalization of labor, dominance of English as the language of business, and the rapid increase in purchasing power of the new middle classes in emerging markets (World Education News and Reviews, 2014). These patterns have propelled the fairly uniform marketing efforts catering to a global community of internationally mobile students, who are seeking similar values and similarities in their representations across cultures. Nonetheless, while the education service is standardized in terms of academic curricula and study programs, marketing strategies, client management, and government affairs also require targeted, culture-wise localized strategies.

What other industry segments are fairly standardized across cultures? How does this standardization influence intercultural marketing efforts?

From Globalization to Ethnocentrism/Xenocentrism

Without a doubt, globalization gives rise to multiculturalism and creates new soft power structures. There is more exposure to differences than ever before and more information is available for the customers to go by. Public policies are also put in place to manage diversity and multiculturalism. However, this does not mean that there is more tolerance for cultural diversity. Globalization does not cancel out cultural differences – in fact, globalization and homogenization are happening in parallel with opposing trends such as ethnocentrism.

Ethnocentrism, originating from the Greek word "ethnos" (έθνος, in Greek), meaning the people, or a nation, implies judging other cultures by our own standards. In marketing, ethnocentrism signifies "the beliefs held by consumers about the appropriateness, indeed morality, of purchasing foreign-made products" (Shimp & Sharma, 1987, p. 280). Ethnocentric consumers tend to apply their attitudes and knowledge about a certain country to form a country image, leading to a country-of-origin effect that shapes

The Globalization Imperative

their response to products from that country. This can sometimes even lead to animosity, or anger toward a country rooted in political, economic, or military conflicts.

Ethnocentrism exerts strong influence on marketing through the use of patriotic appeals. Campaigns using such appeals suggest that domestic products are not only superior, but also that supporting local businesses is an issue of moral and national pride. For this reason, ethnocentric consumers tend to give preference to national companies and local products.

For example, these campaigns using patriotic appeals are often related to food, and concerns over "food miles" – how long does the food have to travel to the consumer – or local eating (Schnell, 2013), which in many countries around the world means giving preference to local food products. In fact, this tendency, named "locavorism," became an emergent consumer ideology. It was so influential that the word "locavore" was the "word of the year" by the Oxford American Dictionary (Oxford University Press, 2007).

Ethnocentrism is also closely connected to political and economic agendas, and it may be expressed through anti-consumption activities such as boycotts of specific country brands, industries, companies, or products. Ethnocentric consumers are proud of their country's brands and symbols, and they are generally less cosmopolitan and less open to foreign products.

The concept of ethnocentrism is also closely related to *economic nationalism*. This implies that the local brands may be seen as representatives of national economy and individual well-being, while the global brands may represent both economic as well as cultural threats. For example, in 2008, when Starbucks Coffee opened an outlet in China's Imperial Palace Museum in Beijing, many Chinese consumers demanded its removal. They saw Starbucks as a Western culture icon offensive for the Chinese culture, since the Museum presents an icon of the Chinese culture. Therefore, Starbuck's presence was highly symbolic. In fact, some consumers even thought that the brand deliberately showed disrespect toward the Chinese culture by establishing a presence at the core of the Forbidden City (Chiu & Cheng, 2007).

It is important to understand potential consequences of ethnocentrism such as brand boycotts, or even its opposite called buycotts. *Boycotts* are consumer ways to express their general opposition to firms and products in the market place, or even to the entire marketing culture of excessive consumption. Most often, the goal of boycotts is to exert economic pressure on specific companies or industries in an effort to change their practices (see, for example, ethicalconsumer.org). Boycotts aim at punishing companies or product categories (micro-boycotting); however, boycotts are often directed at entire countries, called macro-boycotting (Klein, Smith, & John, 2004). Often, boycotts are likely to happen against foreign brands when they are seen as negative symbols of globalization.

Some powerful brands have experienced such boycotts. For example, the #DeleteUber campaign on major social media platforms caused 200,000 users to delete the Uber app around the world, while at the same time Lyft made it to the top of download charts. Similarly, #BoycottTarget campaign in the U.S. led to millions of lost sales and extra expenses.

Buycott is the opposite of boycott and it presents consumer action to reward companies or industries associated with sustainable practices or social justice initiatives. Often, buycotts support local brands. In 2013 a boycott app (boycott.com) was launched in the U.S. to provide information about sustainability practices based on product barcodes, in an effort to support ethical shopping. This platform has supported organized efforts by groups such as Carrotmob (Carrotmob.org) which uses buycotts to reward local businesses committed for making socially responsible decisions.

The opposite concept of ethnocentrism is *xenocentrism*, originating from the Greek word "foreign" (ξενος, in Greek). Consumer xenocentrism implies that preference is given to foreign-based brands. Ethnocentrism and xenocentrism are not entirely mutually exclusive. While in Latin America there is a strong presence of xenocentric orientations, in Asia most often a combination of xenocentric and ethnocentric attitudes could be detected.

For example, in Hong Kong, many consumers may perceive Western culture as superior to the Chinese in certain status attributes such as achievement or competence, while at the same time they may retain positive evaluations of the Chinese culture regarding traditional moral values and solidarity attributes. In Africa, on the other hand, cultural identity is characterized as post anti-colonial, in that African consumers are seeking new expressions of their unique cultural identity, which is no longer defined by anti-colonial and liberation efforts. Thus, this identity may be influenced by both ethnocentric and xenocentric tendencies.

These tensions between globalization and ethnocentrism/xenocentrism provide a framework for categorizing consumers along the scale of local-glocal-cosmopolitan. In response to globalization, some consumers may entrench national or local values and behaviors while others may replace local norms with global alternatives.

The Globalization Imperative

Local consumers may recognize certain attributes of the global culture as superior, while at the same time reverting to traditional values and maintaining their positive evaluations. Local consumers are those that seldom consume foreign products and they are often characterized by ethnocentric tendencies. They have a strong ethnic identity, and this means that they have incorporated ethnicity into their individual self-concept. Ethnic identity in this case is different from ethnic origin, race, or religion. *Glocal consumers* on the other hand are characterized by dual consumption patterns: they buy global products but only on special occasions, and they generally tend to be more focused on the local culture and local brands.

Cosmopolitan consumers present the group that is most open to foreign products. They are generally world-minded and consume global products on a regular basis. They are in fact positively disposed toward consuming products from foreign countries and exhibit an open mind toward foreign countries and cultures. The original Greek meaning of the word cosmopolitan in fact meant "disdain of patriotism," shifting the emphasis onto the individual from the group. In the 18th century, it evolved to mean "the citizens of the world."

In the presence of ethnocentric tendencies, local consumers may in fact be willing to give up on quality and price often affiliated with global brands (Baughn & Yaprak, 1996). Cosmopolitan consumers, on the other hand, are not usually inclined to make this connection and they may gain psychological advantages from acquiring foreign brands as a signal of status.

How can brands solve the challenge of ethnocentrism?

Globalization and Culture

There are diverging views as to how globalization affects culture, and different influences of globalization on culture could be observed. These include *homogenization or "McDonaldization"* of culture, or a process of eliminating cultural diversity; *hybridization of culture,* or blending cultural influences – for example, the emergence of the "global Nollywood"; or *polarization of culture*, or conflict (Holton, 2000). Some studies (e.g., Xie, Batra, & Peng, 2015) argue that consumers assimilate within the global culture, whereby globalization leads to increasing cultural homogenization. Others suggest that consumers could form a hybrid cultural plurality, embracing elements of global culture and integrating them within the local culture (e.g., Steenkamp, 2019). The third stream of research suggests that globalization could collide with forces of localization, and that consumers may reject global influences, leading to cultural conflicts (e.g., Schuiling & Kapferer, 2004).

These tensions between global and local culture are experienced differently in the countries considered to be at the global core, the semi-periphery, or the periphery (Wallerstein, 2004). Furthermore, they are also influenced by religion and geo-politics.

The countries considered to be the *global core* are the developed, industrialized countries, mostly in the Western hemisphere, which are economically stronger and also considered to be more advanced than others. These countries are the ones to set the global technology, educational, and other development standards for the rest to catch up with.

Semi-periphery consists of the countries which are emerging and moving toward the core. Countries on the semi-periphery play an important role in mediating political, social, and economic activities between the *periphery* or the underdeveloped nations, and the core countries, or the nations which are considered strong economically, politically, and in terms of their military power.

The flow of ideas is happening in both directions between West and East. On the one hand, there are concerns over homogenization of cultures as an outcome of globalization, often seen as a result of the Western influence. For example, the concept of "McDonaldization" refers to the global popularity of American fast-food culture. However, this expression is also symbolic beyond food and American culture as such. It reflects a broader concern that contemporary societies are assuming characteristics of a fast-food restaurant, according to sociologist George Ritzer (1996). He suggested this metaphor as a more up-to-date paradigm from that proposed by sociologist and political economist Max Weber over a century ago, who used the concept of "bureaucracy" as a representation of the contemporary society.

The West–East dichotomy is, in fact, misleading, unless we are talking about the two Earth's hemispheres. Nonetheless, this conceptual divide is commonly used to interpret cultural differences, especially when discussing globalization. While the "Western" influences are spreading Eastward, we can also see an opposite trend. The "Eastern" cultural concepts and traditions are equally being transferred, adjusted, and incorporated into the Western societies and lifestyle.

How does globalization affect culture?

The Globalization Imperative

A Case in Point: East Influencing West

We can see a number of examples of the soft cultural power from the East in the Western societies.

One such example is yoga. Over the past thirty years, yoga practice in the U.S. has been adjusted through different and often hybrid styles and practices, and it became "American yoga." It is characterized with the co-existence of spirituality, medical considerations, fitness, and commercial logics, reflecting a different identity from that in its original home market of India (Ertimur & Coskuner-Balli, 2015). It is also followed by an array of commercial books, courses, and publicity campaigns.

Another example includes K-pop, a genre of popular music originally from South Korea that has recently been popularized in the West. K-pop is no longer just a subculture from South Korea. It is now a strong cultural force in some Western countries, much like Beyoncé's army of fans that call themselves Beyhive.

K-pop has in fact become so popular in the U.S. that the company behind the popular Korean boy band, Big Hit Entertainment (BTS), is now valued at $5billioin. It has recently announced its Initial Public Offering (IPO) with support from companies such as JPMorgan, in spite of growing concerns over the stock market performance (Financial Times, 2020).

Do cultures as soft power lose their "essence" when customized to a new market, such as yoga?

New Middle Classes in Emerging and Developing Markets

Population profiles in most countries have undergone a dramatic transformation in the past couple of decades due to the circulation of people and emerging migration patterns. Over 70% of the planet now lives in the non-Western world, and these markets are predicted to account for half of the global economic growth by 2025 (European Central Bank, 2016). New consumer groups in these emerging markets follow distinctly different consumption patterns from those in the West, and their unique ways of consumption are somewhere at the intersection between tradition and modernity (Kravets & Sandikci, 2014).

The contemporary idea of growth is often projected on the middle classes in emerging and developing markets. They are believed to hold the future global spending demand, and their development is seen as crucial for maintaining the global economy growth levels. Estimates suggest that by 2025, there will be 600 million to 2 billion consumers in this group across the globe, and their spending power is expected to reach US$20 billion (Sheth, 2011). It is important to understand their evolving needs and consumer preferences, not only because they follow distinctly different patterns than their Western counterparts, but also because some more mature markets have experienced slower economic growth in recent years.

For example, in the developing countries in Asia alone, there are already about 150 million upper-middle-class consumers, with more than $3 trillion in spending annually (Lim, Jaafar, Wu, & Wastuwidyaningtyas, 2016). Millions are moving from rural to urban areas and they are joining the ranks of the middle class for the first time in history. They are also now seeking products and services that have long been unavailable or unaffordable to them.

The upper middle class already accounts for a quarter of the population of Thailand and more than that in Malaysia, and it is growing quickly in Indonesia and in Vietnam (Lim et al., 2016). China in particular has evolved in less than three decades from being one of the world's poorest economies to a country with a fast growing and affluent middle class (Berger, Herstein, & Mitki, 2013). In 2015, China surpassed the U.S. as the country with the biggest middle class in the world at 109 million. Today, China also has about 52% of urban population, which is expected to increase to 63% in 2022 (McKinsey & Company, 2016).

While the trend of urbanization is seen in all emerging countries, their urbanization patterns are different from one country to another. For example, the Chinese urbanization has led to the development of large cities. China now has over 160 cities with a population of over one million, including the seven megacities with populations of over 10 million. In India, about 40% of the population may be living in urban areas by 2025, and these city dwellers may account for more than 60% of consumption. However, much of this growth is predicted to take place in smaller towns with populations of less than one million, and these cities are projected be the fastest growing in India.

The emergence of these new middle-class urban consumers is creating a new global demand for products and services. Marketers can already detect a shift from customers in these markets wanting to fulfill their basic needs, toward a quest for new experiences. Increasingly, Western products and services are seeking to achieve a hedonistic appeal, incorporating both Western and Eastern, modern and traditional values.

New middle classes in international markets are also much faster than their counterparts in the developed Western markets in adopting digital technology. For example, just within the five years between 2010 and 2015, smartphone adoption rose from 5% to 47% in Latin America. Mobile networks now reach more than 90% of the region's population, and Latin Americans are among the world's most avid users of social networks. They present the fourth largest mobile market in the world, and their social media adoption is surpassing the U.S. (Alaimo, 2017).

What is the relevance of these new middle classes for global marketing?

Service Challenges

Understanding these emerging middle classes and their consumption patterns is particularly challenging when it comes to the global service industries. A number of emerging economies, having previously received a significant percentage of their GDP from manufacturing, have transitioned to service and knowledge-based economies. This shift has enabled new commercial opportunities for international service providers. New middle classes in emerging markets are now, for the first time, becoming consumers of services such as international education, travel, insurance, consulting, or luxury services.

Services are hard to promote to begin with due to their unique characteristics, different from products. Traditionally, this is because of their *intangible* (they cannot be directly perceived by the five senses), *perishable* (they cannot be stored like physical goods), *variable* (they are always performed in different ways), and *inseparable* nature (their production and consumption are happening at the same time) (Fitzsimmons, Fitzsimmons, & Bordoloi, 2014). These characteristics refer to the part that relates specifically to service consumption or use. Service production or delivery can, especially in today's digital environment, actually be stored, used in the same way, and viewed as separate from consumption (McManus, Winroth, & Angelis, 2019). Thus, it is useful to distinguish between service production and delivery, and its later consumption. These are distinct in terms of characteristics and later implications for service use and experience.

The challenges that come with promoting services are amplified in the multicultural arena. In particular, experiential aspects of services are difficult to understand across cultures because experiences are culture-bound. Furthermore, service quality is interpreted differently across cultures, and there are different written and unwritten cultural rules for acquiring and for retaining customers. For example, the nature of a typical proactive restaurant service in the U.S., with waiters frequently attending to the customers, is at times perceived as overtly invasive by Asians. In Asia, the waiters are often expected to remain in the background and only attend to the customers when called to do so.

Pricing is one of the biggest challenges in the services industries because the provider needs to consider various factors that may otherwise not be as relevant for pricing products. These include the *time cost* (the cost of time invested in receiving a service), *convenience cost* (the cost of inconvenience that comes with the effort made to receive the service), the *search cost* (the time and effort invested in the search for the right service provider), as well as the *psychological* cost. Psychological cost involves the fear of not understanding the service, not knowing how to behave during the service provision, and not understanding what one's expected role is as a customer. This is coupled with the fear of uncertainty that comes with receiving the service and enjoying its benefits (Kapoor, Paul, & Halder, 2013).

This complexity is likely to increase across cultures because cultures have a different approach to time, they have different interpretations of convenience, they use different channels for information search, and they are also likely to have a different understanding of psychological costs. For example, while in the U.S. and Europe service hours spent providing service to the customers outside of the agreed service scope are usually billable, this is not the case in the Middle East, Asia, and much of Southeast Europe, for example. There, these extra service hours are expected as an investment in the relationship building which is essential for client loyalty.

Another aspect of service that differs across cultures is the customer's zone of tolerance, or the extent to which customers recognize and are willing to accept variability in service provision. Because services are variable, they may vary across providers, between employees of the same provider, and even between the same service employee on different occasions. The level of expectation from the service provider, and consequently the gap between the expected and the perceived service, can vary greatly depending on the cultural reference points.

For example, a longer wait time may be tolerable in many Asian countries or in the Middle East, cultures that traditionally have a more polychronic approach to time. Conversely, in more monochronic cultures, such as many Western countries, long wait times are generally equated with bad service. These differing approaches to time are discussed in Chapter 6. Tolerance level also depends on a situation, type of service, and personality factors, which all interact with cultural standards and norms. Finally, loyalty is a cultural concept, and it is interpreted by the customers through their cultural lens.

How can service brand loyalty be interpreted differently across cultures?

Industry-Specific Challenges

Every industry segment also poses its own, unique challenges for the marketers across cultures. These challenges are influenced by a host of reasons inclusive of consumer factors, such as personal and cultural drivers of consumption, as well as the current economic and socio-political context in each country or region.

Furthermore, each industry segment has its own developmental pace and it is affected by both local/regional as well as global industry micro and macro factors. For example, some industry segments are developing in a rather uniform fashion across the world, such as technology or tertiary education. Others, like luxury, have had their own unique developmental patterns.

What are the main challenges for the internationalization of service brands?

A Case in Point: Luxury Brands Internationalization Challenges

The luxury industry is one of the top performing industry sectors on a list of 100 companies that also includes technology, consumer goods, automotive, and financial industries (Handley, 2018). Consumer spending on luxury is however shifting toward the emerging markets: Asia will account for more than half of the luxury goods' market by

2023 (Bain & Company, 2014). Emerging markets are big spenders on luxury products which have now become available to a much wider range of consumers than in the past. Growth in luxury spending is encouraging for the luxury brands; however, this segment is not without challenges in the intercultural context.

Luxury brands enable consumers to enact psychological archetypes from Casanova to the Fairy Godmother (Megehee & Spake, 2012), and their function is universal across cultures. However, the symbolism behind luxury brands is culture-specific (Wiedmann, Hennings, & Siebels, 2009). Luxury is interpreted and consumed differently across cultures. Luxury also appeals to different cultural values in different markets, and it is shared differently across cultures. Therefore, traditional segmentation criteria used in the developed markets may not work in these new markets.

Although consumers across the world have similar expectations from luxury brands such as high quality, prestige, and exclusivity, their consumption styles vary from one market to another (Okonkwo, 2007). The idea of selling a hope, a dream, or an aspirational lifestyle attached to luxury products differs across cultures. The experiential dimension of luxury consumption has strong cultural meanings and it is internally driven to satisfy subjective wellbeing (Sussan, Hall, & Laurie, 2012).

New luxury consumers also have different motivations for purchasing luxury products. For example, in the more mature Western markets, consumers may buy luxury for prestige, to express status, for association with a higher class, for reasons of self-esteem, for a sense of accomplishment, to show success, or to seek new experiences or authenticity. Thus, French and Italian consumers view luxury as an integral part of their cultural legacy and lifestyle, while in the Asian countries, luxury is more related to social status and to reputation.

In non-Western markets, new customers may also buy luxury for gifting, as an investment, for stress release, or as an expression of their unique individuality. Buying luxury helps these consumers to feel like they belong to an exclusive cosmopolitan community they were previously not a part of. New luxury consumers sometimes tend to prefer different luxury products than the mature luxury consumers, and these preferences differ by country as well as among different demographic groups. For example, the Chinese Gen Z show shifted preferences amongst luxury consumers toward casual products such as denim, streetwear, or sneakers, while hard luxury products such as watches or jewelry are declining (Bain & Company, 2014).

Considering these differences, global luxury brands face a storytelling challenge in the emerging markets. Legacy luxury brands traditionally thrive on the myths and stories of origin which are brand- and country-specific. Many of them use their brand's country of origin and their own cultural heritage as the core of their storytelling, and they portray a Westernized ideal (Kim, Lloyd, & Cervellon, 2016). Europe is a birthplace of many top luxury brands, many of which have originated from France, the U.K., or Italy. Consequently, their country of origin is an important part of the storytelling narrative, building on the European heritage and legitimacy even in the new, distinctly different luxury markets (Dion & Arnould, 2011).

Storytelling narratives are culturally and socially constituted (Phillips & McQuarrie, 2011). For this reason, it is essential for the global luxury brands to adapt their original concepts to distinctly different markets and "manage growth worldwide while remaining rare enough to be desirable" (Ko, Costello, & Taylor, 2019, p. 412).

How can Western luxury brands expand in the non-Western markets while staying authentic to their origin story from the West?

Brand Promise

Brands present powerful cultural forces, and they offer a promise of a consistent brand identity in all markets. They convey unique ideas that have a strong impact on consumers, and they shape consumer perceptions in powerful ways. Branding symbolism can cut across cultural boundaries, regardless of the unique cultural aspects that brands may convey. Brands strive to leverage these universal connections across cultures, regardless of their origin (Depeux, 2019).

It is, however, difficult for many brands to find the right balance between the universal or home-country themes on one hand, and the local cultural

The Globalization Imperative

themes on the other. *How can global brands deliver their brand promise to diverse global audiences consistently and in a culturally appropriate manner? How can global brands localize while staying true to their core brand essence without diluting it?* These are some of the most commonly recurring questions for intercultural marketers, as well as in this textbook.

A Case in Point: Paco Rabanne and Universal Cultural Codes

Some brands have been more successful than others in using universal cultural codes for their branding strategies. For example, the perfume brand "Invictus" by Paco Rabanne signals a universal message with its brand name, although its original meaning is quite likely only understood by very few consumers.

While many people around the world have never taken Latin at school, or they have forgotten most of what they learnt at best, the brand still evokes its original meaning in Latin: "Invictus,", which means "unbeaten," "unconquerable," or "undefeated." The

Figure 1.1 Paco Rabanne Invictus Perfume.
Source: Courtesy of Labbrand Brand Innovations.

The Globalization Imperative

> brand brings to mind the images of victory, masculinity, and power amongst its diverse global consumers. Figure 1.1 shows verbal and visual representation of the brand, reflecting its original meaning in Latin.
>
> *What other universal cultural codes could brands rely on in their internationalizing strategies?*

Although some cultural themes are fairly universal across cultures, approaches that work for some brands may not necessarily be universally applicable across different cultures and industry segments. For example, concerns over sustainability and environmental protection as well as one's personal health and wellbeing are universal across the globe. Nonetheless, unique manifestations and expressions of these concerns are different across cultures and industry segments.

A Case in Point: Quorn in Asia

Food is one of the most culture-specific segments that requires a high degree of customization. A U.K.-based company Quorn, which produces plant-based meat alternatives, found this to be very true when expanding to Asian markets. Quorn has seen a rapid growth in the U.K. and in the U.S. due to the growing environmental concerns and the popularity of healthy eating trends. These concerns, coupled with the changing social norms, such as those that dictate eating meat, have led to a growing popularity of vegan and vegetarian diets in the West over the past ten years.

However, while the idea of "meatless-meat" has a strong appeal for a growing number of European and U.S. consumers, Quorn found that customers in the Southeast Asian countries were very different from their Western counterparts.

Finding the right value proposition that fits with the local tastes was challenging for Quorn in Asia because consumption habits of Asian

The Globalization Imperative

consumers are rather different than those of their Western counterparts. For example, unlike in the West, taste and texture of plant-based food are some of the top considerations for the Asian consumers, while these are of a lesser concern in the U.K. and the U.S. Asian consumers also expected taste to be balanced with nutritional and sustainability concerns.

Furthermore, Quorn also faced the challenge of overcoming the negative associations that consumers have in Asia with frozen processed food. Perhaps most importantly, the "meatless" aspect needed to be downplayed, because of the high social value of meat and its social significance, which is very strong in Asia. Most Asian consumers find meat to be the key source of protein, and a small population of vegan and vegetarian consumers could not be counted on for promoting the brand. Rather, they had to rely on meat-eaters.

To penetrate the Asian market, instead of referring to its product as "meat-less," or "meat-free," Quorn featured the "mycoprotein" ingredient and emphasized the nutritional value of its products. Figure 1.2 shows how packaging was customized for the Asian market. This helped the brand to stay true to its original values while also customizing toward a distinctly different market.

Quorn UK

Quorn Asia

Figure 1.2 Quorn branding in the U.K. and Asia.
Source: Courtesy of Labbrand Brand Innovations.

Their marketing campaigns also focused on empowering the Asian consumers to make a positive change, as shown in Figure 1.3. This is expressed in the #makeachange brand campaign as an overarching message appealing to this new demographic (reproduced from Koh, 2018).

The Globalization Imperative

Figure 1.3 Quorn promotional campaign.
Source: Courtesy of Labbrand Brand Innovations.

Was Quorn's approach to promoting plant-based food appropriate in Asia? How could they have approached it differently?

Cultural Superstitions

Culture also influences consumer behavior through *superstitions* (Chiu, Kwan, Li, Peng, & Peng, 2012). For example, Chinese consumers may be more inclined to buy a cup of coffee with a price tag of 28 RMB (Chinese currency) instead of an identical cup of coffee from the same coffee shop that sells at 24 RMB, considering that eight is a lucky number and four is considered unlucky in the Chinese culture. This preference for the number eight and aversion toward the number four affects marketing communications messages – the number eight is used much more frequently than the number four in product advertisement in China (Chiu et al., 2012).

Cultural superstitions also affect stock market activity. In the stock markets in Hong Kong, Shanghai, and Shenzhen, the A-shares are more than twice as likely to end with a number eight than with a number four (Rao, Zhao, & Yue, 2008).

Brand Social Impact

Customers expect marketers to engage with cultural diversity while at the same time incorporating the social agenda of the host country. This is a particularly important consideration in the developing markets, because the Western brands are traditionally believed to possess the know-how and capabilities to ignite a positive social change. *Brand social impact* is becoming equally important within the increasingly diverse markets in the developed Western markets. Consequently, brands are increasingly focused on communicating their social impact and relevance. This is an important branding goal because when marketers fail to show their social functions, customers can be frustrated (Vorster, Kipnis, Bebek, & Demangeot, 2019).

However, attempts to appeal to social issues are not always successful across different markets. In fact, these attempts may not be successful even in the home market. Brands can engage with a culture more or less successfully – sometimes campaigns are well received by the customers and at other times they could even backfire. It is important to understand which cultural triggers may prompt customers to appreciate or object to campaigns.

There is much at stake because companies have a lot to gain or lose when engaging with cultural diversity (ibid). Brands should tread carefully when tackling broader societal issues. In particular, they should avoid stereotyping. For example, gender stereotyping remains pervasive in advertising across cultures. Unilever, a British-Dutch food company discovered in a research study encompassing multiple countries that almost 50% of ads across the world show bias when portraying women. Their research suggests that 40% of women don't recognize themselves in advertising, and that 90% of global female consumers believe that women are presented as sex symbols in the ads (Warc, 2016).

This has led to the formation of the "Unstereotype Alliance," supported by companies like Facebook, Google, Alibaba, Mars, and WPP (Hobbs, 2017). They were also joined by the advertising industry bodies such as the U.K.-based IPA (Institute of Practitioners in Advertising) and the U.S.-based ANA (Association of National Advertisers). It is important for the brands to be aware of the nuances and cultural triggers in gender stereotyping as many of them increasingly face backlashes due to their insensitive advertising campaigns.

How can brands avoid stereotyping in their internationalization efforts?

A Case in Point: Coca Cola's Super Bowl Ad

The idea behind Coca Cola's super bowl ad in 2017 was to advocate diversity and unity. The ad was a re-run of an ad originally aired in 2014, titled "America is Beautiful." The super bowl is one of the most popular TV events of the year in the U.S., with an average 30-second commercial spot costing around $4 million.

Coke's ad, also used during the Rio Olympics in 2016, featured people of diverse ethnicities, race, age and religion. The version of the song "America the Beautiful" was sung in many languages other than English, inclusive of Spanish, Tagalog, French, Hindi, Senegalese, Mandarin, Keres, Arabic, and Hebrew.

The main message behind the ad was that America is beautiful, and Coke helps to celebrate shared moments by everyone. The ad was meant to signal optimism and to promote unity. Nonetheless, this campaign was not met with enthusiasm by everyone, and some consumers even took it to Twitter with the hashtag #BoycottCoke. The reason for their dismay was, allegedly, because an American patriotic song was sung in languages other than English.

Some global media outlets commented that the U.S. conservative public could not take diversity, and that many of them confused diversity with patriotism. Comments read that if the public cannot be proud enough to sing the song in English, the country is on the road to perdition. Coca-Cola was even labeled as the official soft drink of the illegal immigrants crossing the U.S. border from Mexico. The critics also accused Coke of singing an American song in a "terrorist language" (Younge, 2014).

Nonetheless, the Super Bowl ad has sparked online discussion, providing a high-profile example of the actual societal debate.

Is it beneficial for brands to spark societal debates regardless of whether they are positive or negative? Do brands have control over these debates?

The Allure of Global Brands

Brands marketed internationally carry a certain allure due to their global presence. As Holt, Quelch, and Taylor (2004) put it, "when a brand is marketed around the world, that fact alone gives it an aura of excellence – and a set of obligations." Global brands are powerful institutions capable of doing great good. However, due to the growing concerns over climate change, sustainability, and corporate social responsibility (CSR) across the world, global brands are often seen as institutions causing considerable harm due to their environmental impact or their corporate practices.

Consequently, global brands are under the spotlight and they are subject to more scrutiny than local brands. Often, they serve as the lightning rods for anti-globalization protests because of globalization's side effects such as exploitative wages, pollution, and cultural imperialism. This is not surprising considering how much economic and political power some of the global brands have, with their annual revenues being greater than the GDPs of small nations. Thus, some global brands are seen as an embodiment of globalization challenges, regardless of their actual impact and their role in the globalization process.

For example, McDonalds is often perceived as a brand that exemplifies globalization and all its negative effects. For this reason, it has been a subject of repeated backlashes and its store fronts were smashed on a number of occasions such as The World Economic Forum meetings in Davos, Switzerland.

Why is there more pressure on the global brands than on the local brands to show cultural understanding and avoid blunders?

A Case in Point: Uber in Asia

Some brands unfortunately fail to strike a chord with international audiences due to a combination of reasons. This failure is often attributed to the brands failing to achieve a successful balance between their global brand promise and local culture, and failing to adequately localize and meet the evolving host country market needs.

Some brands simply fail to stay relevant outside of their home markets long-term, no matter how successful they are at home. Such is the case of Uber, a U.S. ride-hailing company that failed to gain relevance in many international markets. The so called "blue ocean" companies in the sharing economy space, such as Uber and BlaBlaCar, a French online carpooling marketplace, pushed the boundaries of transportation globally. Uber also addressed a universal need for private transportation in the U.S.

However, it failed in Asia because they did not offer additional benefits that the local consumers expected, beyond the basic solution for private transportation needs. They failed to understand that there were unique priorities in different countries in Asia.

For example, some customers preferred ride sharing as a mode of transport. Furthermore, for many Asia customers living in the bustling Asian mega-cities, the immediate availability of transport is more important than other factors due to the difficulties of finding a taxi.

What other comparable brands can you think of, which failed to gain relevance in the international market in spite of success in their home market?

A Case in Point: Club Med in China

Brands are constantly expanding beyond their familiar territory. Many succeed by adjusting their positioning in new markets, or by starting fresh with introductions of new brands. For example, Club Med, a French resort chain offering premium holidays in 30 countries, succeeded to expand in China by helping Chinese consumers solve their current problems. By doing so, it became relevant in that market at a specific point in time.

To meet the evolving tastes and needs of the fast-growing Chinese middle-class consumers, in 2015 Club Med launched a new concept in China, Joyview by Club Med. Joyview offers Chinese urban consumers a chance to experience premium short holidays in China in retreats within two to three hours' drive from the major cities.

One of their main positioning messages is "the whole family together" (一家人在一起, in Chinese), catering to the Chinese consumers who are facing a dynamic period of change which is unparalleled in Chinese history. This change is characterized by the fast pace of the country's development, rapid urbanization, and a never-before-seen speed of technology adoption.

> Due to the pressures experienced in this period of rapid change in China, the customers with their hectic schedules appreciate weekend resort escapes with their families outside of the bustling cities Joyview tapped into that need, offering a compromise solution of premium short holidays in locations that are easy to reach (adapted from Lab-brand Brand Innovations, 2015).
>
> *What other successful brand extension strategies across the cultures can you find?*

Branding Blunders

Today, customers expect culture-wise campaigns from the global brands. They are also more sensitive than are company employees to cultural mishaps. Nonetheless, global brands sometimes work under the assumption that marketing principles that work in their home market would work elsewhere in the world without much localization. Even the brands with large budgets and resources are prone to making cultural mistakes.

These mistakes, commonly known as *branding blunders*, play an important role in understanding the extent of cultural influence. Blunders are usually serious, avoidable mistakes typically caused by carelessness, poor judgment, incomplete analysis, ignorance, arrogance, or simply confusion. They can be related to poor translation of product names, a lack of knowledge of cultural norms, a lack of sensitivity to cultural norms, or even a disrespect of cultural norms.

Many of these blunders happened at the outset of globalization in the 1980s. From today's perspective, some blunders may appear relatively benign or even funny. For example, a Swedish producer of household appliances, Electrolux, allegedly used a slogan "Nothing sucks like Electrolux" when first arriving in the U.S, which apparently caused a pushback because of the negative meaning of the word "suck."

In order to appeal to Chinese customers, Japanese car maker Toyota used the symbolism of Chinese imperial lions when expanding in the Chinese market in the late 1990s. Their advertising showed two imperial lions bowing to a Toyota car. Rather than pleasing the Chinese customers, this triggered a counter campaign launched by the Chinese customers who took it to the media with pictures of the same Chinese lions crushing a Toyota car in return.

In spite of the accumulated cultural knowledge and the wealth of studies focused on cultural influence on consumption in the past couple of decades, blunders continue happening to this day. Arguably, they can no longer be attributed to a lack of cultural knowledge as may have been the case at the outset of globalization. There are different consequences from branding blunders, and some are more benign than others.

Sometimes, poor brand adaptation simply results in the brand being irrelevant because customers cannot relate to its message. For example, The American Dairy Association used its slogan "Got Milk?" in the U.K. with considerably less success than in the U.S., because the slogan simply sounded odd to British consumers.

At other times, the same blunders are funny at best. For example, they translated the "Got Milk?" slogan in the Spanish-speaking countries as "¿Tiene leche?" (in Spanish) which means "do you have breast milk?" or "are you lactating?" Some mistranslations could be amusing, and on occasion they could also help the brands by drawing attention to products that may not be noticed otherwise and would receive little to no coverage. However, blunders are a serious matter as they could alienate customers and lead to long-term negative consequences for the brands.

In some cases, blunders have even caused a serious public outrage due racial and ethnic prejudices or due to gender stereotyping. In the last few years, leading global brands like Pepsi, H&M, and Dove have faced consumer backlash for their insensitive advertisements that offended multicultural communities across the world. For example, Swedish retailer H&M was criticized for featuring an African child as a model wearing a sweatshirt with the phrase "coolest monkey in the jungle." The ad originally appeared on the British website of the retailer and it caused a global outrage.

There are numerous other examples. Nivea, a German skincare brand, had to apologize over its "white is purity" deodorant ad that was seen as racially insensitive. A Manchester-based Co-op supermarket in the U.K. was accused of sexism for its fair-trade Easter egg advertising campaign that read "treat your daughter for doing the washing up," on the basis that gender equality is one of the important Fairtrade principles (BBC, 2017). Unfortunately, we can find many such examples to this day. Some remain more benign, while others carry more serious consequences.

The Globalization Imperative

Some more serious blunders can also be related to political themes. For example, Gap, a U.S. clothing and accessories retailer, had to apologize after it released a T-shirt omitting Taiwan, South Tibet, and South China sea from the map of China printed on its shirts. This was first spotted by the user of Sina Weibo (新浪微博, in Chinese) – a Chinese microblogging site – in a Canadian store. Given the nonlinear global flows of people and the increasingly dense communication networks, blunders travel fast, and far.

Others blunders could simply cause a lack of enthusiasm. For example, when introducing its Pampers brand to Japan, P&G, a U.S. consumer goods company, did not consider the differences in folk traditions between Japan and the West. Storks, used in their advertising campaigns in Japan, do not have the same meaning in the Japanese culture as they do in many Western cultures – in fact, they are seen as scary creatures by most Japanese people. In the Japanese tradition, babies are delivered to the deserving parents inside the peaches floating on the river, and not by storks.

How can brands avoid blunders? Should blunders always be avoided, at all cost?

A Case in Point: Blunders and Superstition – Pepsi in China

Blunders can also sometimes unintentionally tap into the deeply ingrained superstitions and pagan traditions in a host country, upsetting the customers at a much deeper level. These instances are more harmful than when mistranslations happen or when the brands simply fail to integrate cultural symbols or use them in what is seen as an inappropriate way. Some blunders remain to be proven as history vs. just being urban legends; however, the stories remain trapped on the Internet to be seen by consumers, and this could affect the brands long term.

Such is the case with Pepsi in China and the popular branding story that it has apparently mistranslated its slogan "Come Alive with Pepsi Generation" to read "Pepsi Brings Your Ancestors Back from the Grave" (百事使你的祖先起死回生, in Chinese).

In China, the ancestor cult is very important. In fact, it is so present in the people's daily lives that the tradition found its way into online business models: WeChat, a popular Chinese social media app, partnered with the cemeteries to offer people a live video feed of the ancestors worshipping ceremony. This is done during the Qingming Festival, known as the Tomb Sweeping Day, for people who do not get an opportunity to visit their ancestors' graves as is traditional on that day.

Pepsi did not consider just how strong the links are with the world of ancestors in China and how important is the symbolism of the ancestor cult. Pepsi's gaffe, which was a result of mistranslation, has caused a significant pushback and customer dismay at a deeper level, beyond just being a funny linguistic blunder (Baidu, 2011).

Could Pepsi envision such reaction from the Chinese consumers? How can marketers estimate the level of risk when localizing in distinctly different countries?

Brand Globalness

Cultural diversity thrives independently and often in spite of globalization. Global consumers expect campaigns that are both universal and also culture-wise at the same time. Global brands are expected to create a lasting impact by focusing on both universal as well as local cultural values. There is also growing pressure on the global brands to contribute to a more universal human quest for value. Furthermore, global brands are under increased scrutiny to create social impact and to show their sustainability efforts. Thus, many global brands are attempting to move away from their efforts to merely "glocalize" their brands in international markets at a commercial level, and toward a more universal values-based branding in order to engage with local markets.

Marketing task in the international markets is far from simple, because international brands need to reconcile between multiple paradoxical values and needs. While brands attempt to use a local cultural capital for their positioning in order to achieve high cultural relevance and authenticity, consumers also seek the prestige and quality they expect from global brands.

Perceived Brand Globalness (PBG) is a concept used to measure how global the brands are in the minds of consumers. It influences the brand purchase likelihood because of the attributes of quality and prestige that many customers may place on global brands (Steenkamp, Batra, & Alden, 2002). Local customers may value global brands, and they may also seek a prestige that comes with global brands, since consuming them may lead to a higher self-esteem.

Thus, many multinational brands are altering their portfolios to appear more global in their branding efforts in a hope of being perceived as superior to local brands in international markets. This sometimes means replacing local brand names with a uniform global name because such a strategy could enhance a brand image (ibid). For example, the U.K. mobile phone operator Vodafone decided in 2000 to use the Vodafone brand as a single global brand. The name is seen as universal and it means voice+data+phone, deliberately spelling phone as "fone."

Perceived Brand Globalness and the resulting inferences of global brand quality could also be a consequence of a local brand failure. For example, Western baby formula brands were still a preferred choice for Chinese consumers in 2019 according to the Euromonitor International. The share of domestic powder baby formula brands is around 40% and the top six most popular baby formula brands in China are foreign (Hancock, 2019). This was still the case ten years after the melamine (an industrial chemical) scandal had happened in China in 2009. Melamine was found in the locally produced infant baby formula, and it caused six babies to die and some 300,000 to fall ill from complications after drinking the local infant formula in 2009.

A positive association between a PBG and the likelihood of purchase may be weaker for the more ethnocentric consumers (Steenkamp et al., 2002). Nonetheless, PBG is also mitigated by a product type and an industry segment. For example, food is amongst the most culturally-specific product categories and it requires a high degree of localization. On the other hand, tertiary education requires less customization.

Customers relate to global brands at two levels: *utilitarian* and *aspirational*. At the practical, *utilitarian level,* they may hold a perception that global brands are of a higher quality than the local brands. For example, local customers may assume that brands maintain the same quality standard across the world. Global brands are also often able to compete on price and offer cheaper products due to their global presence that comes with product standardization and the economies of scale and scope. Thus, to achieve the effect reserved for global brands, local brands may often signal global presence in their branding strategies in order to increase their value locally. The *aspirational* value seen in global brands is evident through prestige and status symbols that consumers hope to obtain when consuming global brands.

Branding decisions, however, have to be carefully balanced between global and local characteristics. While global brands may be seen as superior, local brands are often cultural icons and they are related to feelings of pride and support of local cultural heritage and national economy. Therefore, local brands may often be seen as a better fit with local traditions. Generally speaking, ethnocentric customers may be less inclined to prefer global brands (Winit, Gregory, Cleveland, & Verlegh, 2014).

No matter whether brands position as global or local, brand identity needs to be reconciled with cultural identity of a host country. While brands embody global standards and present passports to global citizenship to many customers around the world, they also depict the meanings that are unique to cultural groups (Strizhakova, Coutler, & Price, 2008). When brands lack sensitivity to complex cultural identities, the ideas and meanings they convey may have detrimental effects on consumer self-evaluation and on their wellbeing.

It is particularly relevant to understand the impact of brand ownership – the brand's home country – and consumer preferences for global or local brands against the backdrop of possible home-country brand biases. These biases can change over time due to a plethora of factors which may be either cultural or political or economic.

How can brands balance between brand globalness and local culture appeals?

Brand Involvement

Kipnis, Broderick, and Demangeot (2013, pp. 1189–1190) suggest that there are different levels of *brand involvement* or different voices that brands may use in their cultural appeal: brand ignorance, brand tolerance, and brand engagement. *Brand ignorance* happens when brand identity incorporates cultural symbols relevant only to the dominant cultural group while ignoring cultural cues relevant to nondominant groups. Brand ignorance can also occur when a brand portrays particular identities in a derogatory manner.

The authors provide an example of brand ignorance using the example of the "Joy of Pink" fragrance campaign launched in 2010 by Lacoste, a French clothing, footwear, and accessories company. The campaign used fair-skin female models showered in pink ribbons. Notably, this choice of symbols could lower self-evaluations of consumers with darker skin tones.

Another example of brand ignorance could be found in the campaigns of Italian automaker Fiat who launched an advertising campaign featuring Richard Gere driving a car from Hollywood to Tibet. This was a double gaffe: Richard Gere is known for his public support of the Dalai Lama and the Tibetan government residing in India. Furthermore, symbolically, using Tibet and Richard Gere sent a clear message of support for Tibet's independence. Regardless of explanations made by Fiat afterwards, public dismay was strong in China and the company lost quite a bit of sales there.

Brand tolerance suggests that a brand incorporates various cultural clues tailored toward a specific target segment identified mainly in demographic terms. Consequently, it uses models, language, and cultural meanings relevant to a range of groups such as Hispanic or African American. *Branding engagement*, finally, incorporates multiple cultural cues and caters to mixed ethnicities and multiple languages, and it acknowledges a need for their integration (Kipnis et al., 2013).

When taking brands across cultures it is also important to remember that brands have financial value and they present an intangible asset on a company's balance sheet. Many international brands are evaluated in financial terms, for example by Interbrand (www.interbrand.com), an international brand consultancy that publishes a list of the top 100 international brands each year. Interbrand applies a brand valuation process to establish the financial value of brands and how they perform year on year as compared to their competitors. A range of tangible and intangible factors alike can influence a brand's changing position on that list, and its financial value.

How can brands avoid ignorance in multicultural markets?

Integrated Marketing Communications (IMC)

Integrated marketing communications (IMC) refers to the communications functions in marketing. IMC is among the most culture-bound realms of marketing, and it is commonly used to analyze cultural differences and similarities with their relevance in marketing. Today, importance is placed on integration of various marketing communications functions, combining different disciplines for maximum impact.

IMC is increasingly intercultural, and cultural knowledge is crucial for successful IMC. Culture determines how individuals encode messages, their choice of transmission medium, and how messages are interpreted (decoded). The main IMC tactics and their features are summarized in brief, including sales promotion, personal selling, public relations, and advertising. Each of these tools has their own advantages and disadvantages.

IMC Tactics

Sales promotion refers to short-term incentives designed by marketers for the purpose of encouraging purchase of a product. They are aimed at achieving specific objectives such as consumer-product trials. Some of the main business to consumer (B2C) promo tools used as part of sales promotion efforts include samples, coupons, rebates, price packs, loyalty programs, point-of-purchase displays/demos, or product tie-ins. Preferences for specific tools differ across cultures, as does consumer access to various sales channels. The range of discounts and samples that could be offered is also limited in some markets, so knowing the legal environment of a host country is necessary for successful sales promotion efforts.

Personal selling is a form of direct person-to-person communication. A seller attempts to assist or to persuade the prospective buyer to purchase a product or a service in a direct personal interaction. Compared to other IMC tools that present one-way, that is, impersonal communications, personal selling involves a process of two-way personal communications.

Advantages of personal selling include direct contact between a buyer and a seller which allows for more flexibility. This is particularly important in the service industries as it helps to enhance relationships and build trust. A seller can tailor the sales message to specific customer needs, and this tool allows for more direct and immediate feedback. Furthermore, sales efforts can be targeted to specific markets and customers who are the best prospects.

Equally, there are a number of disadvantages of personal selling. This tactic involves high costs per contact, and it presents an expensive way to reach large audiences. It also requires an experienced salesforce, which additionally increases the cost. Furthermore, it is difficult to ensure consistency of messages to all customers, even when efforts are made by the same salesperson. Personal selling across cultures requires a deep knowledge of culture and a high degree of intercultural communications competence.

Public relations (PR) refers to a nonpersonal communication which is not directly paid for by an identified sponsor. Its purpose is not to communicate to the market about the company's products or services but rather to communicate about the company itself. Public relations are IMC efforts focused on building relationships between companies and its publics. It is a cross-disciplinary field that incorporates elements from psychology, sociology, culture, and media studies.

Advantages of PR include credibility, since it should be earned rather than openly sponsored. It is also a relatively low-cost effort compared to advertising or personal selling, and it often results in word-of-mouth. Nonetheless it has its own disadvantages as well. For example, PR is not always under the control of an organization, and it can also be negative.

PR channels or vehicles include news releases – single-page news stories sent to media agencies who might print or broadcast the content; feature articles – longer manuscripts composed and edited for a particular medium, often as an extension of a news release; photo captions – photographs with content identified and explained below the picture; press conferences – meetings and presentations to selected reporters and editors, usually to announce relevant news; or special events – sponsorship of events, teams, or programs of public value. As with other IMC tactics, preferences and usage patterns differ across cultures. PR message development efforts should be informed by cultural analysis.

Are you aware of any PR disasters in international markets due to cross-cultural differences? What was the underlying reason?

Advertising

Advertising is an IMC tactic of calling public attention to something through paid announcements. It presents an audio or visual form of IMC that uses an openly sponsored, nonpersonal message to promote or sell a product, service, or idea. In fact, advertising presents any paid form of nonpersonal communication about an organization, product, service, idea, or cause by an identified sponsor.

We can identify different types of advertising. Advertising to consumer markets includes advertising to increase demand for a specific brand or advertising to increase demand for a product category. An example of product category advertising includes the "Got Milk?" campaign by the California Milk Processor Board in 1993. This campaign was aimed to encourage consumption of milk, unrelated to a specific brand of milk. Business and professional advertising refer to advertising geared toward a specific profession, or trade advertising by the manufacturer to a retailer or wholesaler.

Advertising has a number of advantages. For example, considering that advertising is a paid-for or sponsored IMC tactic, the advertiser controls the message. Ads can also help to communicate with large audiences, and they present an effective way to create brand awareness through symbolic appeals.

Disadvantages of advertising include a high cost of production and ad placement, as well as credibility issues and consumer skepticism that comes with the idea of paid-for IMC tactics. Because of advertising clutter, namely the wealth of advertisements we face on a daily basis, there is also a difficulty in determining advertising effectiveness.

Advertising channels or vehicles include the Internet, social media, newspapers, magazines, radio and TV, direct mail, as well as billboards, cinemas, elevators, and so on.

There are a number of constraints to advertising. These include, for example, the high cost of ad production and media placement, linguistic considerations, differences in processing of stimuli between cultures, availability of media and their reach in different countries, and the availability of reliable data used to determine ad media placement.

Legal constraints to advertising are important to consider because they vary from one country to another as well as from one product category to another. There are particular challenges with Internet advertising due to "banner blindness" because ads are often barely visible, especially on a small screen, due to advertising clutter.

Do all IMC tactics face the same or similar challenges across cultures?

Advertising and Culture

All advertising campaigns across the globe share a universal challenge: they aim to persuade consumers that the product is meant exactly for them. They try to convey to customers that the product brings them a range of benefits inclusive of price, convenience, or status. In other words, ads try to communicate that the product has functional, emotional/psychological, and social value for the customers. This challenge is amplified in the international markets as the notion of value is different across cultures. Furthermore, it is also influenced by the underling socio-political and economic contexts of a host country.

Advertising is an idealized personification and an expression of cultural values (Pollay, 1983). It is a marketing technique that possesses social influence. This influence is not necessarily a positive one if used as a mechanism of control, or for "manufacturing consent," a concept proposed in the popular book by Edward Herman and Noam Chomsky (1988). The authors suggested that the mass media communicate messages, largely through advertising, and thus inculcate individuals with values and beliefs to integrate them into the institutional structures of the larger society.

Cultural values present an overarching backdrop for advertising. Advertisers should not only avoid conflicts with cultural values, they should also appeal to them. Considering that values are a strong driver of consumer behavior (Bardi & Schwartz, 2003), advertising that appeals to cultural values is also more likely to be acceptable for customers than advertising that ignores them (Tai, 2004). While some brands have used a backdrop of universal values to support the case for advertising standardization, a much wiser approach is to localize advertising efforts.

As aforementioned, some product categories and industries are more cultural-specific than others and they require a higher degree of localization in advertising efforts. Such is the example of food. In analyzing food advertisements as a mirror of cultural differences between Greece and the U.K., Theocharous (2015) suggests that the Greek advertisements tend to adopt a more forceful or emotional style. They usually combine formal and factual information with emotional appeals, which are geared toward emphasizing the local origin, nostalgia, and cultural traditions. In the U.K., on the other hand, food companies emphasize the entertainment value of advertisements, and they tend to communicate rational appeals in a more informal register.

Research also suggests that humor is used differently in advertising across cultures (Yue, Jiang, Lu, & Hiranandani, 2016). For example, U.S. consumers may be amused and entertained by a self-mocking or a self-enhancing humor, and consequently, they could have positive reactions to it. Nonetheless, people from Asian cultures generally do not share this orientation (Kuiper, Grimshaw, Leite, & Kirsh, 2004). Because of a smaller private psychological sphere in Asian cultures, the distinction between self-oriented (self-enhancing) and other-oriented (affiliative) humor may be blurred, and it may not be easily understood in these cultures. Generally speaking, people from Western cultures tend to tolerate and use humor more often than those in Asian cultures (Yue, 2011).

Some studies suggest that the Westerners see humor as a positive disposition that makes both the individual as well as others look good (Martin, 2007), while, for example, the Chinese view humor as controversial in social interactions. In fact, humor is seen as a peculiar personality trait reserved for the "humor specialists" (Yue, 2011) in China. This may be somewhat attributed to Confucian values stipulating that a "junzi" (君子, in Chinese) – the closest equivalent of a gentlemen in Western culture – should refrain from loud laughter and from expressing extreme emotions, and should demonstrate restraint and social formality (Xu, 2011).

It is also important to remember that consumers like to see *aspirational values* in promotional campaigns. There may be a difference between desirable (what people think ought to be desired, in line with the general norms of a society) and the desired values (what people actually desire and what they want for themselves). The question also arises as to whether advertising promotes extrinsic or intrinsic values. Extrinsic values are more affiliated with conformity to cultural norms, and intrinsic values remain more personal. Extrinsic values also seek external validations such as opinion of others, whereas intrinsic values are in themselves rewarding (Grouzet et al., 2005).

The Legal Context of Advertising

It is important to analyze cultural factors against the political and legislative environment of a country. Culture is not an independent variable, and it is influenced by other factors – politics, history, and economics. This backdrop also dictates different norms that govern integrated marketing communications, and advertising in particular.

For example, there are differing advertising norms and legislation across countries. While comparative advertising is very common and even encouraged in the U.S., it is either frowned upon or forbidden in some other places such as China, Belgium, France, Germany Japan, Italy, and South Africa. Many countries are known for having very strict principles when it comes to competitive messaging and mentioning competitors directly in ads. Similarly, the use of superlatives such as "the best" or "the most" to describe products in relation to other brands is also often forbidden in those countries and may be punishable by law.

There are also different rules across countries regarding the types of products or services that can or cannot be advertised at all, or at certain times. These include, for example, fast food, cigarettes, or alcohol. The amount of time allowed for advertising also differs, as well as who the advertising can be targeted to. In Sweden, for example, any advertising deemed to be aimed at children under the age of twelve is forbidden altogether. In France, famous for its wine production, any advertising of alcohol is forbidden in the movie theatres and on TV.

Against the different legal backdrops, there are also differing approaches to public relations from one country to another as well as different importance attached to the PR profession across countries. For example, Firestone Tire and Rubber Company, an American tire company, had a safety recall in 2000 after more than 100 deaths were reported in the U.S. due to their defective tires. The Japanese CEO of the U.S. office, in line with his own cultural traditions of personal honor and shame, assumed full personal responsibility. This did not seem to work well in the U.S. Senate hearing, which blamed both Firestone and Ford for telling customers to underinflate the tires.

Different countries also view PR differently. For example, PR has traditionally been rather highly regarded in the U.S. This has been the case since the 1920s when Edward Barneys, the "father of PR," created the first official PR campaign for Lucky Strike, encouraging women to smoke in public as a sign of emancipation. The Chinese Ministry of Labor and Social Security on the other hand, only recognized PR as a profession in 1999 when it also regulated it and instituted a nationwide qualifying exam for PR professionals.

The boundaries between advertising and PR are sometimes blurred. For example, Nike responded with paid ads to negative PR articles that made allegations of child labor and sweat shops in India. As a result, Nike was taken to the Supreme Court by an activist, and the case was settled.

How can brands make the best use of the different integrated marketing communications tactics?

A Word of Caution

Traditionally, the concept of *modernization* in Western management thinking implies that the non-Western countries should catch up with the West which has set the norms for the rest of the world. Increasingly, globalization is seen as an indicator of economic prosperity in the emerging markets. Thus, expectations are placed on non-Western economies to catch up with the global – that is, Western – trends. The underlying assumption is that developing countries should acquire social and political characteristics of the Western industrial societies. This applies to a range of activities such as technology, or the application of scientific knowledge to solve problems in life; agriculture, or a shift to commercial faming; urbanization, namely moving from rural areas to the cities; or telecommunications, or development of the communications infrastructure from the Western perspective.

However, the traditional hegemony or dominance of the West has been questioned with the rise of the BRICS countries. These countries have been collectively referred to as the "Global South," a term that has also been linked to colonialism and neo-colonialism. Today, these countries are challenging the traditional center-periphery (the West and the rest) relationship that the world has been caught up in. They are also questioning the idea of Western dominance in the long run in the economic, political, and cultural sense. These emerging powers may in fact inspire the world to move away from the linear toward more dialectical relationships, in a more balanced political and economic global order (Herdin, Faust, & Chen, 2020).

Mini-Case: Sofitel Hotels & Resorts

Sofitel Hotels & Resorts, a brand within the Paris-based Accor Group, presents a good example of brand promise and brand engagement. It taps into the rich symbolism of its home country brand, France. At the same time, the brand strives to inspire a universal quest for aesthetics and style across the world. Their global storytelling is focused on universal application of French cultural themes. The brand serves as a time-honored ambassador of French "art de vivre" and "savoir-faire," driving on the eternal allure of French style.

The Sofitel brand conveys the sense of enjoying life and appreciating culture, gastronomy, design, and arts, all through a French lens. Put together, these story pillars create a unique customer promise and value proposition that can be translated across cultures, yet still it remains uniquely French. While celebrating its brand's home country and its deep French roots, the brand offers a credible and authentic way for customers to enjoy the universal allure of this lifestyle and aesthetic around the world. This approach has helped the brand to find a unique position in a rapidly growing yet increasingly homogeneous global luxury segment.

Speaking to its French origins is one thing, but making sure it's evident throughout the guest experience is another. Sofitel has imbued its French DNA into all aspects of its guest experience. For example, guests are greeted in French by Sofitel staff around the world wearing made-to-measure designs created by the well-known Parisian-based fashion designer Léa Peckre.

The Globalization Imperative

Senses are awakened by the wafting scent of Essence de Sofitel, a fragrance created by renowned perfumer Lucien Ferrero, which wafts through the hotel lobby and public spaces.

Family and children's programs are inspired by "Le Petit Prince," (*The Little Prince*) the cherished classic French children's book. And guests can also indulge in le goûter (equivalent of the afternoon tea in the U.K), usually consisting of crêpes, cream cakes or pastries or l'apéritif (usually an alcoholic drink enjoyed at the beginning of the meal), in the hotel bars, followed by the "gastronomie Française" (fine dining in French style) in the dining rooms.

Sofitel's recent brand campaign "Live the French Way" caters to its guests who are looking to experience the "chic," and nonchalant French way of life, all while responding to the "Frenchness" in their unique cultural ways. Sofitel explains this unique French style as "modern, elegant, chic, spontaneous and indulgent with a touch of joie de vivre and familiarity" (Accor, 2019). They suggest that "Frenchness" is the most important element mentioned in consumer feedback, and it remains an important part of the brand identity across the world. Figure 1.1 shows Sofitel's advertising as part of the "Live The French Way" brand campaign.

Figure 1.4 Sofitel advertising: Live The French Way.
Source: Courtesy of Sofitel Hotels & Resorts©.

Mini-Case Questions

- What are the key reasons behind Sofitel's success?
- How do they reconcile between their home brand and the host country culture?
- How can cultural values of a country brand be made universal across cultures?
- What are some possible challenges that Sofitel may face with its branding approach?

Chapter 1 Guiding Questions

As you start your project, it is important to analyze your *host country's macro market* first. Cultural factors should be analyzed against the backdrop of the actual political and economic context. Consider some of the following at the outset:

- How would you describe the economic and political climate in your host country?
- Are there any relevant socioeconomic developments in your host region that could influence your marketing efforts?
- Are there any geo-political issues? Security concerns?
- What would a PESTLE framework (political, economic, societal, technological, legal, and environmental climate) show?
- What are the urbanization patterns like?
- How about technology adoption patterns?
- Are there any national development plans or pressing issues that present government development priorities? These could include: developing education infrastructure and boosting skill levels; sustainability and combating pollution; healthcare-related concerns, and so on.
- Which of these issues could present opportunities for your brand's social engagement and corporate social responsibility (CSR)?
- How could this knowledge inform your promotional efforts vis-à-vis the government and the general public?
- Are there any issues or development trends in your host country that affect channel preferences, buying habits, and the use of media and sales channels?
- Are there any legal limitations to advertising?

The Globalization Imperative

You should also assess *attitudes toward globalization* in your selected customer group. Answering some of the following questions:

- Are the customers in your segment likely to be local, glocal, or cosmopolitan?
- Are the customers in your segment likely to express ethnocentric tendencies? What about xenocentric attitudes?
- What are the contexts, roles, or product categories that may evoke ethnic identity in your selected group?
- What is the perception of global brands in your selected market and in your industry?
- Are there any country-of-origin biases in your host country that may affect attitudes toward your home brand? What is a perception of your home-country brand?
- How does your host country respond to globalization? Are there any distinct local responses in terms of hybrid cultures, polarization, or conflict?

References

Accor. (2019). *Celebrating Sofitel's French heritage!* Retrieved from https://group.accor.com/en/Actualites/2019/06/sofitel-live-the-french-way
Alaimo, K. P. (2017). *Tweet, or engage on the street. How to practice global public relations and strategic communications.* New York: Routledge.
Baidu. (2011). 广告中的误译, *in Chinese.* Retrieved from https://wenku.baidu.com/view/b8954543336c1eb91a375ded.html
Bain and Company. (2014). *Luxury goods worldwide market study fall-winter 2014: The rise of the borderless consumer. Luxury spending continues to grow amid demand for tourism and transportation.* Retrieved from www.bain.com/insights/luxury-goods-worldwide-market-study-december-2014/
Bardi, A., & Schwartz, S. H. (2003). Values and behavior: Strength and structure of relations. *Personality and Social Psychology Bulletin, 29*(10), 1207–1220.
Baughn, C. C., & Yaprak, A. (1996). Economic nationalism: Conceptual and empirical development. *Political Psychology, 17*(4), 759–778.
BBC. (2017). *Co-op's "treat your daughter" Easter egg adverts changed.* Retrieved from www.bbc.com/news/uk-england-manchester-39503373
Berger, R. R., Herstein, R., & Mitki, Y. (2013). Guanxi: The evolutionary process of management in China. *International Journal of Strategic Change Management, 5*(1), 30–40.

46

Chiu, C.-Y., & Cheng, S. Y.-Y. (2007). Toward a social psychology of culture and globalization: Some social cognitive consequences of activating two cultures simultaneously. *Social and Personality Psychology Compass*, *1*, 84–100.

Chiu, C.-Y., Kwan, L. Y.-Y., Li, D., Peng, L., & Peng, S. (2012). Culture and consumer behavior. *Foundations and Trends in Marketing*, *7*(2), 109–179.

Depeux, N. (2019). Art of naming: How semiotics and cultural codes can help you to find the right name for your brand? *Labbrand Brand Innovations*. Retrieved from www.labbrand.com/brandsource/art-of-naming-how-semiotics-and-cultural-codes-can-help-you-to-find-the-right-name-for-your-brand

Dion, D., & Arnould, E. (2011). Retail luxury strategy: Assembling charisma through art and magic. *Journal of Retailing*, *87*(4), 502–520.

Eriksen, T. H. (2007). *Globalization: The key concepts*. Oxford: Berg.

Ertimur, B., & Coskuner-Balli, G. (2015). Navigating the institutional logics of markets: Implications for strategic brand management. *Journal of Marketing*, *79*(2), 40–61.

European Central Bank. (2016). *The growing importance of emerging economies*. Retrieved from www.ecb.europa.eu/ecb/tasks/international/emerging/html/index.en.html

Financial Times. (2020). Backer of K-pop's BTS pushes ahead with IPO plans. Retrieved from www.ft.com/content/8a210c70-5785-11ea-a528-dd0f971febbc

Fitzsimmons, J., Fitzsimmons, M., & Bordoloi, S. (2014). *Service management: Operations, strategy, information technology* (8th ed.). New York: McGraw-Hill Irwin.

Grouzet, F. M. E., Kasser, T., Ahuvia, A., Fernández, J. M., Kim, Y., Lau, S. . . . Kennon, M. S. (2005). The structure of goal contents across 15 cultures. *Journal of Personality and Social Psychology*, *89*, 800–816.

Hancock, T. (2019). China's baby formula plan hits foreign producers. *Financial Times*. Retrieved from www.ft.com/content/714ed388-8695-11e9-97ea-05ac2431f453r

Handley, L. (2018). The luxury sector is growing faster than many others and Gucci is in the lead. *CNBC*. Retrieved from www.cnbc.com/2018/10/04/the-luxury-sector-is-growing-faster-than-many-others-and-gucci-leads.html

Herdin, T., Faust, M., & Chen, G. M. (2020). On the need for de-westernization of visual communication and culture in the global south. In T. Herdin, M. Faust, & G. M. Chen (Eds.), *De-westernizing visual cultures: Perspectives from the global south*. Baden-Baden: Nomos Publishing.

Herman, E., & Chomsky, N. (1988). *Manufacturing consent: The political economy of the mass media*. New York: Pantheon Books and Random House.

Hobbs, T. (2017). Unilever teams up with UN Women, Mars and Alibaba to wipe out gender stereotypes. The FMCG giant is launching the new global Unstereotype Alliance at Cannes Lions with the aim of banishing stereotypical portrayals of gender in all major advertising. *Marketing Week*. Retrieved from www.marketingweek.com/unilever-gender-stereotype-alliance/

Holt, D., Quelch, J., & Taylor, E. L. (2004). How global brands compete. *Harvard Business Review*. Retrieved from https://hbr.org/2004/09/how-global-brands-compete

Holton, R. (2000). Globalization's cultural consequences. *Annals of the American Academy of Political and Social Sciences, 570*(1), 140–152.

International School Consultancy Group. (2014). The booming international schools sector. *World Education News and Reports*. Retrieved from http://wenr.wes.org/2014/07/the-booming-international-schools-sector/

Kapoor, R., Paul, J., & Halder, B. (2013). *Service marketing: Concepts and practices.* New Delhi: Tata McGraw Hill Education.

Kim, J.-E., Lloyd, S., & Cervellon, M.-C. (2016). Narrative-transportation storylines in luxury brand advertising: Motivating consumer engagement. *Journal of Business Research, 69*(1), 304–313.

Kipnis, E., Broderick, A. J., & Demangeot, C. (2013). Consumer multiculturation: Consequences of multi-cultural identification for brand knowledge. *Consumption Markets and Culture, 17*(3), 231–253.

Kipnis, E., Broderick, A. J., Demangeot, C., Adkins, N., Ferguson, N. S., Henderson, G. R. . . . Zúñiga, M. A. (2013). Branding beyond prejudice: Navigating multicultural marketplaces for consumer well-being. *Journal of Business Research, 66*(8), 1186–1194.

Klein, J. G., Smith, C. N., & John, A. (2004). Why we boycott: Consumer motivations for boycott participation. *Journal of Marketing, 68*(3), 921–1109.

Ko, E. M., Costello, J. P., & Taylor, C. R. (2019). What is a luxury brand? A new definition and review of the literature. *Journal of Business Research, 99*, 405–413.

Koh, M. (2018). Same but different: Staying true to core brand essence while localizing. *Labbrand Brand Innovations*. Retrieved from www.labbrand.com/brandsource/issue-article/same-same-but-different-staying-true-to-core-brand-essence-while-localizing

Kravets, O., & Sandikci, O. (2014). Competently ordinary: New middle class consumers in the emerging markets. *Journal of Marketing, 78*(4), 125–140.

Kuiper, N. A., Grimshaw, M., Leite, C., & Kirsh, G. (2004). Humor is not always the best medicine: Specific components of sense of humor and psychological well-being. *Humor, 17*135–17168.

Labbrand Brand Innovations. (2015). Labbrand partners with club med to develop new brand Joyview by club med. *Labbrand Brand Innovations*. Retrieved from www.labbrand.com/news/labbrand-partners-club-med-develop-new-brand-joyview-club-med

Landler, M., & Barbaro, M. (2006). Wal-Mart finds that its formula doesn't fit every culture. *The New York Times*. Retrieved from www.nytimes.com/2006/08/02/business/worldbusiness/02walmart.html?mtrref=www.google.com&gwh=4D390E9CE7B321A5BE849BF51CEDA7CA&gwt=pay&assetType=REGIWALL

Livingstone, G. (2018). How quinoa is changing farmers' lives in Peru. *BBC*. Retrieved from www.bbc.com/news/world-latin-america-45008830

Lim, Y., Jaafar, M., Wu, E., & Wastuwidyaningtyas, B. (2016). *Capitalizing on Asia's booming upper middle class*. Boston Consulting Group. Retrieved from www.bcg.com/publications/2016/globalization-growth-capitalizing-asias-booming-upper-middle-class.aspx

Marquardt, M. (2011). *Building the learning organization: Achieving strategic advantage through a commitment to learning.* Boston, MA: Nicholas Brealey Publishing.

Martin, R. A. (2007). *The psychology of humor: An integrative approach.* Burlington, MA: Elsevier Academic Press.

McKinsey & Company. (2016). *Mapping China's middle class.* Retrieved from www.mckinsey.com/industries/retail/our-insights/mapping-chinas-middle-class

McManus, J., Winroth, M., & Angelis, J. (2019). *Service operations management: A strategic perspective.* London: Red Globe Press and Macmillan Publishers.

Megehee, C. M., & Spake, D. F. (2012). Consumer enactments of archetypes using luxury brands. *Journal of Business Research, 65*(10), 1434–1442.

Okonkwo, U. (2007). *Luxury fashion branding: Trends, tactics, techniques.* New York: Palgrave Macmillan.

Oxford University Press. (2007). *Oxford word of the year: Locavore.* Retrieved from http://blog.oup.com/2007/11/locavore/

Peterson Institute for International Economics. (2020). *What is globalization? And how has the global economy shaped the United States?.* Retrieved from www.piie.com/microsites/globalization/what-is-globalization

Phillips, B. J., & McQuarrie, E. F. (2011). Narrative and persuasion in fashion advertising. *Journal of Consumer Research, 37*(3), 368–392.

Pollay, R. W. (1983). Measuring the cultural values manifest in advertising. *Current Issues and Research in Advertising, 6*(1), 71–92.

Rao, P., Zhao, L., & Yue, H. (2008). The lucky number in stock price. *Management World, 11,* 44–49.

Ritzer, G. (1996). *The McDonaldization of society.* Thousand Oaks, CA: Sage Publications.

Rogers, R. (2013). *Digital methods.* Cambridge, MA: MIT Press.

Schnell, S. M. (2013). Food miles, local eating, and community supported agriculture: Putting local food in its place. *Agriculture and Human Values, 30*(4), 615–628.

Schuiling, I., & Kapferer, J.-N. (2004). Real differences between local and international brands: Strategic implications for international marketers. *Journal of International Marketing, 12*(4), 97–112.

Sheth, J. N. (2011). Impact of emerging markets on marketing: Rethinking existing perspectives and practices. *Journal of Marketing, 75*(4), 166–182.

Shimp, T. A., & Sharma, S. (1987). Consumer ethnocentrism: Construction and validation of the CET Scale. *Journal of Marketing Research, 24*(3), 280–289.

Steenkamp, J.-B. E. M., Batra, R., & Alden, D. L. (2002). How perceived brand globalness creates brand value. *Journal of International Business Studies, 34*(1), 53–65.

Steenkamp, J.-B. E. M. (2019). Global versus local consumer culture: Theory, measurement, and future research directions. *Journal of International Marketing, 27*(1), 1–19.

Steger, M. (2009). *Globalization: A very short introduction.* New York: Oxford University Press.

Stelling, O. (2020). *Speed and strategy: Communicating in the Asian century.* Retrieved from www.oliverstelling.com

Strizhakova, Y., Coutler, R. A., & Price, L. L. (2008). Branded products as a passport to global citizenship: Perspectives from developed and developing countries. *Journal of International Marketing, 16*(4), 57–85.

Sussan, F., Hall, R., & Laurie, A. M. (2012). Introspecting the spiritual nature of a brand divorce. *Journal of Business Research, 65*(4), 520–526.

Tai, S. (2004). The relationship of cultural values and message strategies in service advertising. *Marketing Intelligence & Planning, 22*(4), 438–454.

Theocharous, A. (2015). Food advertising as a mirror of intercultural differences: The case of the UK and Greece. *British Food Journal, 117*(4), 1256–1272.

University World News. (2012). *Worldwide student numbers forecast to double by 2025.* Retrieved from www.universityworldnews.com/article.php?story=201 20216105739999

Vorster, L., Kipnis, E., Bebek, G., & Demangeot, C. (2019). Brokering intercultural relations in the rainbow nation: Introducing intercultural marketing. *Journal of Macromarketing, 37*(4), 1–21.

Wallerstein, I. M. (2004). *World-systems analysis: An introduction.* Durham and London: Duke University Press.

Warc. (2016). *Unilever tackles ad stereotypes.* Retrieved from www.warc.com/NewsAndOpinion/News/37208

Wiedmann, K.-P., Hennings, N., & Siebels, A. (2009). Value based segmentation of luxury consumption behaviour. *Psychology and Marketing, 26*(7), 625–651.

Winit, W., Gregory, G., Cleveland, M., & Verlegh, P. (2014). Global vs local brands: How home country bias and price differences impact brand evaluations. *International Marketing Review, 31*(2), 102–128.

World Education News and Reviews. (2014). *The booming international schools sector.* Retrieved from http://wenr.wes.org/2014/07/the-booming-international-schools-sector

Xie, Y., Batra, R., & Peng, S. (2015). An extended model of preference formation between global and local brands: The roles of identity expressiveness, trust, and affect. *Journal of International Marketing, 23*(1), 50–71.

Xu, W. (2011). The classical Confucian concepts of human emotion and proper humour. In J. Chey & J. M. Davis (Eds.), *Humour in Chinese life and letters* (pp. 50–71). Pok Fu Lam: Hong Kong University Press.

Younge, G. (2014). Coca-Cola's super bowl ad showed that some Americans still can't take diversity. *The Guardian.* Retrieved from www.theguardian.com/commentisfree/2014/feb/09/coca-cola-super-bowl-ad-america-diversity

Yue, X. D. (2011). The Chinese ambivalence to humor: Views from undergraduates in Hong Kong and China. *Humor – International Journal of Humor Research, 24,* 463–480.

Yue, X. D., Jiang, F., Lu, S., & Hiranandani, N. (2016). To be or not to be humorous? Cross cultural perspectives on humor. *Frontiers in Psychology, 7,* 1495.

Decoding Culture
The Basics of Cultural Literacy

2

Introduction

Chapter 2 introduces the basics of cultural literacy. It discusses the main definitions of culture and different paradigms for understanding culture inclusive of etic vs. emic and essentialist vs. non-essentialist approaches. It also critically assesses the commonly accepted concept of national culture based on the idea of a culture within nation-states and their geographical boundaries. The chapter also discusses the prevalent "onion" approach to understanding cultures, inclusive of material and immaterial elements of culture. It introduces the concept of "cultural value orientations" as the empirically observable elements of culture. It also sheds light on different degrees of importance of cultural norms, inclusive of cultural imperatives, electives, and exclusives. Case-in-point examples include cultural symbols using the example of hamsa, Bouba, and the Kiki effect as an example of universal sensory experience, and a sensory approach to brand naming. The mini-case included with this chapter is Barbie and Häagen Dazs in China.

Chapter Objectives

- Understand the concept of culture and its main interpretations and definitions.
- Analyze the links between culture and consumer behavior.
- Distinguish between tangible and intangible elements of culture.
- Understand the concept of cultural values.
- Understand the differences between cultural values and cultural norms.

- Analyze the degrees of influence of cultural norms.
- Understand similarities and differences in cultural symbols and sensory perceptions.
- Become familiar with different approaches to studying and understanding culture.
- Critically assess the concept of national culture.

Warm-up question: *What can tell us more about a culture – its openness to change or its ability to retain traditional elements?*

Definitions of Culture

Culture is usually approached as the total sum of beliefs, rules, techniques, institutions, and artifacts that characterize human populations. It represents a set of values, norms, and patterns that are learned and shared, and believed to be common to the members of a given society.

Numerous interpretations of culture exist in the literature. Culture has been approached from the social perspective as a collective phenomenon (Markus & Kitayama, 2010), from the neuroscience perspective as it relates to biology (van den Bos, van Dijk, Westenberg, Rombouts, & Crone, 2011), and from the cognitive perspective as an issue of the mind (Oyserman, 2009). One of the most commonly accepted definitions of culture is Hofstede's (1980, p. 25) view of culture as "the collective programming of the mind which distinguishes one group from another."

American anthropologist Edward Hall (1976) divided cultures according to their communication practices into high-context (most of the information is implicit) and low-context cultures (most information is explicit). Regardless of which approach is taken, culture is commonly interpreted as a shared pattern of values, norms, and beliefs. It is seen as a force that shapes people's motivation, cognition, perception, language use, emotions, and moral reasoning (Heine, 2010).

No matter what the preferred definition is, culture is always interpreted as a collective phenomenon: any group of people that spends time together forms a culture with shared and transferable perceptions, values, or practices. Consequently, culture is also defined as an "evolved capacity for adaptation at a group level" (Hofstede, 2015, p. 547).

Nonetheless, as important culture is in social sciences and management research, it remains rather elusive. Attempts to capture its meaning in words is "like trying to seize the air in the hand, when one finds that it is everywhere except within one's grasp" (Lowell, 1934, p. 115). This is not to discourage the marketers from trying to fully grasp its influence, but rather, to remind them that one has to approach it with an open mind. Most likely, there will always be unknowns left to discover.

Culture Research in International Business

As businesses continue to globalize, awareness of culturally ingrained human behavior around the world is very important for the companies operating in international markets. Cultural knowledge is vital for the success of multinational organizations. In addition to offering opportunities to gain competitive advantages, cultural knowledge can also help the companies as a means to reduce a chance of managerial failure (Asante, Miike, & Yin, 2014). Thus, understanding and dealing with culture is strategically important for organizations and cultural knowledge presents an integral part of strategic management (Hofstede, 2015).

Cultural knowledge is important not just for successful organizational management but also for successful marketing efforts because "of the factors influencing consumer behavior, the most pervasive and thorny is culture" (Cleveland, Laroche, & Hallab, 2013, p. 958). Rather than using culture as an excuse for poor performance, brands are increasingly finding ways to use culture as a bridge to local consumers across the world. Increasingly, companies are recognizing opportunities to use cultural knowledge as a source of competitive advantage.

Culture has become a popular research subject in marketing. It has been researched primarily within the stream of research commonly called Consumer Culture Theory (CCT). This research approach presents an alternative to the traditional psychological-economic model used in marketing for interpreting consumers (Arnould & Thompson, 2005). In contrast to some other fields of marketing research, CCT research has increasingly focused on the sociocultural and symbolic aspects of consumption. These studies adopt a wide range of research approaches, and they assess consumption apart from the usual frames of economics and psychology. The researchers in this field of study suggest that a consumer culture denotes a "social arrangement in which the relations between lived culture and social resources, and between meaningful ways of life and the symbolic and material resources on which they depend, are mediated through markets" (ibid, p. 869).

Fitchett, Patsiaouras, and Davies (2015, p. 155) suggest that CCT is the most successful movement in consumer research, presenting an alternative to traditional approaches and diverging from "the view of the consumer as a utility maximizing, information aggregator, which then held sway, and to a remarkable degree still does in the marketing and consumer behavior fields."

What are the benefits of a sociocultural approach to analyzing consumers, as opposed to the traditional psychological-economic approach?

Culture and Consumer Behavior

American Marketing Association (2018) defines *consumer behavior* as "the dynamic interaction of affect and cognition, behavior, and the environment by which human beings conduct the exchange aspects of their lives." Among other things, this definition stresses the interaction between personal variables and the environment. Understanding cultural aspects of consumption is very important for marketers because most aspects of consumer behavior are believed to be culture-bound (De Mooij & Hofstede, 2011). There is a close link between consumption and culture because people buy products and services in a quest for self-actualization. Through what and how they consume, customers also seek to define their role in society.

Culture is one of the prime determinants of consumers' attitudes, behaviors, and lifestyles (Cleveland & Laroche, 2007). It plays a filtering role in the consumer's experience, determining how they perceive and interpret phenomena (Imrie, Durden, & Cadogan, 2000). Cultural differences impact decision making and they moderate natural human behaviors such as expression of emotions (Matsumoto, Olide, Schug, Willingham, & Callan, 2009). Cultural factors can also shape consumer thinking patterns and they can enhance the role of feelings and metacognitive experiences in consumer decision making. Culture also influences consumer information processing strategies. In sum, culture has a strong influence on consumer behavior, which in turn reinforces the manifestations of culture (Peter & Olson, 1998).

How does culture influence consumption?

Culture Literacy Kit

Hofstede (1991) introduced an *"onion" metaphor of culture*, and this interpretation of culture has become the most commonly adopted approach in culture research (Fang, 2012). The subsequent models proposed by other researchers such as Trompenaars and Hampden-Turner (1997) followed a similar approach.

The "onion" approach to understanding culture suggests that culture manifests through its different levels and layers, which are more or less visible to the observer. These levels represent the skins of the onion that we need to peel off in order to understand the core. The layers are seen in terms of outer, middle, and inner layers of culture.

The outer layer reflects the behavior that can be perceived through the five senses. This refers to the explicit level of culture inclusive of symbols, colors, artifacts, clothes, rituals, food, heroes, and language. The middle layer refers to the essential norms and values held by a certain cultural community. Within this layer, values are considered to be more internal while norms are more external and imposed by society – norms determine how values interact. Together, values and norms stipulate how people behave in a particular culture. The inner layer is the most hidden one, and it consists of basic assumptions and methods that a society has for dealing with everyday universal issues.

Using the "onion" metaphor, we can also distinguish between material and immaterial elements of culture. Material elements include artifacts, practices, food, clothing, or various cultural symbols, while the immaterial elements are values, norms, beliefs, language, heroes, and rituals.

Although this approach to analyzing cultures has been criticized as reductionistic, it may present a handy startup kit or a mental model for approaching cultures. This approach could be used as the first approximation for understanding the more complex, inner workings of culture.

What are the advantages of the "onion" approach to analyzing cultures?

Cultural Symbols and Images

Visual literacy is a very important element for understanding cultures (Herdin, Faust, & Chen, 2020). Visual symbols may signal the deeper, inner workings of a culture. Breninger and Kaltenbacher (2019, p. 51) suggest that our visual system is never unbiased and for this reason, we never perceive cultural differences as being neutral or objective; in fact, our "perception is always already significantly biased and infused with values by past experiences and intrinsic goals." This implies that past experiences are always engrained in the individual's norms and routine behaviors, and they affect how we process cultural symbols.

Cultural symbols work at a sensory level and they present a broad category of objects carrying a meaning that is unique to a particular group of people. Although language is a primary means of communication, visual cues are very important for effective intercultural marketing communication. Customers use a combination of spoken and written language and visual cues such as symbols, colors, and signs to interpret meanings. Some cultural symbols are unique to one culture and they may not exist in other cultures; or, they may exist but their meaning could be different in another culture.

For example, emojis, which first appeared on mobile phones in Japan in the 1990s, have been described as a universal form of visual communication. Nonetheless, they are used rather differently across cultures. For example, while in many Western cultures, an angel emoji – 😇 - is seen as a positive symbol, in others such as the Chinese, it signifies death. A thumbs up emoji – 👍 - seen as a positive and an encouraging symbol in most Western countries, could be considered offensive in Greece or in the Middle East (Rawlings, 2018).

Some symbols are fairly fixed, while others are dynamic and they change over time. For example, the cultural performance known as "luau" is unique to Hawaii and to Polynesia, as is the Yin Yang symbol in the Chinese philosophy and culture. Some other symbols have become more universal across cultures.

What universal cultural symbols could brands use across cultures?

Cultural Icons

Some cultural images are considered iconic, and the concept of iconicity helps consumers to understand the role of images in advertising across cultures. *Cultural icons* are artifacts that are recognized by members of a culture as being representative of that culture. Iconic symbols have a strong, analogical relationship between signs or symbols and the things, ideas, or values that the images represent (Sebeok, 2001). We can observe iconicity in some sounds, too. Such are the example of an onomatopoeia that sounds like a "choo-choo" train, recognizable in the English-speaking countries;

a "boom" as an impact sound recognizable across cultures; or classic music, which is believed to carry a universal sound symbolism. Visual images are, however, characterized by iconicity more than other means of communication.

For example, the Big Ben and a red telephone box are seen as the iconic symbols of England; matryoshka (матрёшка, in Russian) stacking dolls are seen as icons of the Russian culture; the Eiffel tower is perceived as a symbol of France; and a tartan or a patterned cloth found in Scottish kilts presents a cultural symbol of Scotland.

Is it a good idea for global brands to use the iconic cultural images from a host culture in their marketing campaigns?

A Case in Point: Hamsa

Some cultural symbols have been appropriated by multiple cultures, such as the nazars. Nazars are the charms, decorations, and amulets meant to protect from the "evil eye," or bad spirits. Nazars have been used in the Mediterranean, in Asia, and in the Middle Eastern cultures.

For example, "hamsa," a palm-shaped amulet is a symbol believed to protect people from the harm that comes from evil forces. It presents an ancient Middle Eastern talisman that became a protective symbol across cultures and religions. Hamsa is believed to protect from harm and to bring goodness, abundance, luck, wellness, and good health.

In the Arabic tradition, the hamsa hand symbolizes the hand of Fatima, the daughter of the Prophet Mohammed who was the last prophet of Islam. Hamsa means five in Arabic and it also presents five fingers of the hand. In the Sunni Muslim tradition, the hamsa is associated with the Five Pillars of Islam, and for the Shi'ites, it symbolizes the five "People of the Cloak" – Mohammed, his daughter Fatima, his son-in-law Ali, and his two grandsons Hassan and Husayn.

In the Jewish tradition, this symbol is seen as the hand of Miriam. In Hebrew, the number five is "hamesh," and the letter "hei" (ה), the fifth letter of the Hebrew alphabet, is also one of God's holy names in the Jewish tradition. The number five also presents five senses used in an effort to praise God.

Decoding Culture

Hamsa has been appropriated by Muslim, Jewish, Christian, and even Buddhist religions. Similar hand-related beliefs have also been used. In the Christian tradition, the Hand of Mary is used to help with healthy pregnancies and to protect the weak. Figure 2.1 shows the cultural symbol of Hamsa.

Figure 2.1 Hamsa.
Source: Photo by Alex Ringer, FreeImages.com.

Why is it important to understand cultural symbols across cultures? How can this knowledge help with marketing efforts?

Colors

Color is increasingly becoming a variable for marketing decisions involving product design, packaging, branding, and advertising. Different colors are linked to different levels of attention and activation, taste perceptions, and time perceptions (Divard, 2001). Colors also have physiological effects – for example, we can distinguish between the hot colors (red or orange) or the cold colors (such as blue or green) (Déribéré, 1968).

Colors have special meaning and symbolism across cultures, and the same color can evoke different sentiments in different cultures. For example, as a color of clothing, white is used for weddings gowns or for clothing worn on special occasions in the West. In the Arab countries, however, white is worn every day, and white is also used alternately with black as a color of mourning in India and Japan. In China, white is a color of mourning, death, and bad luck, and it is traditionally worn at funerals. Arguably, a lack of success for the white Parker's pens in China could partially be attributed to the Chinese negative attitude toward the color white. Thus, the idea of a white wedding gown is not universal across cultures – Chinese brides traditionally wore red gowns, although these habits have changed with globalization as Western traditions have been incorporated with the Chinese ones.

Cultures are also more or less elaborate with their range of words describing colors. For example, in Liberia, the Bassa people have only two words for color: "ziza" for the red/orange shades, and "hui" for the green/blue shades. On the other hand, the Inuit people living in the Arctic regions apparently have over 15 different words for white, and these colors represent different snow conditions.

Inspired by ancient Chinese calligraphy and the painting tradition called "shan shui" (山水, in Chinese), literally "mountain and water," the traditional Chinese painting style used only black and white to create an impression of depth and 3D effects. A saying exists that there are 10,000 shades between black and white, expressing the idea that we live between the extremes. Languages also use colors differently to describe feelings and states. For example, the expressions "having the blues" or "feeling green with envy" in English language are not directly translatable to other cultures and languages.

Although colors have unique cultural meanings, we can see some universality and associations between words and colors across cultures. Swiss phycologist Max Lüscher suggested that the sensory perceptions of color are fairly universal and shared across cultures, and they are guided at a subconscious level. Research suggests that across different cultures, people have similar associations to certain colors with a fair amount of consistency, while some colors have opposite meanings in different cultures (Jacobs, Keown, Worthley, & Ghymn, 1991).

Are there any important symbolic colors in your host country?

Heroes and Rituals

Heroes are people, alive or dead, real or imaginary, who possess the characteristics which are highly prized in a culture, and who also serve as models for behavior (IRMA, 2014). Heroes are often opinion leaders, celebrities, or people who are positively viewed in a society. They may influence consumer behavior through their association with certain products, brands, or product categories, regardless of their relation to the industry or expertise on the subject.

Some heroes are more directly related to the products they are associated with, such as Michael Jordan, a U.S. NBA player, and Nike sports apparel. Nike teamed up with Michael Jordan to launch the "Jordan Brand" featuring shoes and athletic wear. Others, like the U.S. actress Jennifer Aniston, acted as an ambassador for Smart Water from 2008–2020, without a direct association between the actress with water as a product.

Rituals are important nonverbal behaviors inherent to a specific culture. Rituals are often mistakenly interpreted as behavior of religious or mystical significance. Many cultural rituals may have origins in the ancient religious traditions, but they no longer carry explicit religious meanings. For example, the Feast of St. Anthony in Lisbon, called Lisbon Sardine Festival, celebrated on June 12th, honors St. Anthony, the city's patron saint. Mardi Gras is celebrated across Louisiana in the U.S. with culmination in New Orleans, the day before Ash Wednesday or the start of lent in the Western Christian tradition. This tradition, today mostly secular, dates back thousands of years and it celebrates the pagan spring and fertility traditions. The Surva, or the so-called "masquerade festival" in Pernik, Bulgaria, while a secular tradition today, goes back to the pagan Christian orthodox traditions and rituals aimed at fending off evil spirits.

How can global brands successfully tap into cultural rituals from a host culture?

Signs, Senses, and Brands

Semiotics is the study of signs and sign-using behavior. It is attributed to Swiss linguist Ferdinand de Saussure, who is considered one of its founders. Semiotics can help to explore cultural codes in order to understand how meaning is produced in a given society.

Depeux (2019) suggests that in addition to language, brands use signs and symbols to communicate their story across cultures, and this knowledge is a vital tool used in brand naming. Brand naming is particularly challenging across cultures, because finding universal associations is not always easy. Thus, some brands try to use more universal sound symbols. For example, brands can express their idea of ease by using onomatopoeia (HOP!) or simply by incorporating the word "easy" in their name, as in the EasyJet.

While many brands may seek universal symbols and associations across cultures, some brands also push the boundaries of convention and set new trends across cultures. Some brands have changed the naming landscape altogether as they challenged the long-standing naming norms. Such is the case of Airbnb which made it acceptable to use several consonants together in languages like French – thus, something that had previously felt distant and taboo can now evoke a friendly proximity and it can symbolize modernity (Depeux, 2019).

How can brands find the right balance between universal and culture-specific symbols and associations?

A Case in Point: The Bouba and Kiki Effect

Languages are believed to be connected to more universal human sensory experiences, and some abstract shapes and images may also be fairly universal across cultures. Based on the experiments conducted across several countries by German psychologist Wolfgang Köhler in 1929, we learned that distinctly different linguistic groups of people across the world may associate the same sounds with the same abstract images.

Respondents were presented with two abstract shapes: one of the shapes had softer edges and looked like a blob, and the other had sharp edges and looked spiky, as shown in Figure 2.2. They were asked to match the random onomatopoeic words "bouba" and "kiki" to the corresponding shape. Regardless of the language spoken in each country where the experiment was conducted, "bouba" was closely and repeatedly associated with the round, curvy symbol described as bulbous or blobby, and "kiki" was consistently matched with the sharp-angled shape, described as prickly or spiky.

These findings from the experiment conducted nearly 100 years ago are now recognized as the "Bouba & Kiki effect." This could be attributed to a close connection between language and sensory perceptions of objects and experiences, and it is explained through a sound symbolism that some words naturally evoke in people across cultures. Such is the recurring sound "ma" found in many different words for mother across distinctly different languages (adapted from Moon & Depeux, 2019).

Figure 2.2 Shapes used in the "bouba and kiki" experiment.
Source: Courtesy of Labbrand Brand Innovations.

Should global brands use universal symbolic associations between language, signs, and meanings, or should they use the more culture-specific ones?

Decoding Culture

A Case in Point: Sensory Approach to Brand Naming

Closely connected to the study of signs is the study of sensory perceptions. This knowledge could be used successfully in branding across cultures. Depeux and Rosatti (2019) show how various brands approach brand naming based on the universalities found amongst the sensory perceptions in different cultures. Brands can try to appeal to the five senses, inclusive of touch, sight, hearing, smell, taste, or a polysensorial experience, as shown in Figure 2.3.

TOUCH	SIGHT	HEARING	SMELL	TASTE	POLYSENSORIAL
• Feather • Goop	• Orange • Eclaz • Clearblue	• Crunch • TikTok • BlablaCar	• Rose Tonka • Safran	• NEQTA • Milk Makeup	• La Prairie • Rains • LIME

Figure 2.3 Sensory approach to brand naming.
Source: Courtesy of Labbrand Brand Innovations.

Feather, a Japanese razor brand, picked the word "feather" for their brand name to appeal to the sense of touch. Their goal was to convey a feeling that comes with smooth and caressing effects of the razor as it touches the skin, contrary to the sharpness of a blade.

Orange is a French telecommunications corporation. The color orange they selected for their logo symbolizes brightness and vitality, referring to the company's seamless service and appealing to the sense of sight.

Crunch is a brand of Nestlé, a Swiss food and beverage corporation. The name they selected, Crunch, symbolizes the sound of chewing the product and appeals to the sense of sound while alluding to its rich taste.

Safran is a French multinational aircraft engine, rocket engine, aerospace-component manufacturer and a defense company. Its name evokes a rare, expensive spice used in the old times. It helps to recollect its traditional role in the international trade, aiming to take customers on a far-away, exotic journey by appealing to their sense of smell.

63

> *Milk Makeup* is a U.S. makeup brand which prides itself in being cruelty-free, namely not testing their products on animals. Appealing to the sense of taste, their brand name reflects a taste of softness and simplicity, using milk as a symbol of nourishment and a pleasurable texture of their makeup products.
>
> *Lime* is a U.S.-based electric scooter brand. Its brand name appeals to the polysensory experience and it is meant to evoke both sight and taste. It suggests freshness and vitality, with the term also referring to the green color or lime, sustainability, and environmental protection (summarized from Depeux & Rosatti, 2019).
>
> *How can marketers tap into sensorial experiences in their branding efforts?*

Approaches to Studying Culture

Multiple approaches are used simultaneously to study the influence of culture, including multicultural, cross-cultural, and intercultural. While they sound rather similar, there are some notable differences between them reflecting different approaches to cultural analysis.

Multicultural research focuses on describing a society that has different cultural or ethnic groups seen to co-exist alongside one another; however, they aren't necessarily treated as if they actively interact with each other. Rather, they are understood and approached as relatively independent unities that might overlap, although they are not necessarily analyzed as groups that interact actively on a daily basis.

Cross-cultural research compares and contrasts cultural patterns in order to understand the differences between cultural groups. Most culture research thus far has been cross-cultural in nature. The majority of studies have been conducted at a country level, using national culture as a unit of analysis. This approach departs from the assumption that one dominant culture holds the norm for the entire group in a country.

Intercultural research, on the other hand, explores interactions between cultural groups which overlap and interact more actively. It analyses the cultural changes as well as culture clashes that happen due to their ongoing interactions (Levine, Park, & Kim, 2007).

Even within their home country, marketers need to cater to rather diverse cultural groups. These efforts are most commonly referred to as *ethnic marketing*, especially in the U.S. It is important for marketers to connect with diverse cultural audiences which fall outside of the perceived majority or outside of the mainstream culture in a given market. Often, concepts of multicultural, cross-cultural, and intercultural marketing are used interchangeably with ethnic marketing. Nonetheless, the term ethnic marketing is used most often when targeting diverse audiences within the same home culture.

Ethnic marketing is a commonly used expression for marketing efforts across various cultural groups in the U.S. Ethnic marketing has gained in importance and popularity, with companies and marketing agencies trying to leverage ethnic consumers. This is not surprising since many brands have faced a backlash for insensitive advertising that has been offensive to multicultural communities. Furthermore, according to Nielsen research, 21 of the 25 most populated counties in the United States are already mostly multicultural, and they include "numerically significant pluralities of traditionally minority populations, or are already majority-minority" (Morley, 2016).

We can also distinguish between etic vs. emic and essentialist vs. nonessentialist approaches to studying culture. The *etic approach* to cultural analysis advocates generalization and it focuses on the common issues across cultures, while the *emic approach* focuses on culture-specific traits (Berry, 1989). *Essentialist approaches* to cultural analysis categorize people from a culture based on their essential qualities, which are seen as a part of human nature, such as value systems; on the other hand, *non-essentialist approaches* to culture are rooted in the human conditions (Nathan, 2015). Essential models based on the concept of cultural dimensions have been widely accepted in marketing, likely because they have been relatively easy to test empirically, which has led to a rich body of research. Nonetheless, there are concerns due to an over-reliance on these models because they run a risk of stereotyping and simplifying cultures.

Critical studies based on non-essentialist approaches, on the other hand, examine jointly constructed understandings, reminding us that human conditions vary and that they are not static in any culture (Nathan, 2015). This approach suggests that the reality is socially and experientially based, and dependent on individuals and groups holding the constructs. Thus, knowledge is created in the process of interactions, and it does not exist independently (Holden, 2002). Most studies focusing on cultural influence on consumption have applied etic and essentialist approaches. Concerns due to an over-reliance on these approaches in marketing research are discussed more in-depth in Chapter 8.

The concept of cultural metaphors, discussed in Chapter 8, presents another set of lenses for understanding culture (Gannon, 2011). These include examples such as the Japanese garden or American baseball. These metaphors reflect characteristics of a nation – a phenomenon, activity, or institution that its members find important and with which they identify cognitively and/or emotionally (Gannon, 2011).

How can researchers decide on the right approach for studying culture?

National Culture

In management research, culture is commonly interpreted as a national culture construct. The commonly accepted concept of *national culture* in business has permeated marketing research, and national culture has been used as the primary unit of analysis. This approach departs from the assumption that nations have distinct cultural characteristics. National culture, or a culture of the nation-state defined in its geographical boundaries, is recognized as one of the most enduring components in international business.

This approach is controversial and ambiguous for a number of reasons (Beugelsdijk, Kostova, & Roth, 2017). It should be approached with a critical eye since a country should not be equated with a national culture. Also, cultural values are not static at a country level – researchers should distinguish between country-effect and culture-effects (ibid).

Cultures are also constantly interacting and colliding with one another, and consequently, cultural values are constantly evolving within the same cultural group. There are also variations with acceptance of various cultural values and norms, as well as their different expressions within the same nation-state. Thus, we cannot assume that cultural value orientations are indigenous to all the people from the same city, area, or country.

However, abandoning the concept of national culture appears far-fetched because markets are primarily defined in their geographical boundaries (Kirkman, Lowe, & Gibson, 2017). Thus, although using nations as units of analysis may be a controversial approach, nonetheless, the national culture concept is not entirely obsolete. Researchers have suggested that it could still be used as the "best first guess" about cultures, since the differences between the regions or subcultures within a country do not necessarily cancel out certain national culture traits (Minkov & Hofstede, 2011).

The national culture concept has, however, been challenged on various grounds. In order to really understand cultural identity, marketers need to look at a range of factors beyond being born into a nation, a race, or an ethnicity (Craig & Douglas, 2006). In addition to understanding cultural diversity within a country, marketers also need to consider similarities across the national borders (House & Javidan, 2004). Researchers argue that cultural differences are not only reflected at a national level, but are possible across regions (Kase, Slocum, & Zhang, 2011). Nonetheless, although the relevance of national culture as a unit of analysis has been disputed, the role of nations in international business remains relevant.

What are the advantages and disadvantages of the national culture concept?

Cultural Values

In the 1950s, anthropologist Clyde Kluckhohn suggested that cultures have certain unifying characteristics. These include, for example, a quest for answers to some essential questions in life, preferred patterns of living, and unique ways of dealing with important issues in life. At the core of the quest for understanding these important issues lies the concept of cultural values, and this concept has also been at the core of marketing research. In business and marketing research, values have been interpreted as the most important manifestation of culture, and they have been used to distinguish one culture from another.

Cultural value systems include a broad range of beliefs and attitudes that a group holds. They help people direct their efforts and resources toward achieving desirable goals, and they present standards that transcend specific situations. Values motivate action and serve as the guiding principles in life. Although they are rather stable, they are often unconscious and present the prototypes of behavior.

Values are plural, comparative, and systematic, which allows for their grouping into dimensions. They have hierarchies and a different relative importance in different countries. As enduring beliefs, values have strong impact on behavior, and in particular, values related to tradition have strong correlations with the corresponding behaviors that express them.

What are the main values in your home culture?

Decoding Culture

Research on Values

Value systems include a broad range of beliefs and attitudes that a group holds, and among them, cultural values present the basic predispositions defining human attitudes and behaviors (Meglino & Ravlin, 1998). Values also serve as criteria for identifying differences among social groups (Taras, Rowney, & Steel, 2009).

Values are seen to hold the keys to understanding culture. Commonly, culture researchers suggest that behaviors, attitudes, cognitions, and emotions are largely based on one's values. As enduring beliefs, values are very stable and they form the bedrock of a culture (Bardi & Schwartz, 2003).

Cultural values are also at the root of consumer behavior processes (Arnould, 1989). They present a powerful force that shapes consumers' motivations, lifestyles, and product choices, helping people by directing their efforts and resources toward achieving desirable goals (Kahle, 1983). Values present the commonly held standards of what's acceptable, unacceptable, important, unimportant, right, or wrong – cultural values and norms provide a set of rules for how people communicate, behave, and make decision about what to consume.

Values motivate action and serve as enduring and guiding principles in life, standards or criteria that transcend specific actions and situations (Schwartz, 1994). Being remarkably stable, they present "an enduring belief that a specific mode of conduct or end-state of existence is personally or socially preferable to an opposition or converse mode of conduct or end-state" (Rokeach, 1973, p. 14). Values have also been explained as a centrally held belief which "guides actions and judgments across specific situations and beyond immediate goals to more ultimate end-states of existence" (Rokeach, 1968, p. 161). Values are often unconscious, and they refer to "broad tendencies to prefer certain states of affairs over others" (Hofstede, 2001, p. 5).

Values are also the most abstract of social cognitions that serve as prototypes from which attitudes and behaviors are manufactured, and their influence on behavior is a rather complex process (Homer & Kahle, 1988). Hofstede (2015, p. 548) suggests that history points to a great continuity of values at the societal level: "despite pervasive and ubiquitous change in practices, such as technologies and ways of subsistence, culture at the level of values of entire populations is remarkably stable."

68

Values are plural and comparative to one another, rather than being isolated from one another (Schein, 2010). They are also systematic, and have thus been organized into groups and dimensions (Tsui, Xin, & Wang, 2006) which allows for their analysis.

However, values cannot be empirically observed or analyzed because of their abstract nature. Therefore, we observe values through *cultural value orientations*. They present value expression, which highlights the empirically observable elements of cultural values (Kluckhohn & Strodtbeck, 1961): we cannot observe values that are abstract, but we can observe their expressions. The concept of cultural value orientations has been operationalized in international business and marketing research through the idea of cultural dimensions, discussed in Chapter 6. While it presents a useful construct and a good first approximation for understanding cultures, it should be used with caution (Osland & Bird, 2000). Relying solely on this approach could lead to simplification of complex cultures (Tung & Verbeke, 2010).

What are the main characteristics of cultural values?

Cultural Norms

Cultural norms determine how values interact and they focus on the influence of shared expectations within social environments about what constitutes appropriate behaviors (Chua, Roth, & Lemoine, 2015). They present an expected code of conduct based on the values inherent to a certain cultural group. Cultural norms have different degrees of importance in different cultures. Understanding the norms is particularly important in the so-called "tight cultures." Tight cultures have stronger social norms and consequently, there is a lower tolerance for deviations that come with a consequent degree of sanctioning; on the other hand, the so-called "loose cultures" are less restrictive and have more diverse norms, and their enforcement is also weaker (Gelfand, Nishii, & Raver, 2006). This degree of tightness could affect the strength of value effects – in tight cultures, these effects are stronger (Taras, Steel, & Kirkman, 2016).

Some societal norms and ideals are culture-specific while others are not. For example, Hispanic and Asian women often use bleaching agents to make their skin appear whiter, because white skin is associated with beauty in these cultures. In some other countries, such as Nigeria, some women take fattening agents because skinny is not the beauty ideal for women there, and this is the reverse of the beauty ideal in the West.

Also, while emotions such as anger, joy, or sadness are universal across the globe, their expression, the meaning attached to them, and the commonly accepted intensity of these emotions vary across cultures (De Mooij & Hofstede, 2011). The norms for expressing these emotions are different across cultures too. For example, East Asians tend to control negative emotions such as anger and sadness and they tend to display mostly the positive emotions such as joy and happiness.

Different body parts also play a role in interpreting emotions. For example, in the Japanese culture, people tend to focus more on the eyes in their interpretation of what is communicated, while Americans tend to focus on the mouth (De Mooij & Hofstede, 2011). It goes without saying that these generalizations should not be used in absolute terms, but rather as a guiding framework for a more in-depth cultural analysis.

What are the main norms of behavior in your home culture?

Degrees of Cultural Norms' Importance

We can also assess degrees of importance of cultural norms by distinguishing between cultural imperatives, cultural electives, and cultural exclusives (Cateora, Gilly, & Graham, 2009). *Cultural imperatives* present conditions that must be met and the cultural norms that must be adhered to. They are the customs that one must conform to in a certain culture. One such example is relationship building needed to conduct business in Asian, Middle Eastern, and many Latin American countries, or in Southeast Europe. There, business is not done with companies but with people, and therefore it is a cultural imperative to spend time building relationships before starting or proceeding with business dealings.

Also, it is an imperative not to cause someone embarrassment in many cultures, for example by raising a voice, or by correcting or criticizing someone in public. This is often explained with a concept of "face," which is universally understood as "self-awareness of social evaluation" (Qi, 2011, p. 280). "Face," however, has unique expressions across cultures. In some cultures, such as the Chinese, for example, the concept of face has different contextual connotations based on a situation. In fact, in the Chinese language there are two words representing it: "mianzi" (面子, in Chinese) or a social face indicating a quest for prestige; and "lian" (脸, in Chinese), a moral face, or the confidence of the society in the integrity of someone's moral character (ibid).

Cultural electives are the cultural norms that foreigners may wish to obey; however, they are not required to conform to them. In other words, they are nice to know and adhere to but not a must. In fact, most cultural customs belong in the cultural elective category. For example, alcohol is offered at the start of business meetings in certain cultures regardless of time of day. While this custom may be uncomfortable to some, it is important to learn to politely decline or make a ceremonial or a symbolic attempt to adhere to the norms to the best of one's ability, regardless of how different they may be.

Cultural exclusives are the cultural norms which are reserved exclusively for the locals. These are the customs that are off limits to foreigners or to out-of-group members. Often, these include references to religion or jokes about politics or unique local customs. At times, an inappropriate use of humor using cultural references can lead to the opposite effect and appear disrespectful and sarcastic. For example, a foreign brand of mineral water used an advertisement with a picture of the Ganges River, one of the most sacred symbols of Indian culture with a tagline "Only from clean water." This alluded to the Indian customers that the water from the Ganges river is not clean, and it offended them (Chiu, Kwan, Li, Peng, & Peng, 2012).

Marketers should be careful when it comes to core, or essential, cultural traditions. For example, customers could respond favorably to mixing of elements from different cultures, if they do not infringe with the essential cultural norms. Such are the examples of Häagen-Dazs offering ice-cream in the shape of moon cakes in China, or Starbucks serving moon cakes in Western coffee flavors such as Caramel Macchiato in non-Western cultures. Nonetheless, research also suggests that customers may disapprove of marketing practices that refer to essential cultural traditions: for example, while Chinese consumers may react favorably to a book on Western cuisine to inspire Chinese culinary traditions, they may disapprove of a book about Western philosophy inspiring Confucianism (Chiu et al., 2012).

The influence of norms also differs across product categories. Some normative behaviors are used for habitual, low involvement purchasing decisions. These purchases are made frequently and pose low risk and uncertainty such as everyday items purchased in grocery stores. Consumers are more likely to make decisions based on cultural norms for frequently purchased items. On the other hand, when making high involvement, complex purchasing decisions that carry more risk and require more deliberation, customers may or may not rely on cultural norms. In the case of high involvement purchases, consumers may relate to their cultural norms as just one of the options available to them, though they may not be the main point of reference. For high risk purchases, customers may be more likely to explore other options and to rely on their personal clues (Lee & Semin, 2010).

Is there a strict distinction between imperatives, electives, and exclusives? If so, what is it?

Nonconforming

Traditionally, studies suggested that adhering to commonly accepted social norms brings rewards, while nonconforming may lead to sanctioning and exclusion from social groups. However, *nonconforming* can also create positive inferences in the eyes of observers. Nonconforming refers to behaviors that are inconsistent with the commonly accepted values or norms (Nail, Macdonald, & Levy, 2000). People may want to appear different from others they dislike or disapprove of, and signal their distinctiveness and uniqueness (Simonson & Nowlis, 2000). Also, those who signal that they are unconstrained by normative pressures can also be perceived as having more power than others (Van Kleef, Homan, Finkenauer, Gundemir, & Stamkou, 2011).

People who are visibly nonconforming can also signal freedom, autonomy, or expertise as compared to those who are following cultural norms (Sparkman & Walton, 2017). Thus, deviating from social norms can in fact bring benefits of higher status to individuals, contrary to the traditional perceptions of social rewards for adhering to and sanctioning for deviating from the norms (Warren & Campbell, 2014).

A Word of Caution

Not all consumers behave in a culturally typical manner. Very few individuals in a culture follow cultural norms in all situations. Individuals tend to adhere to cultural norms if they are consistent with their personal values and agendas, and this makes it easier to follow the norms of the majority (Zhang & Chiu, 2012). Traditionally, following cultural norms is important because it leads to social inclusion, brings rewards, and serves as a powerful social mechanism for adhering to group norms (McFerran, Dahl, Fitzsimons, & Morales, 2009).

Although culture research in international business and marketing has primarily focused on values (Earley, 2006), it is worth pointing out that researchers have raised doubts about the usefulness of the value concept.

Notably, there are mixed results in the research suggesting that values may not be sufficient as a concept for understanding cultures (Gelfand et al., 2006).

Mini-Case: Barbie and Häagen-Dazs

The mini-case contrasting Barbie and Häagen Dazs in China offers examples of brand ignorance and brand engagement.

Why Did Barbie Fail in China?

American toy maker Mattel had big plans for its Barbie flagship store in Shanghai when it opened a six-floor store, the world's largest, in China in 2009. Their Shanghai store had one of the largest collections of Barbie dolls in the world, as well as accessories and Barbie-related products such as furniture, clothes, and a café. To celebrate Barbie's 50th anniversary, the company invested over $30 million dollars in the ambitious "House of Barbie" in Shanghai.

With the rapidly developing Chinese middle class who invest more money in their children than most of their counterparts around the world, especially in education (up to 50% of their disposable income), it was hardly imaginable that the House of Barbie could fail. In particular, considering the implications of the one-child policy in China, the investment in the youngest generation in China at that point was unparalleled in history.

The store however closed in 2012, just over two years after it had opened. What happened? Mattel failed to localize the brand in one of the most lucrative and fastest developing retail markets in the world. Did it underestimate China? Or did it overestimate the power of the iconic American brand? A number of reasons could be attributed to this failure.

Primarily, Barbie was not recognized as a lifestyle fashion symbol or as a cultural icon in China. Furthermore, it was not compatible with Chinese cultural values. The ideal of "femininity" in the West that Barbie embodies, was not something that Chinese girls could identify with. There, Barbie was just a doll, and the Chinese consumers didn't care much about all the Barbie-related products. Thus, the experience store concept did not resonate with Chinese consumers because they could not relate to the Barbie symbolism and the values it upholds. The market in China was also not ready for Barbie at that time: although the Chinese economy was booming, Western culture had not yet proliferated everyday life.

Thus, the Chinese could not identify with a 50-year-long Barbie tradition from the U.S. and the story that comes with it. Furthermore, it was only launched in a single store on Shanghai's high street, rather than also across China's second- or third-tier cities. Considering that the company did not source in China, the products were also expensive for the Chinese at the time, and soon after the launch, Barbie knock-offs were available in the local markets across China.

The American nostalgia toward the Barbie doll did not resonate well in the Chinese consumers' minds. They recognized only the Barbie dolls, but not the Barbie brand culture. In fact, many children around the world do not care that Barbie is blond! For example, Rapunzel Barbie was launched in its identical form in 59 countries and half of the global sales came from outside of the U.S. Equally, Mulan and Jasmine dolls sold well across different countries, regardless of not having the traditional Barbie identity (adapted from Labbrand Brand Innovations).

Why Did Häagen-Dazs Succeed in China?

Häagen-Dazs came boldly into China in the 1990s when Chinese consumers were unaccustomed to dairy products. At that time, the idea of having a desert was very different in China than it was in the West. In spite of this situation, Häagen-Dazs charged five times higher prices than in the U.S. and it fast became an iconic desert shop in China. The brand adapted culturally while also retaining its foreign brand identity. Owing to this, it became one the most successful foreign food brands in China ever. Rather than competing with domestic ice-cream producers, Häagen-Dazs catered to the evolving Chinese tastes for luxury foods such as expensive foreign ice-cream. The company used this opportunity and positioned itself in a unique niche of luxury deserts.

Häagen-Dazs also adjusted to the seasonal habits of the Chinese customers and it sold ice-cream mostly during the warmer seasons. They obtained an in-depth knowledge of the Chinese consumers and their cultural habits. For example, the Chinese consumers were less likely to bring ice-cream boxes home but would much rather eat it with others in a store instead.

Thus, Häagen-Dazs created a luxury Western experience across its stores, rather than merely selling its ice-cream products. Their high prices were not a problem either because they signaled quality and luxury elements. Eating Western ice-cream quickly become a status symbol in China.

Häagen-Dazs also adapted to the Chinese gifting culture and offered expensive gift-wrapped ice-cream products. By doing so, it tapped into the Chinese culture of gifting and face saving by offering expensive, luxurious gifts that their customers could purchase for others. It also respected the Chinese holidays by selling moon-cake shaped ice-cream products during the Mid-Autumn festival. It also introduced culture-specific flavors such as Green Tea, and offered a hotpot ice-cream experience combining fruits, chocolate and chopsticks (adapted from Labbrand Brand Innovations).

Mini-Case Questions

- What is the main difference between the approaches taken by Mattel and Häagen-Dazs in China?
- What could Mattel have done differently?
- Would entering the Chinese market later have made a difference?
- Considering the evolving nature of the luxury segment, was Häagen-Dazs right to position as a luxury desert in China?
- Can Häagen-Dazs maintain their luxury status in China over time?

Chapter 2 Guiding Questions

Perceptions of imagery are culturally coded. Consider some of the following as you think about *advertising appeals:*

- What are the main cultural symbols and colors in your host country?
- Are there any issues with impact of colors, brand names, and brand associations?
- Are there any distinct gestures in your host country?
- What are the main rituals?
- How different are the rituals from those in your brand home country?
- What are some cultural imperatives, electives, and exclusives?
- What would imply brand ignorance or brand tolerance?
- What would it take to achieve brand engagement?

References

American Marketing Association. (2018). Retrieved from www.ama.org

Arnould, E. J. (1989). Toward a broadened theory of preference formation and the diffusion of innovations: Cases from Zinder Province, Niger Republic. *Journal of Consumer Research*, 16(2), 239–267.

Arnould, E. J., & Thompson, C. J. (2005). Consumer Culture Theory (CCT): Twenty years of research. *Journal of Consumer Research, 31*(4), 868–882.

Asante, M. K., Miike, Y., & Yin, J. (2014). *The global intercultural communication reader.* New York: Routledge.

Bardi, A., & Schwartz, S. H. (2003). Values and behavior: Strength and structure of relations. *Personality and Social Psychology Bulletin, 29*(10), 1207–1220.

Berry, J. W. (1989). Imposed etics – emics-derived etics: The operationalization of a compelling idea. *International Journal of Psychology, 24*(6), 721–735.

Beugelsdijk, S., Kostova, T., & Roth, L. (2017). An overview of Hofstede-inspired country-level culture research in international business since 2006. *Journal of International Business Studies, 48*(1), 30–47.

Breninger, B., & Kaltenbacher, T. (2019). De-westernization an impossible epistemic shift? Visual research avenues for a genuine paradigm shift in communication studies. In T. Herdin, M. Faust, & G. M. Chen (Eds.), *De-westernizing visual cultures: Perspectives from the global south.* Baden-Baden: Nomos Publishing.

Cateora, P. R., Gilly, M. C., & Graham, J. L. (2009). *International marketing.* New York: McGraw-Hill Irwin.

Chiu, C.-Y., Kwan, L. Y.-Y., Li, D., Peng, L., & Peng, S. (2012). Culture and consumer behavior. *Foundations and Trends in Marketing, 7*(2), 109–179.

Chua, R. Y. J., Roth, Y., & Lemoine, J. F. (2015). The impact of culture on creativity: How cultural tightness and cultural distance affect global innovation crowdsourcing work. *Administrative Sciences Quarterly, 60*(2), 189–227.

Cleveland, M., & Laroche, J. (2007). Acculturation to the global consumer culture: Scale development and research paradigm. *Journal of Business Research, 60*(3), 249–259.

Cleveland, M., Laroche, J., & Hallab, R. (2013). Globalization, culture, religion, and values: Comparing consumption patterns of Lebanese Muslims and Christians. *Journal of Business Research, 66*(8), 958–967.

Craig, S. C., & Douglas, S. P. (2006). Beyond national culture: Implications of cultural dynamics for consumer research. *International Marketing Review, 23*(3), 332–342.

De Mooij, M., & Hofstede, G. (2011). Cross-cultural consumer behavior: A review of research findings. *Journal of International Consumer Marketing, 23*(3), 181–192.

Depeux, N. (2019). Art of naming: How semiotics and cultural codes can help you to find the right name for your brand. *Labbrand Brand Innovations.* Retrieved from www.labbrand.com/brandsource/art-of-naming-how-semiotics-and-cultural-codes-can-help-you-to-find-the-right-name-for-your-brand

Depeux, N., & Rosatti, C. (2019). Art of naming: Conveying sensoriality in naming. *Labbrand Brand Innovations.* Retrieved from www.labbrand.com/brandsource/conveying-sensoriality-in-naming

Déribéré, M. (1968). *La couleur dans les activités humaines.* Paris: Dunod.

Divard, R. (2001). Le consommateur vit dans un monde en couleurs. *Recherche et Applications en Marketing, 16*(1), 3–24.

Earley, P. C. (2006). Leading cultural research in the future: A matter of paradigms and taste. *Journal of International Business Studies, 37*(6), 922–931.

Fang, T. (2012). Yin Yang: A new perspective on culture. *Management and Organization Review, 8*(1), 25–50.

Fitchett, J. A., Patsiaouras, G., & Davies, A. (2015). Myth and ideology in consumer culture theory. *Marketing Theory, 14*(4), 495–506.

Gannon, M. J. (2011). Cultural metaphors: Their use in management practice as a method for understanding cultures. *Online Readings in Psychology and Culture, 7*(1). Retrieved from https://scholarworks.gvsu.edu/orpc/vol7/iss1/4

Gelfand, M. J., Nishii, L. H., & Raver, J. L. (2006). On the nature and importance of cultural tightness-looseness. *The Journal of Applied Psychology, 91*(6), 1225–1244.

Hall, E. (1976). *Beyond culture*. New York: Anchor Books.

Heine, S. (2010). Cultural psychology. In S. T. Fiske, D. T. Gilbert, & G. Lindzey (Eds.), *Handbook of social psychology* (5th ed., Vol. 2, pp. 1423–1464). Hoboken, NJ: John Wiley & Sons, Inc.

Herdin, T., Faust, M., & Chen, G. M. (2020). On the need for de-westernization of visual communication and culture in the global south. In T. Herdin, M. Faust, & G. M. Chen (Eds.), *De-westernizing visual cultures: Perspectives from the global south*. Baden-Baden: Nomos Publishing.

Hofstede, G. H. (1980). *Culture's consequences: International differences in work-related values*. Beverly Hills, CA: Sage Publications.

Hofstede, G. J. (2001). *Culture's consequences: Comparing values, behaviors, institutions, and organizations across nations*. Thousand Oaks, CA: Sage Publications.

Hofstede, G. J. (2015). Culture's causes: The next challenge. *Cross Cultural Management: An International Journal, 22*(4), 545–569.

Holden, N. J. (2002). *Cross-cultural management: A knowledge management perspective*. London: Prentice Hall.

Homer, P. M., & Kahle, L. R. (1988). A structural equation test of the value-attitude-behaviour hierarchy. *Journal of Personality and Social Psychology, 54*(4), 638–646.

House, R. J., & Javidan, M. (2004). Overview of Globe. In R. J. House, P. J. Hanges, M. Javidan, P. W. Dorfman, & V. Gupta (Eds.), *Culture, leadership and organizations. The Globe study of 62 societies* (pp. 9–28). Thousand Oaks, CA: Sage Publications.

Imrie, B. C., Durden, G. R., & Cadogan, J. W. (2000). Towards a conceptualization of service quality in the global market arena. *Advances in International Marketing, 1*, 143–162.

Information Resources Management Association (IRMA). (2014). *Marketing and consumer behavior: Concepts, methodologies, tools and applications*. Hershey, PA: Business Science Reference.

Jacobs, L., Keown, C., Worthley, R., & Ghymn, K. I. (1991). Cross-cultural colour comparisons: Global marketers beware! *International Marketing Review, 8*(3), 21–30.

Kahle, L. R. (1983). *Social values and social change: Adaptation to life in America.* New York: Praeger.

Kase, K., Slocum, A., & Zhang, Y. (2011). *Asian versus Western management thinking: Its culture-bound nature.* New York: Palgrave Macmillan.

Kirkman, B. L., Lowe, K. B., & Gibson, C. B. (2017). A retrospective on culture's consequences: The 35-year journey. *Journal of International Business Studies, 48*(1), 12–29.

Kluckhohn, F. R., & Strodtbeck, F. L. (1961). *Variations in value orientations.* Evanston, IL: Row, Peterson.

Lee, A. Y., & Semin, G. R. (2010). Culture through the lens of self-regulatory orientations. In R. S. Wyer, C.-Y. Chiu, & Y.-Y. Hong (Eds.), *Understanding culture: Theory, research and application* (pp. 299–310). New York: Psychology Press.

Levine, T. R., Park, H. S., & Kim, R. K. (2007). Some conceptual and theoretical challenges for cross-cultural communication research in the 21st century. *Journal of Intercultural Communication Research, 36*(3), 205–221.

Lowell, L. (1934). *At war with academic traditions in America.* Cambridge, MA: Harvard University Press.

Markus, H. R., & Kitayama, S. (2010). Cultures and selves: A cycle of mutual constitution. *Perspectives on Psychological Science, 5*(4), 420–430.

Matsumoto, D., Olide, A., Schug, J., Willingham, B., & Callan, M. (2009). Cross-cultural judgments of spontaneous facial expressions of emotion. *Journal of Nonverbal Behavior, 33*, 213–238.

McFerran, B., Dahl, D. W., Fitzsimons, G. J., & Morales, A. C. (2009). I'll have what she's having: Social influence and body type on food choices of others. *Journal of Consumer Research, 36*(6), 915–929.

Meglino, B., & Ravlin, E. (1998). Individual values in organizations concepts, controversies, and research. *Journal of Management, 24*(3), 351–389.

Minkov, M., & Hofstede, G. (2011). Is national culture a meaningful concept? Cultural values delineate homogeneous national clusters of in-country regions. *Cross-Cultural Research, 46*(2), 133–159.

Moon, S., & Depeux, N. (2019). Art of naming: Making sense of sound – Sound symbolism & naming. *Labbrand Brand Innovations.* Retrieved from www.labbrand.com/brandsource/art-of-naming-making-sense-of-sound-sound-symbolism-naming

Morley, C. (2016). Why focusing on cross-cultural consumers is essential for the growth of your brand. *Forbes Magazine.* Retrieved from www.forbes.com/sites/chrismorley/2016/12/05/why-focusing-on-cross-cultural-consumers-is-essential-for-the-growth-of-your-brand/#4a9b944f3634

Nail, P. R., MacDonald, G., & Levy, D. A. (2000). Proposal of a four-dimensional model of social response. *Psychological Bulletin, 126*(3), 454–470.

Nathan, G. (2015). A non-essentialist model of culture: Implications of identity, agency and structure within multinational/multicultural organizations. *International Journal of Cross Cultural Management, 15*(1), 101–124.

Osland, J. S., & Bird, A. (2000). Beyond sophisticated stereotyping: Cultural sensemaking in context. *Academy of Management Executive, 14*(1), 65–79.

Oyserman, D. (2009). Does culture influence what and how we think? Effects of priming individualism and collectivism. *Psychological Bulletin, 134*(2), 311–342.

Peter, J. P., & Olson, J. C. (1998). *Consumer behavior and marketing strategy*. Boston, MA: McGraw-Hill.

Rawlings, A. (2018). Why emoji mean different things in different cultures. *BBC*. Retrieved from www.bbc.com/future/article/20181211-why-emoji-mean-different-things-in-different-cultures

Qi, X. (2011). Face: A Chinese concept in a global sociology. *Journal of Sociology, 47*(3), 279–295.

Rokeach, M. (1968). A theory of organization and change within value-attitude systems authors. *Journal of Social Issues, 24*(1), 13–33.

Rokeach, M. (1973). *The nature of human values*. New York: Free Press.

Schein, E. H. (2010). *Organizational culture and leadership*. San Francisco, CA: Jossey-Bass.

Schwartz, S. H. (1994). Are there universal aspects in the content and structure of values? *Journal of Social Issues, 50*(4), 19–45.

Sebeok, T. A. (2001). *Signs: An introduction to semiotics* (2nd ed.). Toronto: University of Toronto Press.

Simonson, I., & Nowlis, S. M. (2000). The role of explanations and need for uniqueness in consumer decision making: Unconventional choices based on reasons. *Journal of Consumer Research, 27*(1), 4–68.

Sparkman, G., & Walton, G. M. (2017). Dynamic norms promote sustainable behavior, even if it is counternormative. *Psychological Science, 28*(11), 1663–1674.

Taras, V., Rowney, J., & Steel, P. (2009). Half a century of measuring culture: Approaches, challenges, limitations, and suggestions based on the analysis of 121 instruments for quantifying culture. *Journal of International Management, 15*(4), 357–373.

Taras, V., Steel, P., & Kirkman, B. L. (2016). Does country equal culture? Beyond geography in the search for cultural boundaries. *Management International Review, 56*(4), 455–487.

Trompenaars, F., & Hampden-Turner, C. (1997). *Riding the waves of culture: Understanding cultural diversity in business*. London: Nicholas Brealey Publishing.

Tsui, A. S., Xin, R., & Wang, H. (2006). Organizational culture in China: An analysis of culture dimensions and culture types. *Management and Organization Review, 2*(3), 345–376.

Tung, R. L., & Verbeke, A. (2010). Beyond Hofstede and globe: Improving the quality of cross-cultural research. *Journal of International Business Studies, 41*(8), 1259–1274.

van den Bos, W., van Dijk, E., Westenberg, M., Rombouts, S. A., & Crone, E. A. (2011). Changing brains, changing perspectives: the neurocognitive development of reciprocity. *Psychological Science, 22*(1), 60–70.

Van Kleef, G. A., Homan, A. C., Finkenauer, C., Gundemir, S., & Stamkou, E. (2011). Breaking the rules to rise to power: How norm violators gain power in the eyes of others. *Social Psychological and Personality Science, 2*(5), 500–507.

Warren, C., & Campbell, M. C. (2014). What makes things cool? How autonomy influences perceived coolness. *Journal of Consumer Research, 41*(2), 543–563.

Zhang, A. Y., & Chiu, C.-Y. (2012). Goal commitment and alignment of personal goals predict group identification only when the goals are shared. *Group Processes and Intergroup Relations, 15*, 42–437.

Universal Criteria for Understanding Cultures

Introduction

Chapter 3 discusses the universal criteria for understanding cultures inclusive of Schwartz's groups of universal human values, as well as the concept of Aristotle's triangle as a guideline for universal persuasion efforts. It also discusses universal segmentation criteria across cultures from the perspective of usage and industry segmentation. It also provides additional frameworks for understanding cultural universalities such as the view of cultures as those of honor, achievement, and joy. It also introduces the Intercultural Affinity Segmentation Framework by EthniFacts which is derived from the practice. Case-in-point examples include blockchain, Airbnb, and Oatly in the U.S. The mini-case included in Chapter 3 is Fenty Beauty by Rihanna.

Chapter Objectives

- Understand the basic groups of universal human values.
- Become familiar with the drivers of persuasion through the concept of "Aristotle's triangle."
- Understand alternatives for segmenting cultures such as usage and industry segmentation.

Warmup question: *what are universal segmentation criteria that could be used to understand different cultures?*

Universal Criteria

Universal Human Values

Shalom Schwartz (1994), a social psychologist and cross-cultural researcher, interpreted values as the criteria that people use to justify their own behavior and judge others as well as oneself. He proposed that human values have unconscious nature and serve as abstract prototypes of behavior. Schwartz divided all human values into four basic groups: openness to change; self-transcendence; conservation; and self-enhancement. These *universal human values* are shown and summarized in Figure 3.1.

Openness to change encompasses hedonism, stimulation, and self-direction. *Hedonism* refers to the culture's propensities to enjoy life and receive pleasure, and it shares the elements of both openness to change as well as

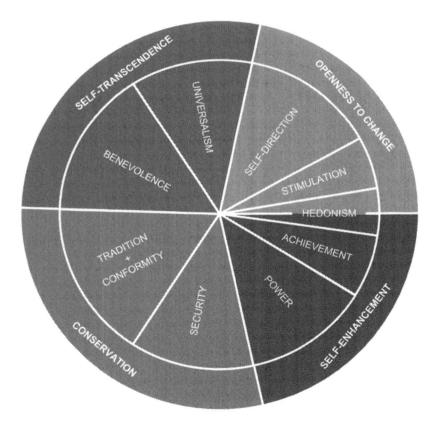

Figure 3.1 Schwartz's theory of basic values.
Source: Gimenéz and Tamajón (2019).

self-enhancement; *stimulation* refers to a need for a variety of experiences and excitement in life, and *self-direction* expresses the desire for freedom, creativity, and independence.

Self-transcendence consists of universalism and benevolence. *Universalism* is the motivation to understand, appreciate, tolerate, and protect the welfare of all people and nature, and *benevolence* means the preservation and enhancement of the welfare of one's family and friends.

Conservation consists of tradition, conformity, and security. *Tradition* refers to respect, commitment, and the acceptance of the customs stipulated by one's culture and religion; *conformity* suggests self-discipline, restraint from harmful actions to others, obedience, and politeness; *security* refers to stability, harmony, and safety.

Self-enhancement includes power and achievement. *Power* represents the attainment of social status and prestige, and *achievement* stands for enjoying personal success, being regarded as capable, ambitious, intelligent, and influential.

While Schwartz offered a comprehensive approach for understanding human values that could be used as a basis for psychographic segmentation in marketing, their application has not been as universally accepted as the dimensional approaches suggested by Hofstede and Trompenaars and Hampden Turner. Nonetheless, dimensional approaches found inspiration in Schwartz's idea that values transcend specific situations, that they are stable over time, and that they are comparative in nature which allows for their systematic grouping and analysis.

How can Schwartz's value model be applied in marketing?

The Art of Persuasion – Aristotle's Triangle

Assuming that some relatively universal values exist across cultures, we can identify universal ways to appeal to these values. We can apply the art of persuasion or rhetoric known as *Aristotle's triangle*. This concept is attributed to the Greek philosopher Aristotle (Ἀριστοτέλης, in Greek), who lived approximately between 384 and 322 B.C.E.

The idea behind this approach is as follows: for any successful persuasion message, we need to identify cognitive and emotional triggers, and also convey a message in a way that signals authority and legitimacy. If we apply the universal art of persuasion to our communication, we are more likely to win both the hearts and the minds of our audience. This approach entails three elements of ethos, pathos, and logos, which present the three core elements of persuasion techniques. Good persuasive technique should balance all three elements, and this refers to both visual as well as verbal messages. While these three aspects of persuasion are universally human, interpretations of these elements are different across cultures.

Ethos (ήθος, in Greek) places focus on the speaker or the "persona." Its origins are found in the Greek word for character and it is used to represent credibility and the values of the speaker, and his or her authority and virtue. Credibility is achieved by promoting factors such as status, achievement, expertise, or simply by appealing to the popularity of the speaker. It is easier to make a decision when someone we respect or simply know of endorses a product, regardless of whether or not the person has product-specific expertise.

When a popular public figure endorses a product, it validates it to the end-consumer. For example, referring to the earlier example, Jennifer Aniston was used to advertise Smart Water by Glaceau, although she is no expert in water. Ethos also means choosing the right language register that is appropriate both for the audience as well as the topic.

Pathos (πάθος, in Greek) shifts the focus from the speaker to the audience. Originating from the Greek words for "suffering" as well as a strong "experience," it is meant to elicit emotions in the audience. It appeals to audience's basic emotions like joy, fear, and envy. These emotions create responses – ideally, the action of buying something. For example, Coke is known for appealing to joy and happiness, and this is shown in their advertising campaigns such as "Open Coke, Open Happiness."

Focusing on pathos can also imply the appeals to negative emotions such as fear. For example, BMW uses an image of a metal leg in its campaign against drunk driving, with a message "spare parts for humans are not original as those for cars." In order to appeal to pathos, companies need to use appropriate language and the emotional tone appropriate to the various cultures. The main idea behind this approach is to establish not only the current emotional state but also the target emotional state that a speaker wants to elicit in the audience.

Logos (λόγος, in Greek), originating from the Greek term for logic, focuses on the message itself. It brings logic into play by using evidence and facts, and by "listening to reason." This is achieved by showcasing cool or new features and by sharing the best reasons to buy the product. Insurance companies in the U.S. often use this approach. For example, Progressive, one of the largest car insurance companies in the U.S., focuses on promoting a range of specific features and offers detailed information on savings and extra service benefits in comparison to its competitors. Its competitor Geico's campaign "15 minutes could save you 15% or more on car insurance" has become one of the most memorable insurance company campaigns and the "one advertiser it is OK to love," according to Griner (2019). Both examples show appeal to logos.

How companies appeal to these three elements differs across cultures. For example, the famous catchphrase by Crest, Procter & Gamble (P&G) brand of toothpaste and other oral hygiene products is, "four out of five dentists recommend Crest toothpaste." This may be suitable in many Western cultures to signal ethos, or the credibility of the source, but in some other cultures, such as the Chinese, their tagline appealing to pathos, "behind that healthy smile, there's a Crest kid," may be more appropriate.

How can Aristotle's triangle be applied in different realms of marketing?

Segmentation and Targeting

Market segmentation presents the key to successful strategy. Marketers depart from the assumption that a mass market consists of many homogenous groups – or segments – that could be identified using various criteria. The main challenge is in selecting some segments, while ignoring groups. Furthermore, the needs of different segments are often conflicting and could even be mutually exclusive.

Therefore, some companies have different brands targeting different customer segments, such as hotels focusing on mass and luxury markets. There are various financial, marketing, and operational advantages of multibranded hotels. We can see multiple examples such as Homewood Suites and Hilton Garden Inn; or Marriott's Downtown, Courtyard, and SpringHill Suites; or the range of Accor Hotel brands from Sofitel and Raffles, to Ibis and Novotel.

The process of segmentation implies dividing a market into distinct groups of customers that have common characteristics and needs. This is followed by targeting, used to analyze how attractive each segment is, all while focusing on the customers most likely to purchase the product. Traditional criteria for segmentation include demographics (age, gender, income, marital status, education, ethnic group, or occupation), psychographics (attitudes, motives, values, activities, interests, opinions, or lifestyle), purchasing behavior (how people shop), benefits (tangible, visible benefits of a product or a service) or geographics (rural or urban, zip code, and similar).

Successful segmentation helps to meet customer needs, identify new niches, gain a competitive advantage, and enable a better use of company resources. It sounds simple, but there are tradeoffs because there are limitations to how many segments a company could target, and many companies are facing a dilemma as to which specific variables/criteria to select.

Targeting, or the decisions about prioritizing, involve a process of analyzing how attractive each segment is based on considerations such as size (how big and valuable each segment is); potential (how stable the segment is, whether it has growth potential, if there are factors hampering its development); whether the company can deliver; and whether it has enough resources to meet the needs of that segment and sustain the same level of production or customer service. Factors such as competitive landscape, as well as general micro and macro market forces, also affect this choice.

The targeting process is challenging enough for marketers in a home market, and these challenges are amplified in international markets. We can also identify a range of universal psychographic segmentation criteria across cultures. We can see that in some industries, a few universal segmentation criteria can cut across cultural boundaries, such as trust.

Universal Segmentation Criteria: Trust and Sharing Economy

Trust, which has different expressions across cultures, is at the core of many companies' business models (Piovesan, 2018). Trust is also behind the idea of collaborative consumption, the concept at the very core of sharing economy (Botsman & Rogers, 2010). This concept has helped companies such as Airbnb, Uber, and Udemy, for example, to reshape how we think of consumption. It has enabled people across the world to work together across geographical, economic, political, and cultural boundaries.

Trust is a universal value and an enabler for people to work together regardless of their backgrounds, and it has always been central to the functioning of modern society. However, trust is a concept that is rather complex to understand because it has both rational and idiosyncratic characteristics (Möllering, 2001). It has been researched by many disciplines and still, there are no common definitions of it. The concept of trust has evolved through history from being confined to immediate and restricted individual networks to third parties deemed to have the authority needed to conduct business transactions, such as organizations, governments, or banks. For example, a shared religion or a shared language may suggest that there is more underlying trust that drives exchange patterns. The three following examples show how trust and humor as segmentation criteria work across different cultures and industry segments.

What other universal segmentation criteria can we identify across cultures?

A Case in Point: Trust and Blockchain

The traditional idea of trust has been revisited, and its complexity has increased significantly in the digital space due to a combination of both technological as well as sociological components. We can see this clearly in the blockchain industry that has managed to cut across cultural, political, and geographical differences. For example, with the development of information technology, blockchain has challenged the assumption about traditional organizations being best suited to manage market transactions or consumers needing a trusted third party to conduct them (Yermack, 2017).

Blockchain systems are transparent, decentralized systems, in contrast to the traditional centrally coordinated monetary systems that contemporary societies are based on. Decentralization in this case leads to more transparency monitored via the public peer-to-peer networks, and each transaction is verified by consensus of a majority of participants. This is very different from the traditional, centralized financial management mechanisms.

Parties without a pre-established trust can conduct transactions safely: security mechanisms are provided by the peers involved in the same activity, rather than by the "trusted" authoritative third party (Freeman, Beveridge, & Angelis, 2019). This redefined notion of trust and its distribution in the crypto world has transformed how we think about organizations across the world, no matter what the underlying cultural value system is (Seidel, 2017).

How has trust contributed to the development of blockchain technology?

A Case in Point: Airbnb

We can see another example of a similar universal segmentation approach with Airbnb, a U.S.-based online marketplace which lets people rent out their properties or spare rooms to guests. Many of us around the world grew up with the "stranger-danger" imperative. We were taught as children that strangers may bring danger and that we should refrain from interacting with people we don't know.

The idea that people who don't know each other want to cooperate based on voluntary trust is at the core of sharing economy, a peer-to-peer activity of acquiring, providing, or sharing access to goods and services facilitated by an online platform. The idea that humans can trust each other no matter where they are in the world, connected through a technology infrastructure, helps to overcome the stranger-danger imperative.

At the core of this approach is design thinking, which, in words of Tim Brown, the Executive Chair of the design agency IDEO, "brings together what is desirable from a human point of view with what is technologically feasible and economically viable."

Airbnb has used the idea of designing for trust in order to provide a sense of belonging anywhere within the global community which is connected through a shared technological infrastructure. They performed a joint study with Stanford exploring people's willingness to trust someone based on how similar they are. The research showed that we prefer to trust people who are like us: the more different somebody is, the less we trust them – a natural social bias. Airbnb's solution was to design a platform for trust where people can share their love of travel and move beyond cultural and other differences. In their words, "the right design can actually help us overcome one of our deepest rooted biases" (Airbnb.com).

Their social campaign launched in January 2015 called #OneLessStranger has sparked significant attention. With its brand vision of bringing the world together, Airbnb dedicated a micro-site, airbnb. cm/one-less-stranger. Airbnb asked the hosts across the world to perform an unexpected kind act of hospitality for a stranger, then take a photo or video with the person to share on social media.

They also donated money to individuals to encourage them to commit a random act of hospitality and take a video or a photo with that person, and then share it using the OneLessStranger hashtag. Three weeks later, this hashtag was trending with over 3 million interactions from around the world (Airbnb.com; Campaign U.S., 2014).

What was the key of Airbnb's success?

Sustainability

Sustainability is another common denominator that increasingly serves as a unifying segmentation criterion across cultures. While there is a global shift toward more sustainable consumption, it is risky to assume that attitudes toward sustainability are the same across cultures. These attitudes are influenced by cultural predispositions, and there are cultural antecedents behind environmental concerns and pro-environmental consumer behavior.

A Case in Point: Oatly in the U.S.

A cultural norm of drinking cow's milk has traditionally been very strong in the U.S. However, over the past ten years, concerns over healthy eating have changed consumer perceptions and plant-based dairy alternatives have seen rapid development. Traditionally, rice and soy milk have served as alternatives to dairy in the U.S., catering to a relatively small segment of society. Although other alternatives such as oat milk have traditionally been popular in Europe, they have been considered fringe products at best in the U.S. until recently.

Companies like Oatly, the Swedish oat drink company, managed to influence the change in social norms in the U.S. Their branding was based on consumer education about the benefits of oat milk. They managed to reconcile between culturally appropriate individual health concerns and universal, societal-focused sustainability concerns across cultures.

Universal Criteria

Their campaign focused on communicating to customers that oat milk requires less water to produce than some other popular plant-based milk alternatives, thus leaving a smaller carbon footprint. At the same time, its nutritional value and smooth texture that resembles whole milk was an important message used to appeal to individual health needs (adapted from Weng, 2019).

Figure 3.2 Oatly's advertising.
Source: Courtesy of Oatly.

> However, it was hard for U.S. consumers to get used to the oat milk taste and texture. To work around this limitation, instead of selling a product, Oatly chose to sell a sustainability vision with a phrase "be human and not a logo" (The Challenger, 2016). To that end, they used humor in advertising to show authenticity.
>
> For example, they embraced the feedback by someone trying oat milk for the first time with the message, "It tastes like sh*t! Blah!" which they used in a prominent ad in the *New Yorker*, shown in Figure 3.2. This approach has helped the Swedish brand to become a challenger brand disrupting the dairy industry in the U.S.
>
> *What drives different attitudes toward sustainability across cultures?*

Cultural Superstitions

Culture also influences consumer behavior through *superstitions* (Chiu, Kwan, Li, Peng, & Peng, 2012). For example, Chinese consumers may be more inclined to buy a cup of coffee with a price tag of 28 RMB – the Chinese currency – instead of an identical cup of coffee from the same coffee shop that sells at 24 RMB, considering that eight is a lucky number while four is unlucky in the Chinese culture. This preference for the number eight and aversion toward the number four affects marketing communications messages – the number eight is used much more frequently than the number four in product advertisements in China (Chiu et al., 2012).

Cultural symbols and superstitions equally affect stock market activity. In the stock markets in Hong Kong, Shanghai, and Shenzhen, the A-shares are more than twice as likely to end with a number eight than with a number four (Rao, Zhao, &. Yue, 2008).

Why is it important for marketers to understand cultural superstitions across cultures?

Other Universal Perspectives of Culture

We can also use a perspective of the world in which only three main cultural groups exist: cultures of honor, cultures of achievement, and joy cultures

(Basanez, 2016). *Cultures of honor* adhere to tradition, value religion, gender roles, and authority. In these cultures, tradition, social, and family values are very important. *Cultures of achievement* on the other hand value egalitarianism, individualism, productivity, and gender equality. *Cultures of joy* value the wellbeing of both individuals and society and quality of life, and they place less importance on hierarchy. While these classifications offer a preliminary framework to interpret cultures, they could not be applied to gain a more in-depth insight of cultures.

Recently, practitioners have proposed more contemporary frameworks for analyzing the new cultural landscape in the U.S. where the majority of the population is either multicultural or directly influenced by intercultural interactions. EthniFacts (2020) is a U.S.-based research company that specializes in ethnic marketing and helps companies to understand consumer behavior at the intersection of personality and culture. Moving past the traditional segmentation criteria and demographic indicators, they suggest that a more realistic market view is necessary to accommodate the growing multicultural influence.

In rapidly evolving multicultural environments, consumers react differently to brand communications – consequently, traditional approaches may not apply. EthniFacts suggest that these contemporary consumers are characterized by a response that is:

Faster – instant reaction to both real and hearsay samples of brand voices and advertising across all traditional and new channels;

Louder and broader – individually and socially, more effective broadcasting of their personal voices on continually expanding channels;

Angrier and more personal – with shorter fuses of toleration and patience that are more difficult to defuse and respond to;

More collective and combative – assertive group identity that reinforces and spreads self-interest reactions and "us vs. them" discourse; and

More likely to "walk their talk" – consumer actions and reactions will speak much louder than their words, with greater impact on purchasing.

(Source: EthniFacts)

Intercultural Affinity Segmentation Framework

EthniFacts also remind us that "in this shifting landscape, there is a convergence of cultures led by individuals who seek new experiences across cultures." One such approach for identifying these individuals and addressing a growing complexity of multicultural consumption is proposed in their "*Intercultural Affinity Model*," shown in Figure 3.3. The framework classifies consumers in five main groups inclusive of monoculturals, sideliners, explorers, enthusiasts, and ambiculturals.

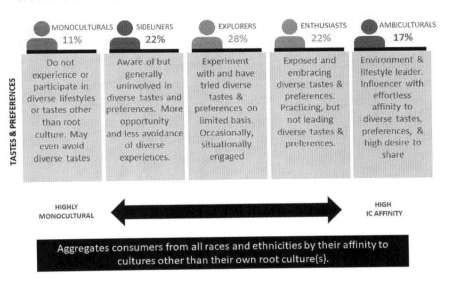

Figure 3.3 Intercultural Affinity Model.
Source: Courtesy of EthniFacts.

How could the Intercultural Affinity Model be applied in other cultures? Which of these segments, if any, could be applicable to your project? How can the framework inspire your segmentation and targeting efforts?

A Word of Caution

Although some of the aforementioned universal segmentation criteria across cultures appear promising, nonetheless it is not easy to apply them in marketing with a high degree of accuracy. They can be used to obtain a more in-depth knowledge of a culture; nonetheless, marketers should not rely on them alone. Multiple universal and culture-specific segmentation criteria should be combined in order to determine the best marketing approach.

Although many human values are universal, some meaningful human variations also exist across cultures. For example, in all cultures people want to remain healthy; however, in some cultures personal health is seen as a core value, whereas for others it may be less of a priority as compared with, for instance, affluence, status, or "face" (most often interpreted as reputation). Some cultures may trust in modern science and medicine, while others may place more trust in their traditional or homespun remedies. Equally, some may believe that they can improve or maintain their health by their own actions, while others may hold a more fatalistic view whereby their own actions are seen to make less of a difference.

It is also important to remember that some product characteristics are fairly uniform across cultures, such as, for example, products for children, technology, or sportswear. Food and beverage, on the other hand, are among the most culture-specific product categories. Services are also generally harder to standardize. They are experiential in nature, and experience means different things in different cultures. However, some services such as higher education are becoming increasingly globalized due to global mobility of students and the internationalization of the workforce.

Mini-Case: Fenty Beauty by Rihanna

Fenty Beauty (stylized FEИTY BEAUTY) by Rihanna was an instant success when it was launched in 2017. In its first 40 days on the market, it made $100 million in sales. Shortly afterwards, it became a global branding icon.

For many years, the global beauty industry has been criticized for its lack of diversity, and for its racial and national bias. At the time Fenty Beauty was launched, the beauty industry had already started to embrace diversity and inclusion. Rihanna recognized that the timing was right to tackle the issue of diversity. There was a need to create fashion products catering to a wider range of skin tones, including the ones that are hard to match using traditional brands. In particular, she saw an opportunity for promoting makeup use across gender lines. Its release was therefore well received by diverse consumers who had previously felt ignored by the mainstream beauty brands.

Because of the inclusivity message, Fenty Beauty has been positively received by consumers across different cultures. It is sold across the world, from China to Saudi Arabia. It has quickly proliferated the popular culture – for example, it was featured in the 2019 song by Ariana Grande. Fenty's ProFilt'R foundation includes fifty skin shades and it was named one of Time Magazine's best inventions of 2017. In fact, it was so successful that some subsequent attempts by the competitors inspired by her idea were not as successful.

What were the key attributes of Fenty Beauty's success? Rihanna offered a solution for some long-standing industry issues that cut across cultural differences, and addressed universal issues faced by all women across the world. By introducing the diversity that was previously unseen in the beauty industry, Fenty Beauty pushed the boundary of the makeup industry toward more inclusivity and diversity regardless of complexion and gender. A year after the Fenty Beauty launch, the rest of the industry followed suit, and there were more shades of makeup than ever launched by all main beauty brands.

The "foundation for all" principle promoted by Fenty Beauty meant that women of any skin shade could find the right makeup, from very dark to women with albinism who could use makeup that did not make their skin look orange. This led to a strong emotional connection with the brand, especially by women who found their perfect makeup shade for the first time ever. This branding inclusivity was so iconic that the term "Fenty effect" was coined to signify chain reaction and other brands launching more than forty shades of makeup, including Dior, Maybelline, and CoverGirl.

This effort to cater to such a wide range of skin tones was met with enthusiasm by conscious consumers outside of the makeup range. Fenty Beauty sent a message that everyone deserves complex options, not just in the beauty industry. This inclusivity was apparent not just in the product line but also in Fenty Beauty advertising and social media campaigns. It featured a range of models from all ethnicities and orientations, and it became one of the biggest beauty campaigns in YouTube history.

This trend of featuring diverse beauty models was later followed by other mainstream brands. The brand also tapped into the global shift toward sustainability, advertising its products as 100% cruelty free, never tested on animals. They didn't even allow suppliers or affiliates to test on animals on their behalf.

Universal Criteria

Figure 3.4 Fenty Beauty by Rihanna.
Source: Courtesy of Labbrand Brand Innovations.

The brand encouraged people to have fun with makeup and to experiment, rather than to wear makeup like a uniform. It also inspired consumers around the world to define their own idea of beauty, and to use makeup to express their unique identity past the idea of uniform beauty standards. It disrupted the traditional brand rules and beauty stereotypes, and created the grounds for social change across cultures (Mackenzie, 2017; Labbrand Brand Innovations, 2019; Time, 2018). Figure 3.4 shows Fenty Beauty advertising.

Mini-Case Questions

- Why was Fenty Beauty an instant success?
- What societal issue did it address?
- How did the brand manage to cut across so many distinctly different culture segments?
- Can you think of other brands that achieved success owing to a similar approach?

Chapter Guiding Questions

Think of your target group in the selected host country, and consider the following elements that would help you craft your *messaging strategy*:

Think of your *culture*:

- What are possible expressions of Schwartz's four groups of basic human values?
- What are the main emotional triggers of your target group?
- What are their main cognitive triggers?
- Who are the heroes in your host country? What is distinct about them?
- What personas could you use to enhance the "ethos" element of the Aristotle's triangle?

Think of your *target segment*:

- Who is your target audience? What demographic segmentation criteria will you use?
- What about psychographic?
- Are there any universal values that you could use for psychographic segmentation?
- How will you target them? How will you position your product?
- What are the similarities/differences (home/host country)?
- What cultural factors are most pertinent to them in regard to packaging, website, communications campaign, and advertising, etc.?

References

Basanez, M. E. (2016). *The world of three cultures. Honor, achievement and joy.* New York: Oxford University Press.

Botsman, R., & Rogers, R. (2010). *What's mine is yours. The rise of collaborative consumption.* New York: Harper Collins.

Campaign U.S. (2014). *Airbnb lets users 'pay it forward' with #OneLessStranger.* Retrieved from www.campaignlive.com/article/airbnb-lets-users-pay-forward-onelessstranger/1327693

The Challenger. (2016). *An interview with John Schoolcraft, the creative director of Oatly.* Retrieved from https://thechallengerproject.com/blog/2016/oatly

Chiu, C.-Y., Kwan, L. Y.-Y., Li, D., Peng, L., & Peng, S. (2012). Culture and consumer behavior. *Foundations and Trends in Marketing, 7*(2), 109–179.

EthniFacts. (2020). Retrieved from www.ethnifacts.com

Freeman, S., Beveridge, I., & Angelis, J. (2019). Ascendants and drivers of digital trust in the crypto industry. In M. Ragnedda & G. Destefanis (Eds.), *Blockchain and web 3.0: Social, economic, and technological challenges.* London: Routledge.

Gimenéz, C., & Tamajón, L. G. (2019). Analysis of the third-order structuring of Shalom Schwartz's theory of basic human values. *Heliyon, 5*(6), 1–7.

Griner, D. (2019). How Geico became the one advertiser it's ok to love. The insurer and the martin agency reflect on 25 years and their best ads. *Ad Week*. Retrieved from www.adweek.com/agencies/how-geico-became-the-one-advertiser-its-ok-to-love/

Labbrand Brand Innovations. (2019). Going deeper than the buzz: Fenty beauty, the brave boundary breaker. *Labbrand Brand Innovations*. Retrieved from www.labbrand.com/brandsource/going-deeper-than-the-buzz-fenty-beauty-the-brave-boundary-breaker

Mackenzie, M. (2017). Fenty beauty is awarded "invention of the year" by Time Magazine. *Allure*. Retrieved from www.allure.com/story/fenty-beauty-invention-of-the-year-2017

Möllering, G. (2001). The nature of trust: From Georg Simmel to a theory of expectation, interpretation and suspension. *Sociology, 35*(2), 403–420.

Piovesan, M. (2018). *A foundation of trust is how the sharing economy thrives.* Retrieved from www.entrepreneur.com/article/315809

Rao, P., Zhao, L., & Yue, H. (2008). The lucky number in stock price. *Management World, 11*, 44–49.

Schwartz, S. H. (1994). Are there universal aspects in the content and structure of values? *Journal of Social Issues, 50*(4), 19–45.

Seidel, M. (2017). Questioning centralized organizations in a time of distributed trust. *Journal of Management Inquiry, 27*(1), 40–45.

Time. (2018). Fenty beauty: Broadening makeup's palette. Retrieved from https://time.com/collection/genius-companies-2018/5412503/fenty-beauty/

Weng, E. (2019). Labbrand brand innovations, going deeper than the buzz: How Oatly became the trendiest plant milk on the market. *Labbrand Brand Innovations*. Retrieved from www.labbrand.com/brandsource/going-deeper-than-the-buzz-how-oatly-became-the-trendiest-plant-milk

Yermack, D. (2017). Corporate governance and blockchains. *Review of Finance, 21*(1), 7–31.

4 Conceptual East–West Differences
Psychological Processes, Philosophical Traditions, Stimuli Processing, and Paradoxical Thinking

Introduction

Chapters 4 and 5 discuss conceptual differences between the two broad groups of cultures commonly referred to as Eastern and Western cultures. Chapter 4 first discusses the mental models and thinking pattern differences between the two. It sheds light on the differences in psychological processes, philosophical traditions, thinking styles, self-construal, perceptions of morality, and tolerance for ambiguity. The chapter also discusses the influence of these differences on processing of stimuli and the preferred information framing patterns. A case-in-point example is a Chinese etymological explanation of a paradox concept, and the mini-case included in Chapter 4 is social media communications in China using the case of WeChat.

Chapter Objectives

- Become familiar with perceived differences in psychological processes, philosophical traditions, and thinking styles between Eastern and Western cultures.
- Understand the differences in self-construal and moral reasoning between them.

- Understand how these differences affect processing of stimuli.
- Understand the concept of paradox and paradoxical thinking.

Warmup question: *How does cultural heritage affect consumption patterns across the world?*

East–West Differences

At the outset, it is important to point out the danger of simplified distinctions between "West" and "East." The polarization between the "core" (the West) and the periphery (the rest) has dictated the global power distribution in the contemporary world. This traditional paradigm has been challenged with the rise of emerging economies. Practitioners and academics have increasingly questioned these binary conceptualizations of the "West and the rest.", Nonetheless, research in cross-cultural psychology has established some notable differences and unique characteristics between the two groups, which could inform marketing efforts.

We can identify different approaches to philosophy, logics, self-construal, and perceptions of morality. We can analyze the differences in philosophical (stability/change) and mental frames (linear/holistic; analytical/associative) between these two cultural groups (Nisbett, Peng, Choi, & Norenzayan, 2001). We can also see the differences in psychological, philosophical, and ethical concepts such as self-construal (independent/interdependent) (Heine, 2008) and morality (morality of justice/ethics of community) (Shweder, Much, Mahapatra, & Park, 1997).

These differences can inform marketers because they affect how people process promotional information, and how they relate to brands and brand extensions. They also determine whether consumers may attribute what they perceive as negative information to the brands internally, or to the broader set of external reasons.

These ingrained cultural differences also affect patterns of WOM (word-of-mouth) and a level of peer to peer interactivity, considering that cultures differ in the level of interactivity desired by consumers. WOM is not only used differently across cultures, but it is also generated in a different manner in different cultural contexts (Lai, He, Chou, & Zhou, 2013). These differences could also be used to explain why some brands succeed or fail in international markets. For example, eBay failed in the Chinese market in the face of Taobao. It appears that eBay overlooked some important Taobao unique features. Taobao facilitated interactions between buyers and sellers via instant messaging as a way to build trust, which eBay failed to do.

How could these differences manifest in consumption?

Psychological Processes

Research in cultural psychology has revealed that psychological processes are not hardwired into the brain. Therefore, they do not appear in identical ways across different cultural contexts. Rather, as Heine (2010, p. 1423) explains, "psychological processes are seen to arise from evolutionarily shaped biological potentials becoming attuned to the particular cultural meaning system within which the individual develops." This suggests the strong influence of culture, or nurture.

Psychological processes that drive behavior are related to meaning; because meanings vary across cultures, so do these processes that drive behavior (Heine, Proulx, & Vohs, 2006). For example, studies have shown that self-concept relates to orientations of individualism-collectivism (Triandis, 1989). In the Western cultures, people tend more often to describe themselves in terms of their inner characteristics (an independent self-concept), whereas people from Eastern Asian cultures most often describe themselves in terms of their roles and memberships (an interdependent self-concept) (Heine, 2008).

Research also suggests that there exist consistencies across cultures in a range of consumer behavior patterns beyond differences in the self-concept (Markus & Kitayama, 1991). These include differences in personality (Church et al., 2006), identity and image (Etcoff, Stock, Haley, Vickery, & House, 2011), motivation and emotion (De Mooij, 2010), mental processes such as abstract or concrete thinking (Hsieh, 2004), patterns of categorization of objects or concepts, and information processing (De Mooij, 2010). Although some research exists on these topics, we still have rather limited knowledge of these cultural differences and how they affect marketing. One of the reasons is that many of these concepts have been explained primarily in the context of the individualism/collectivism dichotomy, which has been a dominant concept in culture research in marketing.

Philosophical Traditions

Philosophical traditions also reflect the differences between Eastern and Western worldviews: Western philosophy has embraced the sense of stability and logic in line with the Greek philosophical traditions of Aristotle and Plato, rather than the concept of change suggested by the Greek philosopher Heraclitus. Au contraire, the concept of change is central to Asian or Eastern, and especially the Chinese philosophy that views change as the essence of life.

The traditional Eastern philosophy emphasizes integration of contradictions and paradoxes, and the idea that the mutually opposing elements are dependent on one another and cannot be separated. The focus on change suggests that contradictory elements should be embraced and integrated because the world is constantly changing (Peng & Nisbett, 1999). On the other hand, Western philosophy emphasizes separation between paradoxical elements, rather than their integration (Chen, 2009).

Thus, while there is a low tolerance for ambiguity in the Western philosophical tradition, Eastern philosophical thought has traditionally had high tolerance for ambiguity, embracing paradoxes as necessary and beneficial. This implies that in the Western tradition there is a lower tolerance for contradictory information in communication, and consumers tend to choose one correct solution or a piece of information over the other. Conversely, in Eastern cultures, there is a high tolerance for contradictory information.

These differences could be traced to the fundamentally different origins of the two cultures, namely the agricultural roots of the traditionally isolated East, and the traditional hunting, and then trading-oriented Greek and Roman societies in the West (Graham, 1989).

De Bary (1988, p. 70) points at the distinctly different growth patterns of the historically expansive West, in contrast with China as a representative of the Eastern cultures: it was "land – bound, agrarian . . . preoccupied with intensive cultivation of the soil, self-cultivation of the person." Adapting to the cyclical changes of nature was essential for a Chinese farmer and it has had a profound influence on mental frames.

The Western world on the other hand was more driven by trading considerations. Thereby the differences had to be established in order to determine the value of exchange (ibid). This resulted in the essential differences in the philosophical quest between the two: the quest for one "truth" is at the core of the Western tradition, while the Chinese philosophers have been occupied with seeking the "way," explained in the concept of "dao" (道, in Chinese), rather than the one absolute truth (Graham, 1989).

Thinking Styles

There are some notable *thinking style* differences between Eastern and Western cultures. Researchers distinguish between what is broadly referred to as holistic vs. analytic thinking styles (Nisbett et al., 2001). Thinking styles refer to how one interprets an object and its relationship to other objects in a context. Broadly speaking, people who think holistically tend to emphasize inter-connectedness between the individual objects and their context, and they attribute a lot of importance to context as a predictor of outcomes. The main attribute of the analytical thinking style focuses on individual objects as separate entities, classifying them according to their attributes or categories, and stressing the information about the object.

Research has drawn parallels between these two thinking styles, attributing the holistic style to Eastern and the analytical style to Western cultures. This difference has also been linked to the collectivistic or individualistic orientations whereby perceptions of self are either more interdependent or dependent on others (Markus & Kitayama, 1991). This thinking style influences how decisions are made: cultures with an analytical thinking style focus on the dominant attribute in the products, whereas in cultures with a holistic thinking style there is more of a compromise approach between different attributes.

There are culturally driven differences in the decision-making processes influenced by these two thinking styles. For example, these differences affect resource allocation – people with an analytical thinking style concentrate their resource allocation according to the current demand, and people with holistic thinking styles spread out or disperse their resource allocation (Li, Masuda, Hamamura, & Ishii, 2018).

Faure (2003) used the concept of the "oriental argument development" to describe the Chinese reasoning as a representative of the holistic thinking style commonly found in Eastern cultures. This implies a thinking pattern which moves in concentric circles and includes digressions. This is to distinguish from the Western approach characterized by formal logic and causal relationships developing linearly and using either inductive (from facts to conclusion) or deductive (from general principle to particular case) approaches. Analytical thinking typically attributed to the Western culture is interpreted as that focused on objects which exist independently of their context. They are viewed in terms of their attributes, whereas holistic thinking relates to context, as associative thinking where people seek relations between all variables (Nisbett et al., 2001).

Language could also be used to illustrate these differences. For example, the nature of the Chinese language presents one of the main reasons for a different worldview. Language has also influenced the "circular" thinking pattern commonly affiliated with the Chinese, as opposed to the "linear thinking" in the West (Nakamura, 1964). The Chinese characters are simplified visual representations of reality; in order to understand a specific meaning, one has to capture the root of the whole character first (Faure, 2003). To illustrate this nonlinear thinking pattern, a traditional Chinese saying has it that "only devils move on a straight line" (Faure, 1999, p. 202).

Thinking Styles and Consumption

Differences in thinking styles can also influence how individuals recall brand information and brand stories, and how they use brand information. This is important when brands are affiliated with blunders, recalls, or other negative information. How consumers respond to this negative information differs across cultures. For example, cultures characterized with analytical thinking are more likely to use the information about the object and its category to respond to the information presented about the brand's failure. For this reason, they may be more affected by this negative information than consumers characterized with holistic thinking styles, because they are likely to attribute this failure to brand internal reasons rather than to the external context. On the other hand, consumers characterized with holistic thinking styles are more likely to attribute brand failure to a broader set of external reasons (Monga & John, 2008).

Differences in thinking styles also affect how customers respond to brand extensions and new product introductions. If there is a negative perception of a brand, cultures with analytical thinking styles are less likely to positively evaluate brand extensions. On the other hand, cultures with holistic styles may be more inclined to consider the broader contextual reasons when formulating their response to brand extensions (Ahluwalia, 2008). Some industry segments are exceptions to this rule of thumb, such as luxury products and products affiliated with prestige. In these cases, the difference between the two thinking styles is not as distinct. This is because luxury brands are symbolic and they appeal to abstract values, and their storytelling is characterized with metaphors.

These underlying thinking style differences may also affect how consumers perceive price fluctuations. Because consumers from cultures characterized with a more holistic thinking style tend to see interrelationships between the object and its context, they are less likely to make assumptions of stability of an object over time, and change is accepted as a natural expression of this interdependence (Nisbett & Masuda, 2003). On the other hand, consumers characterized with analytic thinking styles expect more consistency in an object's attributes.

Self-Construal

We can also observe *self-construal* differences between the two groups. Western cultures are generally characterized with an independent self-construal, and the self is conceptualized as an autonomous, independent person (Markus & Kitayama, 1991). Broadly speaking, in these cultures people are more likely to focus on unique personal traits and attributes, rather than on relationship with others. Eastern cultures on the other hand are more likely to be characterized by interdependent self-construal where one's perception of self tends to focus on the interpersonal domain, opinions, or reactions of others. The relationship itself, rather than the individual, becomes the fundamental unit of consciousness (ibid).

The independent vs. dependent self-construal affects preferences for persuasion messages. For example, consumers with an independent self-construal may be more likely to value messages that emphasize potential gain, rather than messages emphasizing potential loss. Messages which are loss-framed may on the other hand be more effective with consumers that have interdependent self-construal (Aaker & Lee, 2001).

These differences influence the nature of expression. People in Western cultures strive to achieve singularity and authenticity in expression, showing preference for uniqueness (Kim & Markus, 1999). Conversely, in the Eastern societies which hold Confucian values, people tend to conform to others, be humbler in expression, attend to the needs of others, and consider how their actions affect the group balance (Yang, 1981).

This ability to adopt the perspective of others varies across cultures and it is linked to how people perceive themselves vs. the group (Wu & Keysar, 2007). For example, while both Western and Eastern cultures can distinguish between their own perspective and that of others, Westerners make be likely to make more egocentric errors when reasoning about others and interpreting their reactions (Holyoak & Gordon, 1983).

Consumers with an independent self-construal are also more likely to engage in impulse purchasing behavior, in contrast to consumers from cultures with independent self-construal (Kacen & Lee, 2002).

Moral Reasoning

Although some universality in *moral reasoning* has been shown across cultures, there appear to be differences in approaches to morality between different cultural groups (Snarey, 1985). Western morality relies on the wider principles than just a morality of justice (Haidt, Koller, & Dias, 1993. In non-Western cultures, morality is often derived from fulfillment of one's roles and interpersonal obligations (Shweder et al., 1997). The Eastern moral systems entail the ethics of community or the ethics of divinity; Western morality is characterized with the ethics of autonomy and it stresses the individual's right of choice rather than the enforced sense of duty or a deontological concern (Hwang, 2015).

For example, the Chinese concept of "guanxi" (关系, in Chinese) represents a web of reciprocal interpersonal connections and it is one of the most prominent traits of the Chinese culture. It represents a web of moral obligations beyond merely being a system of interpersonal relationships (Leung, 2004). Guanxi are connections built with the purpose of influencing or securing resources, and this exchange of mutual favors is seen as an asset (Berger, Herstein, & Mitki, 2013). Thus, relationships are often ranked higher than the law, referred to in China as a "rule of man" that may favor relationships over legal contracts. Derived from the Confucian philosophy, this approach has prevailed throughout Chinese history over the "rule of law" (Fung, 1966).

Looking at the historic origins of this concept, Jacobs, Gao, and Herbig (1995) noted that in the West, the combination of contractual relations used for the serf system and church support exercised control over behavior, and this served as a disciplinary mechanism. Conversely, ancient China had neither contractual relations nor religion. The tradition society did not have a code of civil law similar to the Roman law, and it only had the criminal law and imperial decrees (Hendryx, 1986). In the Western societies, governance systems depend on legally binding written contracts; conversely, Chinese businesses tend to rely more on trust-based networks of social relationships, that is, guanxi (Yen, Barnes, & Wang, 2011).

Stimuli Processing

There are notable differences in cognition between East Asians and Westerners in their *stimuli processing* (Medin, Ross, & Markman, 2005). These differences stem from the aforementioned differences in mental frames (analytical/holistic; independent/context-dependent; categorical/relationships) (Nisbett & Masuda, 2003). Advertising is the most culture-bound element of the marketing mix, and differences in stimuli processing patterns have a particularly strong influence on advertising preferences (De Mooij, 2010). Advertising appeals congruent with thinking styles are likely to be more persuasive.

Analytical vs. holistic information processing style affects the type of connections that are drawn and how they are categorized. Generally speaking, in the Western cultures, there is more focus on central or individual objects which are detached from a context and classified according to rule-based categorical memberships. Less attention is paid to the background or the context and more attention is placed on product attribute information as the predominant factor influencing evaluation and purchase decisions.

Conversely, in the Eastern tradition people tend to classify events or objects according to their relationships, and they spend more time on the background and relate to the context as a whole – individual elements cannot be understood without understanding their interconnectedness (Ji, Zhang, Usborne, & Guan, 2004). People from Eastern cultures spend more time on the background of the image, processing information in a context-dependent fashion, which leads to "field dependency," that is, more difficulty in separating a focal object from its original context (Chua, Boland, & Nisbett, 2005). These differences determine how visual images and advertising appeals are customized across cultures.

How can different patterns of thinking and stimuli processing inform marketing strategy?

Paradoxical Thinking

Recent research has pointed out that *paradoxical thinking* – namely, the ability to embrace paradoxical orientations – is a useful trait in business. Approaches that involve managing rather than suppressing paradoxes are increasingly seen as beneficial for managers. In fact, adequately managing paradoxes and conflicting demands is believed to lead to long-term success for organizations (Smith, Binns, & Tushman, 2010). Paradoxes are viewed as opportunities for organizational learning and for helping companies understand that many apparent opposites are dynamically interrelated over time (Dameron & Torset, 2014).

Traced back to Greek folklore, the Greek word paradox (παράδοξο in Greek) refers to something that is contrary to intuition or to common sense (adjective), or a logical dead-end whereby all the steps in one's reasoning seem logical but the conclusion is implausible/false (noun). Already in the 6th or 7th century b.c., the Greek philosopher Epimenides of Knossos (Crete) was associated with a version of the "liar paradox," namely a statement of a liar who states that they are lying. This paradox, known as the "Epimenides paradox" (το παράδοξο του Επιμενίδη in Greek), is expressed in his known maxim "the people from Crete are always liars."

Western research tradition is founded on the idea that only one correct solution exists, and thus the mutually opposing or contradictory solutions cannot be embraced simultaneously. From the Western perspective, paradoxes are traditionally seen as obscure, absurd, irrational, and negative. Research suggests that Westerners tend to reduce cognitive dissonance by rejecting one contradictory concept in favor of the other, seeking one correct side over the other (Nisbett et al., 2001).

Paradoxes have been interpreted as the "contradictory yet interrelated elements – elements that seem logical in isolation but absurd and irrational when appearing simultaneously" (Lewis, 2000, p. 760). The paradox concept centers on the notion that "polar, opposite conditions can simultaneously exist, or at least can be potentiated, in the same thing" (Mick & Fournier, 1998, p. 124).

From the management perspective, semantic or logical paradoxes of the "liar's paradox" nature are not of primary interest in management research. It is the other type of paradox defined as the "pragmatic paradox" which arises from observations of human behavior rather than from semantics, which is of primary interest for managers (Dameron & Torset, 2014).

Why do we need to understand paradoxes in marketing? Paradoxes are pervasive across all aspects of marketing practice. For example, paradoxes are at the core of many successful brands. We can no longer adhere to the old ideas that a brand stands for one thing and one thing only, such as the USP/share-of-mind argument of the traditional positioning theory; these

Conceptual East–West Differences

ideas are replaced by an appreciation of brands as inherently ambiguous, equivocal, and polymorphic in nature (O'Driscoll, 2008).

Ambiguity is central to the personality and aura that surround the legendary brands (Brown, 2006). Brands appeal to mutually opposing consumer needs. They carry a paradoxical essence, or a "paradessence," promising to satisfy simultaneously opposing consumer desires. As Shakar (2001, p. 61) suggests, every brand has "two opposing desires that it can promise to satisfy simultaneously. The job of a marketer is to cultivate this schismatic core, this broken soul, at the center of every product." Many iconic brands have been successful because they addressed some fundamental underlying contradictions in a society (Holt, 2004). Brands try to appeal to paradoxical values that can be found in different cultures through their advertising campaigns (De Mooij, 2005).

There are many other paradoxes which underpin marketing theory and practice. These include, for example, paradoxes of centralization/decentralization, cultural heritage/contemporary relevance, and global/local that influence corporate brand management. We also see these paradoxes in the process of technology adoption, where customers can gravitate between positive and negative experiences and tensions they experience when they adopt technology (Johnson, Bardhi, & Dunn, 2008). For example, these include tensions such as assimilation/isolation, control/chaos, efficiency/inefficiency, fulfilling/creating needs, engaging/disengaging, competence/incompetence, freedom/enslavement, and new/obsolete (Mick & Fournier, 1998). Today, we can also see paradoxes in the media and popular culture such as, for example, the "meat paradox," or the psychological conflict between preference for meat and consumer moral response to animal suffering (Shaw, 2019).

Slater, Hult, and Olson (2010) explored a paradox of marketing strategy creativity and marketing strategy implementation, suggesting that various cultural tensions and resource competition may make it difficult, if not impossible, to reconcile the two. Other marketing scholars have explored tensions inherent in the coopetition (cooperation and competition) paradox. The emotional state of simultaneously experiencing positive and negative emotions underlies tension in coopetition, which can lead to positive action (Raza-Ullah, Bengtsson, & Kock, 2014).

Consumer experience changes in their expectations, values, and identities when they come in contact with other cultures (Steenkamp, 2019). These tensions between global and local cultures could result in various paradoxes expressed in their attitudes and behaviors. Adopting a paradox perspective to study consumers could help the marketers better understand the long-standing tensions between globalism and localism.

How can a paradox lens be beneficial for marketers?

Cultures and Paradoxical Inclinations

Some cultures may be inclined to use paradoxical frames more than others (Jarvenpaa & Lang, 2005). Notably, East Asians are more likely than Westerners to tolerate contradictions. They tend to categorize conditions using both of the two opposing categories, instead of choosing one over the other. Thus, for example, Asians tend to categorize themselves as both shy and outgoing, cooperative and competitive, or even both happy and sad (Lu, Au, Jiang, Xie, & Yam, 2013). This is in contrast to people from Western cultural backgrounds who tend to categorize conditions using one rather than both of the two opposing categories (Spencer-Rodgers, Williams, & Peng, 2010).

This is best illustrated with the philosophical and cosmological concept of Yin and Yang inherent in the Chinese culture. Yin (阴, in Chinese) and Yang (阳, in Chinese) are the opposing but complementary elements that are in the constant process of interaction, and they undergo transformation through this interaction. Any identity or a phenomenon can only exist as the coexistence of its opposite (Fang, 2012). The traditional Yin-Yang symbol presents the opposites contained in one another which together form a perpetually changing and a harmonious unity as shown in Figure 4.1.

Cultural conditioning exerts a strong influence on how consumers manage paradoxes and on their tolerance for ambiguity. This inclination affects their ability to process contradictory information. For example, Asian philosophies view change as the essence of life, and this change is seen as a process achieved through constant reconciliation between paradoxes, or the opposing elements symbolized through Yin and Yang.

Consequently, the use of paradoxical mindsets differs between Western and Eastern cultures: Western philosophy emphasizes separation between paradoxical elements, whereas traditional Eastern philosophy emphasizes their integration. Holistic thinking inherent in the Eastern cultures explains why consumers value and process contradictory pieces of information, contrary to the Westerners who favor one over the other (Aaker & Sengupta, 2000). Similarly, people from the Eastern cultures are more comfortable with contradictory statements and try to find the truth on both sides, while the

Conceptual East–West Differences

Figure 4.1 Yin-Yang symbol.
Source: Photo by Ba 1976, FreeImages.com.

Westerners try to reduce cognitive dissonance by rejecting one in favor of the other (Peng & Nisbett, 1999).

How would you characterize your host country's culture in regard to its approach to paradoxes? What about your home country?

> **A Case in Point: Chinese Approach to Paradox – A Spear and a Shield**
>
> A closer look at the Chinese language further reveals the Chinese tendency and ability to tolerate paradoxes. The Chinese word for

"contradiction" (maodun, 矛盾 in Chinese), illustrates the Chinese approach to paradox. When broken down, 矛 (mao) means a "spear," while 盾 (dun) stands for "shield." The Chinese idiom 自相矛盾 (zix-iang maodun, or "mutually contradict/ing") is said to have originated from a story of a craftsman who advertised his spears and shields at a market by suggesting that "no spear can penetrate my shield," followed by "no shield could fend off my spear."

Challenged by a passerby who asked "What if I used your spear to penetrate your shield?", he was left speechless. This story illustrates the Chinese approach to paradoxes, suggesting that even the most contradictory concepts form a unity or a state of completeness in the Chinese tradition.

What can we learn from these distinctly different cultures about paradoxes? How can this learning be applied in marketing?

A Word of Caution

Notably, most theories in marketing rely on Western cognitive frames. Traditionally, Western frameworks have been used to research the differences between East and West. The differences between the two cultural groups have also been interpreted in rather binary terms. For example, Asians are often seen as interdependent, dialectic thinkers, while Westerners are seen as analytical and independent thinkers (Markus & Kitayama, 1991).

When using these tools, it is important to remember that these classifications are not to be taken in absolute terms, and that socioeconomic status can moderate cultural traits. For example, research shows that more people who belong in the middle class of the social strata are likely to be independent thinkers than those who belong in the poor societal class because they have greater access to capital and more mobility options (Grossmann & Varnum, 2011). Although the effects of one's culture are persistent across generations and should not be underestimated, even when migrating to another country, the culture effects interact with the socioeconomic status and need to be analyzed in a socioeconomic context.

Mini-Case: Social Media in China – The Example of WeChat

Chinese consumers have embraced digital technologies very fast. Today, the majority of the Chinese use the Internet from their mobile phones. This development was fostered by notable advancements in digital innovation by the three Chinese tech giants known as "BAT" (Baidu, Alibaba, Tencent), arguably underappreciated by their Western counterparts, which go by the acronym "FANG" (Facebook, Amazon, Netflix, and Google).

WeChat dominates life for many in China. It is the most popular social media platform, which contributes to $1.76 billion in lifestyle spending in China (Statista, 2019). From a mere messaging app launched in 2011, WeChat has become a complete digital ecosystem that has transformed professional and private lives in China. As the main social media and messaging platform in China, WeChat provides a combination of email features, instant messaging, and social media "moments" viewed instantaneously by large groups of users (Papa, Santoro, Tirabeni, & Monge, 2018).

WeChat is used instead of email, which never really took off in China, serving as a single platform combining "WhatsApp plus Facebook plus PayPal plus Uber plus GrubHub plus many other things" (Li, 2019); in fact, the percentage of Internet users with a personal email address is in decline in China (Bailey, 2015). WeChat facilitates both one-on-one as well as group interactions, and most companies in China use their official WeChat account as the main, and often as the only, social media vehicle.

Cash is quickly becoming obsolete and it is replaced by WeChat wallet (Jones, 2017). WeChat serves as the main and often the only payment method in China, suggesting a very high level of trust from its users (Statista, 2019). This is somewhat attributed to the design of the platform – the formation of group chats is a process that involves actions that are more conscious than simply adding members, and consequently there is a greater degree of familiarity resulting in higher trust among the group members (Harwit, 2016).

WeChat is illustrative not only because of the profound influence it exerts on its billion people user-base but also because it reflects idiosyncratic characteristics of technology adoption in emerging markets. Social media adoption is influenced by the broader socioeconomic context of a country. For example, in China, higher connectivity is attributed to the loneliness of the one-child generation and a rapid process of urbanization that has caused separation of families when moving to the cities.

The level of trust in WeChat has caused envy by its Western peers – in spite of privacy concerns in China, its users place a great amount of trust in WeChat. They not only share their personal information but also conduct financial transactions and essential business. In fact, WeChat is one of the main tools for doing business in China. While WeChat adoption and its popularity in China is certainly related to the fact that other social media tools are not available in China, the level of trust by its users can also be attributed to cultural factors. Owing to the Chinese mindset that embraces paradoxes and contradictory propensities, its users place an unparalleled level of trust in an app that does not guarantee their privacy.

Mini-Case Questions

- How did WeChat become so popular in China in spite of privacy concerns?
- What explains such a high level of trust by WeChat users?
- Why is it that Chinese consumers don't mind sharing private information on a platform that is not private?
- Are there differences in how people relate to privacy across cultures?
- Why is WeChat envied by its Western peers?

Chapter Guiding Questions

Focus on *advertising appeals* and *personal selling* elements of your plan, and think of the influence of cultural factors on stimuli processing patterns. What best describes your country:

- Analytical or holistic thinking?
- Independent or interdependent self-concept?
- Ethics of community or morality of justice?
- High or low context pattern of communication?
- Should you focus on categorical relations or context-independent presentation of your product?
- What are the likely space orientations?
- What is the likely degree of tolerance for ambiguous promotional messages?

References

Aaker, J. L., & Lee, A. Y. (2001). "I" seek pleasures and "we" avoid pains: The role of self-regulatory goals in information processing and persuasion. *Journal of Consumer Research, 28*(1), 33–49.

Conceptual East–West Differences

Aaker, J. L., & Sengupta, J. (2000). Additivity versus attenuation. *Journal of Consumer Psychology, 9*(2), 67–82.

Ahluwalia, R. (2008). How far can a brand stretch? Understanding the role of self-construal. *Journal of Marketing Research, 45*(3), 337–350.

Bailey, D. (2015). Email marketing won't resonate with Chinese consumers, but WeChat will. *Jing Daily.* Retrieved from https://jingdaily.com/wechat-is-more-effective-than-email-to-reach-chinese-consumers/

Berger, R. R., Herstein, R., & Mitki, Y. (2013). Guanxi: The evolutionary process of management in China. *International Journal of Strategic Change Management, 5*(1), 30–40.

Brown, S. (2006). Ambi-brand culture: On a wing and a swear with Ryanair. In J. Schroeder & M. Salzer -Mörling (Eds.), *Brand culture*. London: Routledge.

Chen, G. M. (2009). Beyond the dichotomy of communication studies. *Asian Journal of Communication, 19*(4), 398–411.

Chua, H. F., Boland, J. E., & Nisbett, R. E. (2005). Cultural variation in eye movements during scene perception. *Proceedings of the National Academy of Sciences of the United States of America, 102*(35), 12629–12633.

Church, A. T., Katigbak, M. S., Del Prado, A. M., Ortiz, F. A., Mastor, K. A., Vargs-Flores, J., . . . Cabrera, H. F. (2006). Implicit theories and self-perceptions of traitedness across cultures: Toward integration of cultural and trait psychology perspectives. *Journal of Cross-Cultural Psychology, 37*(6), 694–716.

Dameron, S., & Torset, C. (2014). The discursive construction of strategists' subjectivities: Towards a paradox lens on strategy. *Journal of Management Studies, 51*(2), 291–319.

De Bary, T. W. (1988). *East Asian civilizations. A dialogue in five stages.* Cambridge, MA: Harvard University Press.

De Mooij, M. (2005). *Global marketing and advertising: Understanding cultural paradoxes.* Thousand Oaks, CA: Sage Publications.

De Mooij, M. (2010). *Global marketing and advertising: Understanding cultural paradoxes* (3rd ed.). Singapore: Sage Publications Asia-Pacific.

Etcoff, N. L., Stock, S., Haley, L. E., Vickery, S. A., & House, D. M. (2011). Cosmetics as a feature of the extended human phenotype: Modulation of the perception of biologically important facial signals. *PLoS One, 6*(10), e25656.

Fang, T. (2012). Yin yang: A new perspective on culture. *Management and Organization Review, 8*(1), 2–50.

Faure, G. O. (1999). The cultural dimension of negotiation: The Chinese case. *Group Decision and Negotiation, 9*(3), 187–215.

Faure, G. O. (2003). *China: New values in a changing society.* China Europe International Business School (CEIBS), Academia Sinica Europæa, Euro China Forum Dublin, Shanghai, China.

Fung, Y.-L. (1966). *A short history of Chinese philosophy.* New York: The Free Press.

Graham, A. C. (1989). *Disputers of the Tao: Philosophical argument in ancient China.* La Salle, IL: Open Court.

Grossmann, I., & Varnum, M. E. W. (2011). Social class, culture, and cognition. *Social Psychological and Personality Science, 2*(1),81–89.

Haidt, J., Koller, S., & Dias, M. (1993). Affect, culture, and morality, or is it wrong to eat your dog? *Journal of Personality and Social Psychology, 65*, 613–628.

Harwit, E. (2016). WeChat: Social and political development of China's dominant messaging app. *Chinese Journal of Communication, 10*(3), 1–17.

Heine, S. J. (2008). *Cultural psychology*. New York: W. W. Norton.

Heine, S. J. (2010). Cultural psychology. In S. T. Fiske, D. T. Gilbert, & G. Lindzey (Eds.), *Handbook of social psychology* (5th ed., Vol. 2, pp. 1423–1464). Hoboken, NJ: John Wiley & Sons, Inc.

Heine, S. J., Proulx, T., & Vohs, K. D. (2006). Meaning maintenance model: On the coherence of social motivations. *Personality and Social Psychology Review, 10*(2), 88–110.

Hendryx, S. (1986). The Chinese trade: Making the deal work. *Harvard Business Review, 78–84.*

Holt, D. B. (2004). *How brands become icons*. Boston, MA: Harvard Business School Publishing.

Holyoak, K. J., & Gordon, P. C. (1983). Social reference points. *Journal of Personality & Social Psychology, 44*(5), 881–887.

Hsieh, M. H. (2004). Measuring global brand equity using cross-national survey data. *Journal of International Marketing, 12*(2), 28–57.

Hwang, K. K. (2015). Morality "East'" and "West": Cultural concerns. In J. D. Wright (Ed.), *International encyclopedia of the social & behavioral sciences* (2nd ed., Vol. 15, pp. 806–810). Oxford: Elsevier.

Jacobs, L., Gao, G. P., & Herbig, P. (1995). Confucian roots in China: A force for today's business. *Management Decision, 33*(10), 29–34.

Jarvenpaa, S. L., & Lang, K. R. (2005). Managing the paradoxes of mobile technology. *Information Systems Management, 22*(4), 7–23.

Ji, L. J., Zhang, Z., Usborne, E., & Guan, Y. (2004). Optimism across cultures: In response to the severe acute respiratory syndrome outbreak. *Asian Journal of Social Psychology, 7*(1), 25–34.

Johnson, D. S., Bardhi, F., & Dunn, D. T. (2008). Understanding how technology paradoxes affect customer satisfaction with self-service technology. *Psychology & Marketing, 25*(5), 416–443.

Jones, B. (2017). Cash is quickly becoming obsolete in China. *Business Insider.* Retrieved from www.businessinsider.com/china-cashless-alipay-wechat-2017-10

Kacen, J. J., & Lee, J. A. (2002). The influence of culture on consumer impulsive buying behavior. *Journal of Consumer Psychology, 12*(2), 163–176.

Kim, H., & Markus, H. R. (1999). Deviance or uniqueness, harmony or conformity? A cultural analysis. *Journal of Personality and Social Psychology, 77*(4), 785–800.

Lai, J., He, P., Chou, H.-M., & Zhou, L. (2013). Impact of national culture on online consumer review behavior. *Global Journal of Business Research, 7*(1), 109–115.

Leung, T. (2004). A Chinese-United States joint venture business ethics model and its implications for multi-national firms. *International Journal of Management, 21*(1) 58–66.

Lewis, M. (2000). Exploring paradox: Toward a more comprehensive guide. *Academy of Management Review, 25*(4), 760–776.

Li, M. W., Masuda, T., Hamamura, T., & Ishii, K. (2018). Culture and decision making: Influence of analytic versus holistic thinking style on resource allocation in a fort game. *Journal of Cross-Cultural Psychology, 49*(7), 1066–1080.

Li, Y. (2019). To cover China, there's no substitute for WeChat. *The New York Times.* Retrieved from www.nytimes.com/2019/01/09/technology/personaltech/china-wechat.html

Lu, S., Au, W. T., Jiang, F., Xie, X., & Yam, P. (2013). Cooperativeness and competitiveness as two distinct constructs: Validating the cooperative and competitive personality scale in a social dilemma context. *International Journal of Psychology, 48*(6), 1135–1147.

Markus, H. R., & Kitayama, S. (1991). Culture and the self: Implications for cognition, emotion, and motivation. *Psychological Review, 98*(2), 224–253.

Medin, L. D., Ross, B. H., & Markman, A. B. (2005). *Cognitive psychology* (4th ed.). Hoboken, NJ: John Wiley & Sons.

Mick, D., & Fournier, S. (1998). Paradoxes of technology: Consumer cognizance, emotions and coping strategies. *Journal of Consumer Research, 25*(2), 123–143.

Monga, A. B., & John, D. R. (2008). Cultural differences in brand extension evaluation: The influence of analytic versus holistic thinking. *Journal of Consumer Research, 33*(4), 529–536.

Nakamura, H. (1964). *Ways of thinking of Eastern people.* Honolulu: East-West Center Press.

Nisbett, R. E., & Masuda, T. (2003). Culture and point of view. Proceedings of the *National Academy of Sciences of the United States of America, 100*(19), 11163–11175.

Nisbett, R. E., Peng, K., Choi, I., & Norenzayan, A. (2001). Culture and systems of thought: Holistic versus analytic cognition. *Psychological Review, 108*(2), 291–310.

O'Driscoll, A. (2008). Exploring paradox in marketing strategy: Managing ambiguity towards synthesis. *Journal of Business and Industrial Marketing, 23*(2), 95–104.

Papa, A., Santoro, G., Tirabeni, L., & Monge, F. (2018). Social media as tool for facilitating knowledge creation and innovation in small and medium enterprises. *Baltic Journal of Management, 13*(3), 329–344.

Peng, K., & Nisbett, R. E. (1999). Culture, dialectics, and reasoning about contradiction. *American Psychologist, 54*(9), 741–754.

Raza-Ullah, T., Bengtsson, M., & Kock, S. (2014). The coopetition paradox and tension in coopetition at multiple levels. *Industrial Marketing Management, 43*(2), 189–198.

Shakar, A. (2001). *The savage girl.* New York: HarperCollins.

Shaw, J. (2019). What the 'meat paradox' reveals about moral decision making. *BBC.* Retrieved from https://www.bbc.com/future/article/20190206-what-the-meat-paradox-reveals-about-moral-decision-making

Shweder, R. A., Much, N. C., Mahapatra, M., & Park, L. (1997). The "big three" of morality (autonomy, community, divinity) and the "big three" explanations of suffering. In A. M. Brandt & P. Rozin (Eds.), *Morality and health* (pp. 119–169). New York: Routledge.

Slater, S. F., Hult, G. T. M., & Olson, E. M. (2010). Factors influencing the relative importance of marketing strategy creativity and marketing strategy implementation effectiveness. *Industrial Marketing Management, 39*(4), 551–559.

Smith, W. K., Binns, A., & Tushman, M. (2010). Complex business models: Managing strategic paradox simultaneously. *Long Range Planning, 43*(2), 448–461.

Snarey, J. R. (1985). Cross-cultural universality of social-moral development: A critical review of Kohlbergian research. *Psychological Bulletin, 97*(2), 202–232.

Spencer-Rodgers, J., Williams, M. J., & Peng, K. (2010). Cultural differences in expectations of change and tolerance for contradiction: A decade of empirical research. *Personality and Social Psychology Review, 14*(3), 296–312.

Statista. (2019). *Number of monthly active WeChat users from 4th quarter 2011 to 4th quarter 2018 (in millions)*. Retrieved from www.statista.com/statistics/255778/number-of-active-wechat-messenger-accounts/

Steenkamp, J.-B. E. M. (2019). Global versus local consumer culture: Theory, measurement, and future research directions. *Journal of International Marketing, 27*(1), 1–19.

Triandis, H. C. (1989). The self and social behavior in differing cultural contexts. *Psychological Review, 96*(3), 506–520.

Wu, S., & Keysar, B. (2007). The effect of culture on perspective taking. *Psychological Science, 18*(7), 600–606.

Yang, K. (1981). Social orientation and individual modernity among Chinese students in Taiwan. *Journal of Social Psychology, 113*(2), 159–170.

Yen, D. A., Barnes, B. R., & Wang, C. L. (2011). The measurement of guanxi: Introducing the GRX scale. *Industrial Marketing Management, 40*(1), 97–108.

Conceptual East–West Differences

Intercultural Communication and Religious Beliefs

Introduction

This chapter expands on the conceptual East–West differences discussed in Chapter 4. The first part of the chapter focuses on different approaches to communication between the two, and it discusses the concept of intercultural communication competence from the perspective of Western communication theories as well as through the Eastern theory lens. In the second part, the focus is on the influence of religious beliefs and religious conditioning on consumption preferences. Both the similarities as well as the differences among the world's five main religions are illustrated. The case in point examples included in this chapter are Sulwhasoo branding, modest fashion, and Islamic art. The mini-case included in Chapter 5 is Islamic finance.

Chapter Objectives

- Understand the notion of communications competence from Western and Eastern perspectives.
- Understand the importance and the influence of religious beliefs on marketing.
- Learn about similarities and differences among the world's main religions.

Warmup question: *What does it take to be a successful communicator across cultures?*

119

East–West Divide

Researchers have increasingly echoed their concerns over the Western-centric nature of communications and culture study. Arguably, Western domination and bias have permeated these study fields. Traditionally, most communications theories relied on Western cognitive frames, and they were developed by Westerners with Westerners in mind (Gunaratne, 2010). Against this backdrop, researchers have suggested that culture and communications study fields would benefit from the plurality of views and from novel and more dynamic methods and approaches for grasping the nuances across cultures (Herdin, Faust, & Chen, 2020). Consequently, studies have called for the development of new, non-Western approaches to the study of communication (Asante, Miike, & Yin, 2007).

One such approach is an *Asia-centric communication paradigm*. This approach is based on the ontological assumption of interconnectedness between all people and things across space and time. This paradigm implies that one's sense of self is more deeply rooted in the web of human relationships than in the ego (Miike, 2006). In Asian tradition, everyone and everything are interrelated across space and time and therefore the core focus of communication is on the interdependence. On the other hand, in Western theory, the independent self is at the core of the analysis, while relationships remain in the background (Kincaid, 1987).

This Asian dialectical approach to communication and culture emphasizes a persistence of paradoxical tensions which are seen as a natural part of reality. This is illustrated through the ongoing process of interactions between the opposing elements of Yin and Yang.

From this perspective, the existence of all things is thus interpreted through a dynamic interplay between these two opposing yet complementary forces, much like all of life is also produced from the unification of Yin (female) and Yang (male) elements. This approach is based on the idea of duality, where the opposites are seen as interdependent; this is contrasted with the traditional dualistic approach where the opposites are seen as mutually exclusive and one option is chosen over the other (Faure & Fang, 2008).

These opposite elements transform each other in the process of constant change which presents the fundamental principle of the Universe, as well as the central idea in the Chinese culture (Lai, 2008). These ideas are also central to concepts in the Asian approach to communication. Communication is seen as an evolving, non-linear process focused on achieving an equilibrium between the opposites (Chen, 2011).

From the Asia-centric perspective, not only are people, objects and events interrelated, but they also only become meaningful in relation to others. In the Indian philosophical tradition, similarly, everything is seen as united at a higher ontological level and it can only be understood in relation to one another (Dissanayake, 1983). This also implies connectedness of different time dimensions inclusive of past, present, and future. The Japanese model of communication proposed by Ishii (1984) is based on the Buddhist concept of a predestined connection or "en" across space and time. In Asian tradition, communication is also highly context-specific and communicators adjust their messages to maintain interpersonal and situational harmony based on specific situations.

How can marketers move past the traditional East–West divide in communications studies and make the best use of different approaches?

Communicating Across Cultures

Considering these differing approaches to communication in general terms, the idea of competent communication also differs between what is commonly perceived as "Western" and "Eastern" cultures.

Communication competence (CC) and intercultural communication competence (ICC) are used interchangeably in the literature, differing in their emphasis on a cultural context (Chen & Starosta, 1996). *Intercultural communication competence* is usually interpreted as the ability to think and act appropriately with people from other cultures (Friedman & Antal, 2005), and it has been approached both from culture-general as well as culture-specific perspectives (Dai & Chen, 2014).

The ICC concept involves a range of interpretations beyond just the ability to interact effectively in different cultural contexts. Various dimensions of ICC are interpreted differently, from the angle of empathy, experience, motivation, positive attitude toward other cultures, or listening (Arasaratnam & Doerfel, 2005).

Generally speaking, ICC has been classified into three broad dimensions inclusive of affective, cognitive, and behavioral aspects. Chen and Starosta (1996) delineated these three constructs into intercultural awareness of how other cultures act and behave (cognitive), intercultural sensitivity and motivation to understand other cultures (affective), and intercultural adroitness, that is, effectiveness in terms of attaining communication goals in interactions (behavioral aspect). All three are important for successful ICC.

Traditional Western communication theory usually conceptualizes communication competence in terms of communication effectiveness and appropriateness (Chen, 2009). Intercultural communication competence is thus interpreted as the ability to communicate with people from different cultures effectively and appropriately. "Effectively" means that the goals are being accomplished, and "appropriately" refers to communicating with respect to the values, norms, and expectations of others.

This approach to communication is primarily efficiency-oriented and individualistic, and it is based on positivistic theory and research (Ishii, 2001). The positivistic epistemology – theory of knowledge – suggests that only the facts derived through scientific methods can be counted as legitimate knowledge claims. Thus, our knowledge is meant to be confined to empirical facts only. The main epistemological approaches relevant for intercultural research are discussed in Chapter 8.

How can we identify the cultural differences that drive communications approaches? For example, we can distinguish between different approaches to conflict resolution – one is anchored in the Western tradition of a debate (and winning it), and the other, Asian approach involves a compromise solution, reflected in the concept of harmony. This is also reflected in the attitude toward nature, whereas we can see the difference between dominance over nature, vs. an attempt to be in harmony with nature, reflected in the Chinese concept of feng shui, discussed in Chapter 6. Thus, a successful communicator from the Western perspective may be someone who presents a winning argument, while from the Asian perspective this may refer to a person who proposes the best compromise solution.

We can also relate to differences in time orientations between cultures. For example, the cultures that are more present-oriented may seek more flexibility, whereas those that are more future-oriented may prefer predictability of the process.

What is the main difference between Western and Eastern approaches to communication?

Asian Perspective of Communication

Asian theory and practice of communication revolves around the idea of *harmony*. Harmony is a central concept in Asian thought and it has a strong influence on how communication competence is interpreted. In the Chinese tradition in particular, harmony (和, in Chinese) is an elaborating symbol that provides people with cognitive and affective orientations (Chen, 2011). This concept perhaps best reflects the broad East–West cultural differences (Leung, Brew, Zhang, & Zhang, 2011).

In ancient Greek philosophy, harmony was seen to have a quantitative tendency and it referred to a linear, rational, and mathematical order through an orderly alternation of odd and even numbers. The original meaning of harmony in Chinese comes from music and it refers to balance, peace, and coordination. The Chinese character 和 (he), which stands for harmony or peace, is also a conjunction in the Chinese language that is equivalent to "and" in English (Chen, 2011), pointing to the idea of mutual interdependence and interrelatedness of all things.

In the Asian tradition, establishing a harmonious relationship is the ultimate goal of all human communication (Chen & Starosta, 1996). Harmony moderates a mutual dependency between opposite but complementary forces. Similarly, human interactions are interpreted as a process in which the interacting parties constantly adapt and change in order to achieve a state of harmonious relationship with others. From the Asian perspective, harmony is a goal of all human interactions and a measure of social competence – communication competence is the ability to achieve harmony in the ongoing process of interactions, the success of which is not being measured as a static communication output (Chen, 2011). Achieving harmony is also seen as a moral responsibility – if harmony between people is achieved, harmony in the world will be achieved according to the Asian approach (Chen, 2009).

Harmony is also seen as a process of "harmonization," rather than as a fixed, static state. The goal of perpetual change is to achieve a temporarily balanced but permanently dynamic status through the constantly changing process of harmonizing (Chin & Mao, 2010). Thus, harmony is not interpreted as a stagnant or a temporary concordance. Rather, it is a dynamic process which is sustained by the energy generated through the interaction of different, opposing elements in a creative tension.

Sharing their insights from the practice, communication professionals suggest that we can learn from the Asian wisdom. For example, we need to learn how to reconcile the seemingly opposing considerations, from the Western perspective at least, of speed and strategy, in order to be successful intercultural communicators. Stelling (2020) reminds us that due to the

Conceptual East–West Differences

rapid global changes we are facing, ultimately, "how we interact with one another, the tools and channels we use, the content we share: nothing will remain the same."

In other words, we may have to move past the traditional frameworks we hold eternally as valid and embrace complexity and perhaps even ambiguity in communications. This approach that embraces a reconciliation between contradictory orientations is illustrated in a quote by Alibaba's CEO Jack Ma, who said, "one must run as fast as a rabbit, but be as patient as a turtle" (Doebele, 2000, pp. 74–75).

How does a different interpretation of communication competence as efficiency in the Western theory and a dynamic process of harmony from the Eastern perspective affect marketing efforts through branding, PR, and advertising?

A Case in Point: Sulwhasoo Branding

This ideal of harmony is transferred to the relationship between humans and nature, which also suggests the ideal of beauty. Sulwhasoo, a high-end Korean natural skincare brand, emphasizes that a "pursuit of true beauty is a journey that begins with Asian wisdom, embodying the harmony and equilibrium with Nature." Across its different communications messages, verbal and visual, the brand stresses

Figure 5.1 Sulwhasoo's advertising.
Source: Courtesy of Labbrand Brand Innovations.

a "holistic beauty of the body and mind, as well as inner and outer beauty" (Sulwhasoo, 2020).

This process of harmonization between the opposites is seen in Sulwhasoo's communications messages as well as through its branding symbols. The opposites are also seen in the blend of cutting-edge technologies and the traditional holistic Asian wisdom which the company considers as its main value proposition (Sulwhasoo, 2020). Their advertising often depicts opposite images that blend in harmony, such as square and round drops on the image in Figure 5.1.

Do you know any other brands that use a similar approach?

Religious Beliefs and Marketing

Religion exerts strong influence on international business. Religion also influences migration patterns: 60% of migrants move to a country with the same major religion. *Religiosity* is an individual's commitment and adherence to religious values and beliefs, and it presents a degree of commitment with which a person adheres to religious teachings and beliefs. While the significance of the *religious value systems* has been studied extensively in social sciences, our knowledge of this domain in marketing remains somewhat limited. This could be attributed to methodological challenges in tackling this sensitive topic (Essoo & Dibb, 2004). It is rather challenging, using traditional quantitative methods in marketing, to assess religiously motivated antecedents and drivers of consumer behavior across cultures.

Religious beliefs and conditioning have strong influence on consumer preferences and consumer behavior. Religion affects its believers on multiple levels, and it influences their consumer consumption patterns and their perception of brands and products (Fam, Erdogan, & Waller, 2004).

More than eight out of ten people around the world identify with a religious group. Religious attitudes affect consumer choice and they influence consumers' lifestyle, purchase patterns, risk avoidance, or retail store patronage (McDaniel & Burnett, 1990). Studies found that in some countries like Malaysia, for example, religious consumers were less likely to make impulsive purchases and they were also more concerned with quality and price (Mokhlis, 2006). In other cultures, such as South Korea, highly religious

Conceptual East–West Differences

consumers were less likely to switch brands or retail providers than their counterparts (Choi, 2010).

As shown in Figure 5.2, today, religion and spirituality have adapted to consumer society and to a rapid technology adoption – even in the holiest of places! Faith is mixed up with business in many different ways. Consequently, many religious groups act like commercial organizations. We can

Figure 5.2 Shwedagon Pagoda, Yangon, Myanmar.
Source: Author.

Conceptual East–West Differences

see the emergence of mega churches and religious best sellers. It is not surprising, then, that marketers try to endow nonreligious goods and services with a mystical or magical aura.

More than in any other realms of marketing, we can see the use of religious themes and symbols in advertising. Religious beliefs have a strong influence on advertising, especially in regards to the so-called controversial products and services. These products are often referred to as "unmentionables" or "socially sensitive products" (Wilson & West, 1981, p. 1) which, "for reasons of delicacy, decency, morality, or even fear tend to elicit reactions of distaste, disgust, offense, or outrage when mentioned or openly presented."

Generally speaking, people with higher religiosity are more likely to be offended by advertising for controversial products. These products are divided into categories of addictive products, such as alcohol or gambling; gender-specific and sex-related products such as underwear, female hygiene products, and contraceptives; political and society-related products and services such as political parties, extremist groups, religious denominations and sects, or weapons; and health-related products focused around sexual disease or weight loss (Fam et al., 2004). Marketers should consider degrees of controversy that these products can cause in different countries when advertising these products across cultures.

How does religion influence marketing?

A Case in Point: Modest Fashion

We can see the growth of faith-based products and services such as halal or kosher meat or religious travel. Some faith-based products and industries in particular are developing at a rapid speed.

Such is the example of "modest fashion," or Islamic fashion. It is one of the fastest-growing consumer markets globally and a multi-billion-dollar industry that has stepped onto the global fashion mainstage. In 2017, the first ever Modest Fashion Week (MFW) was held at the Saatchi Gallery in London, showcasing fashion items from over 40 designers across the world.

Modest fashion is rapidly gaining in popularity – for example, Google searches for the term were up 500% between January and April 2019 alone (The Independent, 2019).

> Modest fashion is a good example of a religious-based product that has crossed religious and cultural boundaries. While the clothing is primarily worn due to religious or cultural reasons, it is also adopted by women who want to look more modest and stylish at the same time. This type of clothing conceals the body shape, rather than accentuating it which is often the case with other types of clothing. It also offers new clothing options to Muslim women across the world.
>
> This opportunity was spotted not just by Muslim designers but also by the mainstream fashion brands. For example, DKNY launched its first Ramadan collection in 2014, and in 2015 H&M featured its first hijab-wearing model. In 2016, the first hijab was worn in the Miss Minnesota Pageant by a young model, Halima Aden. She also became the first hijab-wearing model to appear on the cover of *British Vogue* magazine in 2018, the first time in its 100-year history (adapted from The Independent, 2019).
>
> *What helped modest fashion to gain popularity? Why is it attractive to non-Muslim women?*

Religion and Sanctioning of Marketing Campaigns

Various degrees of sanctioning could happen in advertising across cultures due to religious considerations. For example, Chick-fil-A, a U.S. fast food provider has made a name promoting Christian principles, such as being closed on Sundays. However, it encountered controversy in 2012 after its CEO Dan Cathy suggested in public that he opposed same-sex marriage. Although this caused dismay by many consumers who do not share the same views, it did not damage the company's sales owing to its religious customers.

Unilever, a British-Dutch producer of fast-moving consumer products saw its ads for Lux soap featuring Sarah Jessica Parker being banned in Israel. Their billboards were taken off within 24 hours due to opposition from the Orthodox Jewish community constituting 11% of the population in Israel. On the other hand, when Ikea, the Swedish manufacturer of furniture and home accessories tailored its catalogues to cater specifically for that religious community in Israel, their efforts were met with dismay from the rest of the population.

In spite of being widely criticized for some bold choices, advertisers continue to use religion, sometimes in a deliberately controversial way. For example, Benetton, an Italian clothing brand, has released a number of controversial adverts dealing with religion. Their "Kissing Pope" campaign as a part of the "Unhate" campaign released in 2011 featured the world's leading politicians and religious authorities kissing each other. Although it was deemed controversial by global authorities, it resulted in increased brand awareness among its customers, and it made it to the top five trending topics worldwide on Twitter and Google. Owing to this campaign, Benetton's Facebook fan numbers increased by 60% and the brand enjoyed extensive media coverage. More than 3,000 articles were published with over 600 TV reports aired in 60 countries.

How can brands avoid sanctioning and backlash when using religion in marketing?

Similarities Between the World's Main Religions

The five of the *world's main religions* include (in their chronological order) Judaism, Christianity and Islam (Western religions); and Hinduism and Buddhism (Eastern religions). These main global religions have some distinct overarching similarities which are, however, expressed differently through their unique rituals and religious practices.

For example, every major religion teaches good values and humanism: there are good people and bad people. There is a common belief across religions that being good will benefit oneself and the community. To illustrate this belief, all major religions have a being or beings and idols of their worship, such as: God/Allah in Judaism, Christianity, and Islam; Moses, in Judaism and Christianity; Jesus in Christianity; Mohammed in Islam; Buddha, or bodhisattvas in Buddhism; various saints in Christianity; walis (saints) in Islam; tzadikim (saints) in Judaism; and deities in Hinduism. They also all have "holy men" such as rabbis, priests, imams, or monks. All major religions also have a say in life after death, they have sacred places, and they engage in practices of charity, sacrifice, prayer, and fasting.

The three Western religions (Judaism, Christianity, and Islam) practice monotheism, or a belief in only one God. Arguably, Hinduism began this way while Buddhism is not centered on the concept of God. All religions have prayer as a form of devotion; however, the expression and praying rituals differ among them: Muslims pray five times per day; Jews may pray three times a day. In Christianity, there are no prescribed times for prayer. Ordinary Christian believers (not clergy) have abandoned the original form of prayer. Buddhist and Hindus have no prescribed time for prayer either, but many pray at dawn and dusk.

All major religions encourage fasting. Fasting is one of the pillars of Islam, especially during the month of Ramadan, and traditional Jews fast six days every year. In Western Christianity most people do not fast but according to the Bible, Jesus did fast for 40 days. Orthodox Christians still fast for a few weeks before major holidays and also throughout the year. Hindus fast two to three times a week, and fasting is considered a form of treatment in Ayurvedic medicine. In the Buddhist tradition fasting is a way of practicing self-control by going without food for an extended period. It is believed that Buddha advised monks not to take solid food after noon, and many observe full moon to determine fasting patterns.

Giving alms to the poor and needy presents another unifying theme across all major religions. While in Hinduism there is a practice of giving to the poor ("dana") by the higher cast, in Buddhism ordinary people give alms to the monks. "Zakah" is one of the pillars in Islam – giving money which is later distributed to the poor, to pay for education, or to get businesses out of trouble. A similar concept called Tzedakah also exists in Judaism.

All religions also encourage their followers to go on a pilgrimage, and they all have different sites. For Muslims, it is Mecca at least once in a lifetime if they can afford it physically and financially. For Christians, it could be Jerusalem (in the medieval times it was Rome) as well as many local sites across the world. For the Jews, the place of pilgrimage is Jerusalem three times a year, and for the Hindus it is the river Ganges hosting millions of people who go there to be purified. Buddhists have four holy sites believed to produce the sense of spiritual urgency – one in Nepal (Lumbini in today's Nepal, believed to be the birthplace of Buddha) and three in India (such as Bodhgaya).

The idea of sacrifice also exists across religions, although it has different expressions and manifestations. In some religions, for example, sacrifice of animals has been abandoned. In some others, such as Buddhism, the idea of sacrifice has a rather different meaning – Buddhists are often vegans which means that they sacrifice themselves to save animals. Their idea of sacrifice implies a self-sacrifice for personal liberation in order to help others.

Conceptual East–West Differences

What similarities among the world's five main religions are relevant for marketers?

Unique Features of the Worlds' Main Religions

Inasmuch as the world's main religions share many common features, they have their idiosyncratic expressions and traditions. Followers of Judaism believe in One God and reject the doctrine of original sin. Atonement for the sins committed is made by seeking forgiveness from God in prayer and repentance. The Day of Atonement, or Yom Kippur (יום כיפור, in Hebrew) is set aside especially for this purpose. Ideas of the afterlife in Judaism vary widely among different groups and different time periods; for the most part, Judaism does not emphasize the afterlife.

Christians believe in one eternal God who is the creator of all that is. He is viewed as a loving God who offers everyone a personal relationship with himself now in this life. Christians believe that all people sin, and therefore sin is demystified and not strictly punishable. Jesus is believed to be the savior, the Messiah who was prophesied by all the prophets of the Old Testament. Jesus, out of love for humanity, has paid for the sins of all of humanity.

For the followers of Islam there is only one almighty God – Allah – who is infinitely superior to humankind. Allah is viewed as the creator of the universe and the source of all good and evil. Everything that happens is believed to be Allah's will. He is seen as a powerful and strict judge, who will be merciful toward his followers depending on their life's good works and religious devotion. Muhammad is believed to be the last prophet and his words and lifestyle are the ultimate authority for the followers of Islam. Allah is worshiped through good deeds and disciplined religious rituals.

Most Hindus worship one Being of ultimate oneness (Brahman) through infinite representations of gods and goddesses. They believe that various deities become incarnate within idols, temples, gurus, rivers, or animals. A Hindu's goal is to become free from the law of karma and from the continuous reincarnations, and to free the soul from the perpetual cycle of rebirths. Hinduism suggests that one's position in the present life is determined by the actions in the previous life, thus offering a possible explanation for suffering and evil in this life.

Buddhists do not worship any gods or a single God. Buddha (Siddhartha Gautama) never claimed to be divine. He is viewed by the Buddhists as having attained the ideal that they are also striving to attain – spiritual

131

Conceptual East–West Differences

enlightenment and, with it, freedom from the continuous cycle of life and death. A person is believed to have countless rebirths which are a result of the person's cravings, attachments, and delusions. Rebirths inevitably include suffering, and a Buddhist seeks to end them. Thus, the goal of a Buddhist is to purify one's heart and to let go of all sensual desires and attachments. Meditation is an important religious practice in Buddhism. It is different than praying or focusing on God; rather, it implies self-discipline. Through practiced meditation a person may reach Nirvana – "the blowing out" of the flame of desire. To its followers, Buddhism offers a framework for personal discipline.

The main premises of the world's five major religions are summarized in Table 5.1. These general characteristics influence how consumers make decisions, in particular when it comes to the high-involvement products.

Are the differences bigger than the similarities among the world's main religions? Which are more important for marketers across cultures?

Table 5.1 Similarities and differences among Western and Eastern religions.

Western Religions: Judaism, Christianity, and Islam	Eastern Religions: Hinduism and Buddhism
One God	Freedom to choose God(s)/no-God
God's message revealed through prophet	Direct contact with God/self
Nonmystical (God chooses prophet)	Mystical (human experience)
Congregational (society is essential)	Individual
Scripture has ultimate authority	Scripture has limited/no authority
Human suffering – disobedience of God's will	Human suffering – soul's ignorance
	Philosophy of Karma
Eternal Hell/Heaven	No eternal Hell/Heaven
	Universe exists in endless cycles
	Continuity of life (reincarnation)
	Liberation (moksha)
	No Judgment day

Religion and Attitudes Toward Trading

Historically, different religions have held different attitudes toward trading, placing differing importance on trading and the position of traders in society. Thus, shared attitudes toward trading derived from religious beliefs may

Conceptual East–West Differences

enhance trust and reduce transaction costs between the trading partners, because they imply similar value systems. Religious preferences may also influence consumer protectionism – a belief that one religion is superior to the other, or loyalty to one's own religion. This is similar to the concept of ethnocentrism discussed in Chapter 1.

There are some historic differences between the main religions and their attitudes toward trade, even within the same groups of Western or Eastern religions. For example, Judaism provides an appropriate framework for economic exchange, and also the incentive to build up trade relations without discriminating between Jews and non-Jews. Christian thinking recognizes the market system, but places some constraints on it, which are defined by Christian ethical standards. Trade is not treated explicitly in Christianity, and it is probably seen more as a necessity than a contribution to economic well-being. Islam is a very trade friendly religion and trading is explicitly recognized as a welfare. Traditionally, the quality of products was emphasized over quantity, which is likely one of the reasons why many non-Muslims buy halal meat as a recognition of its quality today.

Hinduism takes a rather ambiguous stance toward international trade, and trading is traditionally reserved to a specific caste. In the past, for people from religions other than Hinduism, it was difficult to find the appropriate Hindu trading partner. Buddhist countries historically had a general disincentive to trade, and there are considerable differences among Buddhist countries practicing different streams or versions of Buddhism. Accumulation of wealth is generally not seen as positive – Buddhists restrict the acquisition of wealth to the necessary, because it may hamper the attainment of enlightenment (Helble, 2007).

A Case in Point: Islamic Art

Religions are different in their approach to art. We can see this in the example of Islamic art. Unlike the Christian artistic tradition, Islamic art is not limited to just the religious themes. Rather, it includes all the broad artistic traditions in the Muslim culture. It uses a unique artistic language and a strong aesthetic appeal that aims to transcend differences between languages and cultures practicing Islam. One of the most common features of Islamic art is the use of geometric

Conceptual East–West Differences

patterns and ornamentation. In Islamic art, geometry is seen to reflect the universal language of the universe, helping the believer to reflect on creation and on the divine.

Geometry is believed to be spiritual or divine – circles have no end and they are infinite; complex geometric shapes create the impression of endless repetition; and repeating patterns demonstrate that in the small part one can find the infinite which is meant to represent the divine. Such use of geometric patterns in Islamic art is meant to represent nature and objects through their spiritual qualities, rather than through their physical and material qualities (Hussain, 2009).

By looking at Islamic art, for example, Figure 5.3, we can see a deep connection between the West and Islam. We can thus interpret the Muslim world as a variant of the Western experience, and not as the exotic "other world" (Malik, 2018).

Figure 5.3 Vakil Mosque in Shiraz, Iran.
Source: Image by Mira Pavlakovic, Freeimages.com.

What can artistic religious tradition tell us about a culture? How can marketers apply their knowledge of artistic traditions from different religions?

A Word of Caution

Although brands sometimes use religion deliberately to create awareness for their nonreligious products or to spark a controversy, religion needs to be used with caution. It is very easy to offend consumers unintentionally by referring to their religious beliefs and symbols in inappropriate ways. Furthermore, religious beliefs are often affiliated with ethnocentrism. Thus, unless selling religious products and services, it may be a good idea to refrain from using religion – while it may increase the value of ordinary consumer brands, it is also a high-risk approach.

Mini-Case: Islamic Finance

Ideas from one religion can cross cultural and religious boundaries. We can see this in the example of Islamic, or shariah (الشريعة, in Arabic) finance. Much like with halal meat that has been increasingly popular with nonbelievers of Islam due to its perceived high quality, somewhat similar trends are happening in finance. Why is shariah finance increasingly attractive to non-Muslims?

One in three customers of Al Rayan Bank, Britain's biggest sharia-compliant retail bank by assets are non-Muslim, up from one in eight in 2010 (D'Urbino, 2018). This is reflective of a broader trend of non-Muslims becoming increasingly attracted by the features offered by Islamic finance without attaching religious significance to it. By definition, Islamic finance is sharia-compliant, which means that it presents banking or a financing activity that complies with sharia or the Islamic law. These governing laws stipulate how financial transactions are conducted. They are derived directly from the Q'uran which prohibits interest on loans, or riba (الرّبا, in Arabic) which means interest, or an unjust, exploitative gain.

Traditionally, Islamic banks should not offer personal or business loans with interest. Rather, they should enter into partnership with their clients on a profit-sharing basis. For example, Islamic banks invest deposits and take a cut of the profits. Thus, they assume a share of the profits and losses – when the loan is repaid, the lender collects the agreed upon percentage of the profits (or deducts if there are losses). An underlying idea behind this approach is that the borrower must not bear all the risk of a failure.

Shariah finance also prohibits charging extra for late payments. Sometimes late fees may be charged if they are donated to charity, or if the buyer has deliberately refused to make a payment. It also prohibits any form of alleged gambling, which is used to mean "speculation" in general. This refers to the contracts hinging on the occurrence of an uncertain event in the future.

In this banking tradition, derivatives and futures are also prohibited because they involve excessive risk and they may lead to fraudulent behavior. They are also prohibited because they lack material finality – they need to be linked to a real economic transaction. Similarly, day trading or short-term buying and selling of financial instruments is also considered un-Islamic, because this short period of ownership means that the traders do not genuinely own what they trade.

With the growing resistance against the Western financial institutions, it is not surprising that these features of Islamic banking appear attractive to 8consumers, not only because of its inherent features.

Case Study Questions

- What is the key incentive for non-Muslim consumers to select Islamic banks?
- What were the main factors of success for Islamic banks in the West?
- Should the shariah financing religious principles be separated from the secular banking principles in order to attract non-Muslim consumers?

Guiding Questions

Think about the *communications* differences between your home and host countries:

- What is the ideal of communication competence in your brand's home country?
- What about the host country?
- How would you have to adjust your communication approach to be considered a competent communicator in your host culture?

Think about *religious considerations* and their effect on your marketing efforts:

- What is your host country's religion? How much does it influence daily lives?
- What is a home country religion?

- What are the similarities between two religions?
- How could religion influence your intercultural marketing efforts in your host country?
- How do religious preferences influence your specific product and industry in your host country?
- Are there any religion-related issues, taboos, and controversies you should be aware of in your marketing efforts?
- What main religious considerations could drive positioning for your selected product?
- How risky is it to use religion explicitly when selling your product?
- Are there any benefits of appealing to religious values?

References

Arasaratnam, L. A., & Doerfel, M. L. (2005). Intercultural communication competence: Identifying key components from multicultural perspectives. *International Journal of Intercultural Relations, 29*(2), 137–163.

Asante, M. K., Miike, Y., & Yin, J. (Eds.). (2007). *The global intercultural communication reader.* New York: Routledge.

Chen, G. M. (2009). Beyond the dichotomy of communication studies. *Asian Journal of Communication, 19*(4), 398–411.

Chen, G. M. (2011). An introduction to key concepts in understanding the Chinese: Harmony as the foundation of Chinese communication. *China Media Research, 1*(4), 1–12.

Chen, G. M., & Starosta, W. J. (1996). Intercultural communication competence: A synthesis. *Communication Yearbook, 19*, 353–384.

Chin, T., & Mao, Y. (2010). *Understanding harmonious spirit, the humanistic-caring value in Chinese organizational behavior.* Paper presented at the Academy of Management Annual Meeting, Montreal, August 6–10. Retrieved from http://program.aomonline.org/2010/submission.asp?mode1-4ShowSession&SessionID1/4 1544

Choi, Y. (2010). Religion, religiosity, and South Korean consumer switching behaviors. *Journal of Consumer Behavior, 9*(3), 157–171.

Dai, X. D., & Chen, G. M. (2014). *Intercultural communication competence: Conceptualization and its development in cultural contexts and interaction.* London: Cambridge Scholars Publishing.

Dissanayake, W. (1983). Communication in the cultural tradition of India. *Media Development, 30*, 27–30.

Doebele, J. (2000, July 17). Fast as a Rabbit, patient as a turtle. *Forbes,* 74–75.

D'Urbino, L. (2018). Why non-Muslims are converting to sharia finance. *The Economist*. Retrieved from www.economist.com/britain/2018/10/20/why-non-muslims-are-converting-to-sharia-finance

Essoo, N., & Dibb, S., (2004). Religious influences on shopping behaviour: An exploratory study. *Journal of Marketing Management, 20*(7–8), 683–712.

Fam, K. S., Erdogan, B. Z., & Waller, D. S. (2004). The influence of religion on attitudes towards the advertising of controversial products. *European Journal of Marketing, 38*(5/6), 537–555.

Faure, G. O., & Fang, T. (2008). Changing Chinese values: Keeping up with paradoxes. *International Business Review, 17*(2), 194–207.

Friedman, V. J., & Antal, A. B. (2005). Negotiating reality: A theory of action approach to intercultural competence. *Management Learning, 36*(1), 69–86.

Gunaratne, S. A. (2010). De-westernizing communication/social science research: Opportunities and limitations. *Media, Culture & Society, 32*(3), 473–500.

Helble, M. (2007). On the influence of world religions on international trade. *Kyklos, 60*(3), 385–413.

Herdin, T., Faust., M., & Chen, G. M. (Eds). (2020). *De-westernizing visual cultures: Perspectives from the global south*. Baden-Baden: NOMOS Publishing.

Hussain, Z. (2009). Islamic art. *BBC*. Retrieved from www.bbc.co.uk/religion/religions/islam/art/art_1.shtml

The Independent. (2019). What is modest fashion and why is it becoming mainstream? Retrieved from www.independent.co.uk/life-style/fashion/modest-fashion-asos-hijab-range-design-islam-religion-a8875636.html

Ishii, S. (1984). *Enryo-Sasshi* communication: A key to understanding Japanese interpersonal relations. *Cross Currents, 11*(1), 49–58.

Ishii, S. (2001). An emerging rationale for triworld communication studies from Buddhist perspectives. *Human Communication: A Journal of the Pacific and Asian Communication Association, 4*(1), 1–10.

Kincaid, D. L. (1987). Communication East and West: Points of departure. In D. L. Kincaid (Ed.), *Communication theory: Eastern and Western perspectives* (pp. 331–340). San Diego, CA: Academic Press.

Lai, K. L. (2008). *An introduction to Chinese philosophy*. New York: Cambridge University Press.

Leung, K., Brew, F. P., Zhang, Z., & Zhang, Y. (2011). Harmony and conflict: A cross-cultural investigation in China and Australia. *Journal of Cross-Cultural Psychology, 42*(5), 795–816.

Malik, K. (2018). Look at art for the deep connection between Europe and Islam. *The Guardian*. Retrieved from www.theguardian.com/commentisfree/2018/jul/08/look-to-art-for-connection-europe-and-islam

McDaniel, S. W., & Burnett, J. J. (1990). Consumer religiosity and retail store evaluative criteria. *Journal of the Academy of Marketing Science, 18*(2), 101–112.

Miike, Y. (2006). Non-Western theory in Western research? An Asiacentric agenda for Asian communication studies. *The Review of Communication, 6*(1/2), 4–31.

Mokhlis, S. (2006). The effect of religiosity on shopping orientation: An exploratory study in Malaysia. *Journal of American Academy of Business, 9*(1), 64–74.

Stelling, O. (2020). *Speed and strategy: Communicating in the Asian century.* Retrieved from www.oliverstelling.com

Sulwhasoo Website. (2020). Retrieved from www.sulwhasoo.com/sg/en/about/sulwhasoo.html

Wilson, A., & West, C. (1981, January/February). The marketing of "unmentionables." *Harvard Business Review, 51*, 91–102.

Frameworks for Interpreting Cultural Differences

Introduction

Chapter 6 focuses on the main frameworks for understanding cultural differences. It discusses the traditional frameworks of context, time and space. It also introduces the concept of cultural dimensions, the most popular research approach used to analyze the influence of culture in international business and marketing. It then discusses Hall's (1976), Hofstede's (1991) and Trompenaars' and Hampden-Turner (1997) frameworks, which have traditionally been used to analyze the influence of culture in business. Critical views regarding these frameworks are also offered, reminding researchers that an over-reliance on these frameworks could run a risk of over-simplifying culture. The case-in-point examples include Ikea's web design and processing of nutritional information. The mini-case included in Chapter 6 is Disney Land in Paris and Hong Kong.

Chapter Objectives

- Learn the traditional variables for understanding cultures inclusive of context, time, and space.
- Understand the concept of cultural dimensions.
- Learn the main premises of Hofstede's and Trompenaars and Hampden Turner's work.
- Become familiar with other categorizations of culture.

Warmup question: *Is it more important to understand cultural differences or cultural similarities to internationalize brands successfully?*

ers. Thus, paraverbal cues become an integral part of the
Traditional Variables for Understanding Cultures

The traditional variables for understanding cultures include those of context (high/low), time (monochronic/polychronic), and space orientations, and they were introduced by the American anthropologist Edward Hall (1976). They are often used as preliminary frameworks for understanding cultural differences.

Cultures and Context

Context signifies the situation in which something happens. It refers to the setting, or the set of conditions that exist where and when something happens. Hall (1976) proposed this framework for understanding cultures based on their preferred communication styles, suggesting that people in different countries encode and decode messages based on their cultural wiring. Thus, Hall suggested that cultures can be compared based on their preferred communication styles, dividing them into high- and low-context cultures.

In *high-context cultures*, such as, for example, Arab nations, Greece, France, or China, most information is already contained in the person, and very little communication is explicit. In these cultures, people are deeply involved with each other and social hierarchy is respected, while individual inner emotions are kept under strong self-control. Information is shared through simple messages that have a deep meaning, and communication style is more implicit than explicit. A precise style containing no more or less than what is required is used, with long pauses and silences which are meant to convey meanings.

These cultures also tend to use a lot of metaphors and clues that are understood by the members of that society. In fact, contextual clues that surround the actual message are as important as the message itself. Often, this type of communication style is based on hinting at a message through what is left unsaid. In high-context communication, most information is already contained "in the physical context or internalized in the person" (Hall, 1976, p. 79).

High-context cultures use many communicative cues such as body language and silences. Thus, paraverbal cues become an integral part of the message. In-person communication relies on nonverbal strategies such as proximity, tone of voice, body language, gestures, facial expressions, or deliberate silences. Things aren't spelled out explicitly because most members of the cultural group are assumed to understand them already. Individuals from a high-context culture are more sensitive to nuances in advertising, and thus fewer words are better than many.

In high-context cultures, a lot of hinted, unspoken information is implicitly transferred during the communication process, which is geared toward building relationships with others. These relationships tend to be more important long-term for doing business than in the low- context cultures. Therefore, there is less structure and fewer rules in this type of communication. High-context cultures also do not rely much on written, or formal, information as do low-context cultures. Instead, face-to-face meetings are preferred, because the physical presence is necessary for effective nonverbal communication, which is a very important element in communication.

Low-context cultures on the other hand have preferences for a straightforward and explicit communication style. This style is more common in cultures where people are highly individualized, and they also place lesser importance on social hierarchy, which is generally not seen as imposing on individuals' lives.

In the low-context cultures, communication is predominantly explicit and consists of direct statements and verbal speech. Conversations are also less animated and the meaning is most often encoded in the spoken word. Rich and expressive language is often used in an elaborate verbal style. The choice of words is less important than in high-context cultures: what is meant is what is said. The context of the message usually plays a little role, and communication is more direct and nonpersonal. Low-context communication style implies that very little is left implicit and hidden, and communication is more task-oriented.

How can these concepts be applied in marketing successfully?

Implications for Marketing

There are implications for marketing from these communications style differences. For example, high-context communication tends to be more connotative – most of the information is not expressed directly through words, and the words that are used are more metaphorical. Facial expressions, tone, background, actions, and body movements are needed to get the full meaning. Low-context communication is, on the other hand, more denotative. In most situations, thoughts, opinions, needs, and feelings are communicated in a straightforward way. Thus, background and tone are less important, and the literal meaning of the words is usually preferred. These differences are relevant across all realms of marketing.

These two different modes of communication also have implications on how conflict and confrontations are managed in a culture. In high-context cultures, people tend to personalize their disagreement with others and they prefer to avoid confrontation. By showing one's disagreement and anger in public, the person is admitting a loss of control, which may then lead to a loss of face. What is said is taken personally, and maintaining social harmony is key. In the low-context cultures, repression of views is unreasonable and most people believe that everyone has their own right to express opinions. Explicit criticism has nothing to do with interpersonal relationships – rather, it is believed to be solution-oriented.

High- and low-context cultures also use language differently. In high-context cultures metaphoric and expressive language is used more often, whereas in the low-context cultures a precise language style is more commonly used. In high-context cultures, there are long pauses and more silences, and the silence is meant to have a meaning; metaphors are used more often than in the low-context cultures. Also, high-context cultures emphasize visuals over text, and the context carries more weight than the actual words. In low-context cultures, on the other hand, there is a strong emphasis on the actual words and the written text.

How could these differences affect advertising considerations? What about PR and personal selling?

A Case in Point: Ikea Web Design

These considerations should be taken into account with web design and website localization. For example, IKEA's website in high-context cultures like Japan looks different from its website in a low-context country, such as the Netherlands.

Ikea's Japanese homepage has heavy, bright, and colorful graphics and less text. It also uses scrolling graphics and a slideshow, using various hints that may resonate with high-context cultures such as the Japanese. On the Netherlands IKEA homepage, there are no metaphors or bright colors – tables are stacked and functional products are emphasized, and the text is also more explicit.

Interpreting Cultural Differences

The Dutch Ikea site shows explicit information about the products, with a range of prices and options, while IKEA in Japan uses metaphors and symbolic images. This shows that cultures may have different preferences regarding visual stimuli. This affects web design, amongst other marketing channels.

Figure 6.1 IKEA Holland web page.
Source: IKEA.

Figure 6.2 IKEA Japan web page.
Source: IKEA.

> Although the Internet is a low-context medium, its adaptation is recommended in high-context cultures. Some research suggests that people in high-context cultures prefer more interactivity on the website as it enables a better experience for them (e.g., Wurtz, 2005). It is therefore important to consider the visual aspects of website localization and adjust it across cultures, including color codes, animation, flash, and interactive features. Figures 6.1 and 6.2 show IKEA's web pages in Holland and Japan.
>
> *What other realms of marketing are affected by the differences between high- and low- context cultures?*

Cultures and Time

Cultures also have different perceptions of time. Using time as a lens for analysis, we can make a distinction between monochronic and polychronic cultures. The terms come from the Greek words "chronos" (χρόνος, in Greek), meaning time, "mono" (μονό, in Greek) or single, and "poly" (πολοί, in Greek) meaning many or multiple. People coming from cultures characterized with a *monochronic* approach to time are generally considered to have a preference for doing one thing at a time; they value a certain orderliness and they do not value interruptions. They tend to divide time into smaller units and are generally seen to prefer concentrating on the job at hand and one task at a time.

Cultures with a *polychronic* approach to time tend to do multiple things at once, they tend to manage interruptions well, and they may be willing to change plans often and easily. Perceptions of time are linked to how people approach relationship building, which is seen as necessary for business interactions, and building them takes time. Often, a monochronic time approach is more dominant in the low-context cultures, whereas a polychronic approach is found more often in high-context cultures (Cateora, Gilly, & Graham, 2009).

Using time as a framework to analyze cultures, we can also identify linear-separable, circular-traditional, and procedural-traditional time (Graham, 1981). The *linear-separable time* is similar to a monochronic approach to time, and it is more prevalent in Europe (with exceptions of some countries) and North America, which are predominantly low-context cultures.

This approach implies that a clear separation is made between the past, the present, and the future. In those cultures, that time is considered to be a valuable investment toward future gains. The *circular-traditional time* approach follows a cyclical approach to time whereby the future is seen as a repetition of the past. Finally, in the case of *procedural-traditional time*, the activity or procedure is more relevant than the amount of time that is spent on performing it. Time and money are seen as separate, and monetary value is determined by a task rather than by the time spent doing it (ibid).

In which marketing disciplines can these frameworks be used successfully?

Cultures and Space

Space orientations also differ across cultures. They relate to the concept of personal vs. public territory, divisions between private and public, and what is considered to be a comfortable personal distance between people in a given culture. This concept also relates to comfort or a lack of comfort with physical touch and direct physical contact, and expectations about where and how contact will take place. For example, certain cultures, such as French, Spanish, or Greek, allow cross-gender touching or kissing, and greeting rituals fit with these patterns.

Eye contact has a strong role in interpersonal interactions. This importance of eye contact in social communication is expressed through various metaphors, such as "eyes are the windows to the soul." Space orientations also relate to comfort with eye contact, and what is attributed to direct eye contact or a lack of direct eye contact.

However, these interpretations also differ across cultures. In some cultures, direct eye contact is taken as a sign of reliability and trustworthiness, while in others it is disrespectful and inappropriate. For example, in many Asian cultures, looking down is usually interpreted as a sign of respect, whereas in Western cultures looking away or not looking someone in the eye is disrespectful and suggests that the person may not be trustworthy.

In many Western cultures, people tend to relate to others who make direct eye contact as more likable, credible, or dominant when compared with those who avoid direct eye contact. However, in some other cultures, excessive eye contact may make an observer feel uncomfortable regardless of the situation (Kleinke, 1986). Thus, people from East Asian cultures may interpret someone who is making a direct eye contact as being less approachable, or even angrier, in comparison to individuals from Western cultures.

There is variability in how people relate to facial expressions and in particular the direct eye contact across cultures (Elfenbein & Ambady, 2002). The total amount of time that people maintain direct eye contact in conversation varies between cultures. Studies have shown that in Western cultures, it is much more important to maintain eye contact during social interactions than in East Asian cultures (Argyle, Henderson, Bond, Iizuka, & Contarello, 1986).

Studies have also shown that facial expressions – such as fear or disgust – could be recognized and interpreted differently across cultures due to the underlying differences in eye fixation patterns (Jack, Blais, Scheepers, Schyns, & Caldara, 2009). For example, people from some Asian cultures such as Japanese tend to use facial information from eye movements and expressions, while Americans and British tend to focus more on the mouth (Yuki, Maddux, & Masuda, 2007).

This also influences how people make inferences about age across cultures. For example, non-Asians have difficulties determining the age of Asian people, whereas many people from Eastern Asian cultures engage in more holistic face processing which helps them to process both their own faces as well as faces of other races and ethnicities in order to gauge a person's age (Tanaka, Kiefer, & Bukach, 2004).

Recent development of neuroscience has enabled researchers to obtain a more in-depth knowledge of responses to stimuli. This is done with help of the fMRI studies that investigate the effect of culture on neural processing. Research shows that people respond differently to the same facial expressions from those who belong to the same race, vs. those who belong to a different race.

Marketers need to consider these cultural differences in the perceptions of facial expressions and expression of emotions when devising advertising campaigns across cultures. These differences also affect personal selling.

How can we translate the difference in space orientations between cultures to marketing tactics?

Hofstede's Dimensions of Culture

Hofstede originally suggested that cultures differ along four main dimensions inclusive of Power Distance, Uncertainty Avoidance, Individualism/Collectivism, and Masculinity/Femininity. Later, the additional dimensions of Long-/Short-Term Orientation were added as well as a sixth dimension of Indulgence/Restraint with others (Hofstede, Hofstede, & Minkov, 2010). Hofstede's research has identified a range of primary dimensions, building on the previous work (e.g., Kluckhohn & Strodtbeck, 1961). Following this line of thinking, Triandis (2004) suggested that some dimensions are primary and others secondary, and that secondary dimensions evolved from the primary dimensions.

The national level analysis of culture became the most popular approach in management research, mostly due to the popularity and the contribution of Hofstede's work in the 1970s and the 1980s, and the research conducted by Hall (1976) and Glenn and Glenn (1981). Cultural dimensions of Hofstede have been the dominant approach in the studies of national culture in both organizational as well as marketing research (Kirkman, Lowe, & Gibson, 2017). The use of nation as the primary unit in cross-cultural analysis has been defended by researchers from a range of disciplines, including cross-cultural psychologists, political scientists, and economists. In spite of the growing criticism of this approach, the use of national culture as a unit of analysis has been defended on the grounds that it shapes values of a larger group and presents a critical factor in business, politics, and economic development (Inglehart & Baker, 2000).

Hofstede's Six Dimensions of Culture could be summarized as follows (Hofstede, 2011, p. 8):

- Power Distance, related to different solutions to the basic problem of human inequality;
- Uncertainty Avoidance, related to the level of stress in a society in the face of an unknown future;
- Individualism vs. Collectivism, related to the integration of individuals into primary groups;
- Masculinity vs. Femininity, related to the division of emotional roles between women and men;

- Long-Term vs. Short-Term Orientation, related to the focus of people's efforts on the future or the present and past; and
- Indulgence vs. Restraint, related to gratification vs. control of basic human desires related to enjoying life.

The *power distance index (PDI)* indicates how much the less powerful people accept and expect that power is distributed unequally in society. It reflects the fundamental question: *how much inequality should there be among people?* In the higher power distance cultures, hierarchy is clearly established in a society. Most people don't question it, and parents teach their children to be obedient. Inequality between people and an uneven power distribution are generally tolerated. In the lower power distance cultures on the other hand, people question authority and they may attempt to distribute the power more equally. In the words of Hofstede (2011, p. 9), inequality (more vs. less power) is "defined from below, not from above," suggesting that "society's level of inequality is endorsed by the followers as much as by the leaders."

In the cultures characterized with a higher power distance index, strong hierarchies exist and for this reason decisions are often made by the heads of families and top managers. Thus, marketing should appeal to the leadership by emphasizing how products create benefits for the whole family, the company, or the society as a whole. For the cultures that are generally characterized with a low power distance index, marketing messages are better suited toward a broader range of ordinary people who will discuss the products and make decisions based on their personal preferences.

Individualism vs. collectivism (IDV) reflects the degree to which people in a society are integrated into groups. It is important to note, though, that this should be interpreted as a societal, rather than an individual trait. In the so-called "individualistic societies," people have loose ties between them, and are often usually actively engaged with immediate family and friends. The societies considered to be more collectivistic on the other hand have more tightly-integrated relationships. In those cultures, people are more integrated in the immediate as well as within broader groups, and they tend to express loyalty and support for in-group members when a conflict arises.

Thus, in the cultures characterized with high individualism, marketing messages are often tailored to emphasize benefits for individuals – for example, individual freedom, saving time, and rewarding yourself. On the other hand, for cultures characterized with low individualism, it may be more suited to emphasize strong community ties, market to the whole community, and explain how if its members buy the products, the community will also see the benefits and everyone will reap the rewards. This difference can be understood by answering: *how much do we depend on our extended family people?*

Uncertainty avoidance (UAI) reflects society's tolerance for ambiguity and its willingness to embrace something unexpected, unknown, or different from the status quo. This concept is not the same as simply avoiding risks: rather, it illustrates a comfort level with uncertain or unstructured situations. Countries with a high uncertainty avoidance score give preference to more strict codes of behavior, guidelines, and laws, and generally they tend to rely on the idea of the "absolute truth," or one correct solution. Such cultures try to minimize ambiguous or uncertain situations by "strict behavioral codes, laws and rules, and disapproval of deviant opinions" (Hofstede, 2011, p. 10).

A lower uncertainty avoidance score implies that there is more acceptance of differing thoughts or ideas. Such cultures tend to impose fewer regulations, ambiguity is more accepted, and the environment is more free-flowing rather than being tightly structured. The difference between the two could be understood by answering the question: *how reluctant or afraid are we of new people or ideas?*

Cultures characterized with a low tolerance for uncertainty prefer to have product characteristics and advantages spelled out clearly in the packaging and in advertising. On the other hand, those that have higher tolerance for uncertainty and for ambiguity may be more open to accept lifestyle promotions, generalizations about products, implied benefits, and references to positive change which may be unknown. Such product promotions are less likely to stir negative emotions affiliated with uncertainty.

In high uncertainty avoidance cultures, marketers tend to use more structured and serious, detailed visuals along with demonstrations regarding the use of a product. Such a style is called Germanic style. On the other hand, more humor in advertisements is used primarily in the low uncertainty avoidance cultures.

Masculinity vs. femininity (MAS) is also a societal, rather than an individual characteristic. It describes the common division of emotional roles between genders in a society. It reflects some commonly held perceptions of how a man or a woman should look, feel, and behave in a society. Societies high on masculinity value achievement, heroism, strength, assertiveness, and material rewards for success. In societies that score high on femininity there is a preference for cooperation, modesty, sympathy, caring for the weak, and the quality of life, and women share roles and views equally with men. The fundamental difference between the two can be understood by asking the question: *how should men and women behave in a society?*

Because cultures that are characterized with a relatively high masculinity differentiate between the roles of men and women, it is important for marketers to ensure that marketing targets the correct gender for the product as understood by the particular culture. Cultures characterized with low masculinity tend to promote gender equality. They may respond negatively to gender-oriented promotions, and thus a more neutral approach appealing to both men and women may be more effective. In both cultures, however, it is important to avoid gender stereotyping.

Long-term orientation vs. short-term orientation (LTO) describes a culture's connection between the past and current and future actions/challenges. In countries with a lower degree of this index (short-term orientation), traditions are honored and kept, while in those cultures with a high degree in this index (long-term orientation) adaptation and change are viewed as a necessity. Marketers may try to fit the promotions into traditional structures for markets with high long-term orientation, while emphasizing short-term benefits for low-scoring markets. The fundamental question that helps us to understand the difference between the two is: *do we focus on the future, the present, or the past; do we separate between them or see them as connected?*

Indulgence vs. restraint (IND) is a measure of whether or not the simple joys of life are fulfilled and gratified freely. Societies characterized with higher indulgence allow a relatively free gratification of the basic and natural human desires related to enjoying life and having fun. Societies characterized with a high restraint tend to control gratification of needs and regulate them by means of strict social norms. The differences between the two CVOs could be answered with the question: *is life serious or fun?*

Cultures characterized with high indulgence value leisure time and sports and they have more relaxed sexual representation standards. This allows for more freedom when promoting products. Online interfaces such as websites or social media spaces could be designed to enable more casual, fun interactions, and encourage more user-generated content.

In low indulgence cultures, there are tight social restrictions. Thus, marketers may like to promote the social benefits of their products, their usefulness, or how they fit into the existing social order. In the low-indulgent cultures, marketers also may want to emphasize opportunities to save money or serve the community, in more organized, formal, and structured forms of interaction.

What is the biggest contribution of Hofstede's work to marketing?

Trompenaars' and Hampden-Turner's Dimensions of Culture

Building on Hofstede's work, Trompenaars' and Hampden-Turner (1997) framework includes *universalism vs. particularism*; *individualism vs. communitarianism*; *specific vs. diffuse*; *neutral vs. emotional*; *achievement vs. ascription*; *sequential time vs. synchronous time*; and *internal direction vs. outer direction*.

The dimension of *universalism vs. particularism* reflects how cultures relate to laws and obligations. Cultures characterized with higher universalism place a high importance on laws, rules, societal values, and obligations. The rule of law is strong in these cultures and it comes before relationships. People are dealt with fairly based on common, universal guidelines and not on contextual situations or relationships. Particularism, on the other hand, reflects a tendency to believe that circumstances and relationships dictate the rules that people live by. Thus, individual response to a situation may change based on what's happening in the moment, and the specific circumstances.

The *individualism vs. communitarianism* dimension reflects a degree to which people value personal freedom. In cultures characterized with higher individualism, people hold strong beliefs in personal freedom and achievement. They believe that they must make their own decisions, and that they must take care of themselves. In cultures that score higher on communitarianism, on the other hand, people may believe that a group is more important than the individual, and that it provides help and safety in exchange for loyalty.

The *specific vs. diffuse* dimension illustrates how people relate to their personal and public lives. In cultures that express more specific tendencies,

152

Interpreting Cultural Differences

people tend to keep work and personal lives separate. As a result, they may believe that relationships don't have much of an impact on their work objectives, and they believe that people can work together without getting along personally. In diffuse cultures, on the other hand, people see a strong overlap between their work and personal lives. They may believe that good relationships are vital to meeting business objectives, and thus they tend to spend time outside of work with colleagues and clients.

The *neutral vs. emotional* dimension relates to regulation of emotions. In the cultures seen as having a more neutral expression, people make a great effort to control their emotions, especially in public. They do not tend to reveal what they're thinking or how they're feeling to others. In cultures that are more emotional in their expression, on the other hand, people tend to express their emotions, even spontaneously, at work. It is generally welcome and accepted to show emotion to others, even in public.

The *achievement vs. ascription* dimension illustrates how people value each other. In the achievement-oriented cultures, people may believe that you are what you do, and they may base your worth accordingly. Performance is valued in these cultures, no matter who you are. In cultures that are characterized with ascription, people may believe that you should be valued for who you are, not necessarily by your own merit. Power, title, and a position matter very much in these cultures, and these roles define people's behavior toward others.

The *sequential vs. synchronous* view of cultures helps to understand how people manage time. In sequential cultures, people have a general preference for events to happen in a logical order. They place a high value on punctuality, planning, and sticking to plans, and staying on schedule. Similar to the monochronic cultures, people in sequential cultures go by "time is money," and they don't appreciate it when their schedule is changed. In the synchronous cultures, on the other hand, people see the past, present, and future as interwoven periods. They often work on several projects at once, and view plans and commitments as moveable. This approach to culture is similar to the cultures having a polychronic approach to time.

The *internal vs. outer direction* view of cultures helps to understand how people relate to their environment. In the internal directed cultures, people may believe that they can control their environment in order to achieve their goals. This may also suggest patterns of team work within organizations. In the outer-directed cultures, on the other hand, people believe that either

153

nature, or their environment, controls them. At work and in their personal life, they may be more likely to focus their actions on others, and to avoid conflict where possible.

How could you combine Trompenaars' and Hampden Turner's framework with Hofstede's dimensions for your project?

Synthesis of Dimensional Approaches

Cateora et al. (2009) offer a framework that presents a synthesis of the aforementioned characterizations. In their view, all cultures could be divided broadly into information-oriented (IO) and relationship-oriented (RO) cultures. *Information-oriented cultures* are characterized with low-context orientations, individualism, low power distance, low distance from English, linguistic directness, monochronic time, propensity for the use of technology interface for communication, and competition.

Relationship-oriented cultures, on the other hand, are viewed as high-context, collectivistic, characterized with high power distance, higher distance from English, linguistic indirectness, polychronic time, preference for face-to-face interactions, focus on the background of an image, and a propensity to reduce transaction costs.

Context and cultural dimensions are often combined to analyze cultural influence. For example, direct, low-context communication style is characterized with the use of personal pronouns, that is, "I" in individualistic cultures. On the other hand, high-context communications style, which focuses more on the "we" pronoun, drawings, symbolism, and metaphors is pertinent in the collectivist cultures. By looking at both, for example, low power distance and individualistic cultures, we can identify a direct, explicit, and personalized advertising.

Horizontal and Vertical Cultures

Grounded in the ideas of individualism/collectivism and power distance, some researchers made a distinction between horizontal vs. vertical cultures. This approach expands on the traditional individualism/collectivism dimension suggested by Hofstede (Shavitt, Johnson, & Zhang, 2011). For example, cultures with *horizontal orientation* are seen to value equality while cultures with a more vertical orientation tend to emphasize hierarchy.

Interpreting Cultural Differences

Thus, we may infer that advertising in cultures with vertical orientation may emphasize status and achievement, while in cultures with horizontal orientation, marketers may want to focus on interpersonal support and on achieving group goals.

Similarly, in *vertical cultures*, ads may use spokespeople portrayed as high achievers or label the brands as "award-wining." In horizontal cultures, on the other hand, unique and personal benefits of purchasing a brand may be emphasized. Research across cultures has also established that magazine ads in the vertical cultures (for example, in the U.S. or South Korea) place more emphasize on luxury and prestige as status signals than they do in horizontal cultures such as Denmark or Sweden (ibid).

How would you combine different cultural dimension approaches in your project?

Brands and Culture

Global brands should adopt cultural orientations in their host markets. Much like in their home markets, brands are viewed as possessing human-like characters and traits. Brands have personalities, and consumers relate to brands as if they were people. The interpretations of what constitutes a certain trait – such as Apple's "Think Different" slogan – vary greatly across cultures, as does the idea of thinking "differently."

Brands are more likely to be successful if they resonate with the dominant values in a host culture (Allen, Gupta, & Monnier, 2008), for the most part. This may not apply to certain fringe products or nonconforming consumers. This is important across all aspects of marketing practice.

A Case in Point: Processing of Nutritional Information

Cultural mindset affects information processing references, or cognitive schemas that are culturally congruent (Oyserman, 2011).

For example, cultures affect consumer reactions to nutritional information and how it is presented on products. Gomez and Torelli (2015) suggest that, for example, French consumers tend to focus on food enjoyment more than on the nutritional information. Enjoying food is a central aspect of the French culture. Therefore, when the values associated with food enjoyment are made salient, the customers tend to evaluate food more favorably.

On the other hand, they may evaluate it less favorably when the nutritional information is present. Equally, they tend to have more difficulties reading and processing nutritional information because it is seen as the opposite of food enjoyment, and as something practical and utilitarian that may hamper their enjoyment.

This suggests that marketers should appeal to the dominant cultural values across all aspects of marketing practice; in this example, product packaging and promotion. In this case, nutritional aspects of food should not be overemphasized in cultures that tend to focus on food enjoyment.

How can brands use the knowledge of cultural clues to inform their efforts?

A Word of Caution

While studies using Hofstede's cultural dimensions have played an important role in informing marketing science over the past four decades, a growing body of research echoes worries about an overreliance on this approach. Many mixed results have appeared in these studies. Thus, although the cultural dimensions approach has been the most common in intercultural marketing, it is important to retain a critical outlook when applying this framework. This approach is helpful for understanding broad trajectories of thinking within a culture; however, it should not be applied in absolute terms. Moreover, assessing individuals based on the country-level scores is tricky – these frameworks seek to determine behavioral patterns of groups, not of individuals belonging to these groups.

However, relevant insights could be obtained from these frameworks that serve as the best first approximation. There are plenty of studies and examples available for researchers and practitioners. These studies have been used to inform a range of marketing channels and tactics inclusive of message development, advertising, or web design. It is important, however, to remember that these frameworks are originally created for organizations in order to understand organizational behavior, rather than for understanding consumers.

Interpreting Cultural Differences

These models also do not take into account the differences between regions or subcultures. Many external and internal factors influence how marketers should communicate with their consumers across cultures. Ford (2018) suggests that an absolute application of any cultural scale that is based on the assumptions of exact equivalence is problematic, because cultures are not static and thus any scale that attempts to frame them is problematic.

Mini-Case: Disneyland in Paris and Hong Kong

When Disneyland opened its first European theme park, "Euro Disney," in 1992 near Paris, it had rather high ambitions to make it one of the most lavish theme parks anywhere in the world. Unlike their previous success with Tokyo Disneyland in Japan where nearly 70% of the customers were repeat visitors, European visitors did not share the same sentiment. The location near Paris won over many other sites in Southern Europe, and the French government provided numerous incentives for the company to anchor there. Projections were ambitious considering how many visitors come to Paris each year, and the proximity to other European locations within just a few hours of driving distance.

This situation was so dire in fact, that in 2014 Disney announced its "22-year money-losing failure" with a $1.25 billion bailout plan (Pozzebon, 2014). A number of factors lead to its strategic and financial failure. These included macro factors such as the European recession in the late 1980s, changeable weather with a lot of rain, the price that proved too high for European audiences, poor cost management, and many others.

Primarily though, from the cultural perspective, the French tourists saw Disney as an American icon, and in many ways, as an expression of American cultural imperialism. Even the name chosen – Euro – was associated with the currency, and it was not seen as an abbreviation for the continent. The French consumers thought that Mickey Mouse was promoted at the expense of local childhood cartoon icons such as Asterix, which later became a competing park in the relative proximity of Disney.

Disneyland Paris was at times also seen as somewhat of a cultural disaster. Much like in the U.S., Disney's advertising messages focused on glamour and grandeur. However, the French audience was more interested in understanding specific details of various rides and attractions. Many were put off by the emphasis of size and glitz, seen as another expression of cultural imperialism. The actual park layout as well as the amenities on offer did not appeal to the local culture either. In Europe, people prefer to walk around for their leisure activities, rather than to be taken by train. They also tend to consume healthier snacks rather than fast-food, and they prefer local flavors. For example, in Euro Disney, the local sausage was originally unavailable and alcohol was forbidden at the park.

Some other details also did not appeal to the European audiences – such as not providing kennels in a culture where people frequently travel with dogs. This clash of cultures was also seen internally – for example, a Euro Disney employee apparently wrote on a suicide note that he did "not want to return to working for Mickey" (The Independent, 2010).

With lessons learnt in Paris, Disney was determined not to repeat the same mistakes in Hong Kong. To that end, feng-shui (风水, in Chinese, literally wind and water) rules were observed. Feng-shui is a traditional Chinese practice of geomancy, or the use of energy to achieve harmony between individuals and their physical environment. A feng-shui master was brought to observe planning and construction of the park in Hong Kong, in order to ensure that objects were arranged in harmony with nature to achieve health and prosperity, in the old Chinese tradition. The position and the direction the park, as well as all buildings and objects were arranged according to the feng-shui principles. They even followed the old Chinese belief that a number four is unlucky and thus there were no fourth floors in the park either.

An auspicious date for the park opening was chosen too – September 12, 2006 – and the traditional good-luck opening ceremony was observed at the outset. Although this was not an easy formula for cultural acceptance either, because many Disney characters were still new in China at that point, even so, by observing the main cultural imperatives, Disney at least avoided the strategic disaster it faced in Paris for many years.

Mini-Case Questions

- What was the reason for Disney's failure in Europe?
- How could Disney have avoided the problems in Paris?
- To what extend did they correct some of the mistakes in Hong Kong?
- Was their approach in Hong Kong a guarantee for success?
- How different would Disney's experience been in Europe have been had they selected another location?

Chapter Guiding Questions

As you work further on your advertising appeal, think of the *Unique Advertising Proposition (UAP)* and the cultural factors it hinges on. Consider the following questions:

- What unique cultural characteristics need to be taken into account in order to increase advertising appeal for your target audience?
- How can dimensional frameworks inform your marketing efforts, especially advertising?
- Which cultural dimensions may be applicable as the best first guess about your host country? How do they differ from your brand's home market?
- Which of them could inform your marketing strategy?
- What imagery should be avoided? Promoted?
- Are gender representations in your host country influenced by cultural value orientations?
- What are the dominant values? Are there any latent values that are important to your specific segment, or in your industry of choice?

References

Allen, M. W., Gupta, R., & Monnier, A. (2008). The interactive effect of cultural symbols and human values on taste evaluation. *Journal of Consumer Research*, *35*(2), 29–308.

Argyle, M., Henderson, M., Bond, M., Iizuka, Y., & Contarello, A. (1986). Cross-cultural variations in relationship rules. *International Journal of Psychology*, *21*, 287–315.

Cateora, P. R., Gilly, M. C., & Graham, J. L. (2009). *International marketing*. New York: McGraw-Hill Irwin.

Elfenbein, H. A., & Ambady, N. (2002). On the universality and cultural specificity of emotion recognition: A meta-analysis. *Psychology Bulletin*, *128*, 200–235.

Ford, J. B. (2018). Major mistakes made in cross-cultural marketing research. *Projectics/Proyéctica/Projectique*, *3*(21), 13–21.

Glenn, E. S., & Glenn, C. G. (1981). *Man and mankind: Conflict and communication between cultures*. Norwood, NJ: Ablex.

Gomez, P., & Torelli, C. J. (2015). It's not just numbers: Cultural identities influence how nutrition information influences the valuation of foods. *Journal of Consumer Psychology*, *25*(3), 404–415.

Graham, R. J. (1981). The role of perception of time in consumer research. *Journal of Consumer Research*, *7*, 33–42.

Hall, E. (1976). *Beyond culture*. New York: Anchor Books.

Hofstede, G. (1991). *Cultures and organizations: Software of the mind*. London: McGraw-Hill.

Hofstede, G. (2011). Dimensionalizing cultures: The Hofstede model in context. *Online Readings in Psychology and Culture*, *2*(1). Retrieved from https://scholarworks.gvsu.edu/cgi/viewcontent.cgi?article=1014&context=orpc

Hofstede, G., Hofstede, G. J., & Minkov, M. (2010). *Cultures and organizations: Software of the mind* (Rev. 3rd ed.). New York: McGraw-Hill.

The Independent. (2010). Losing the magic: How Euro Disney became a nightmare. Retrieved from www.independent.co.uk/news/business/analysis-and-features/losing-the-magic-how-euro-disney-became-a-nightmare-2132892.html

Inglehart, R., & Baker, W. E. (2000). Modernization, cultural change, and the persistence of traditional values. *American Sociological Review*, *65*(1), 19–51.

Jack, R. E., Blais, C., Scheepers, C., Schyns, P. G., & Caldara, R. (2009). Cultural confusions show that facial expressions are not universal. *Current Biology*, *19*(18), 1543–1548.

Kirkman, B. L., Lowe, K. B., & Gibson, C. B. (2017). A retrospective on culture's consequences: The 35-year journey. *Journal of International Business Studies*, *48*(1), 12–29.

Kleinke, C. L. (1986). Gaze and eye contact: A research review. *Psychology Bulletin, 100*, 78–100.

Kluckhohn, F. R., & Strodtbeck, F. L. (1961). *Variations in value orientations*. Evanston, IL: Row, Peterson.

Oyserman, D. (2011). Culture as situated cognition: Cultural mindsets, cultural fluency, and meaning making. *European Review of Social Psychology*, *22*(1), 164–214.

Pozzebon, S. (2014). *Why Euro Disney is a 22-year money-losing failure. Business Insider*. Retrieved from www.businessinsider.com/euro-disney-announces-1-billion-crisis-plan-2014-10

Shavitt, S., Johnson, T. P., & Zhang, J. (2011). Horizontal and vertical cultural differences in the content of advertising appeals. *Journal of International Consumer Marketing*, *23*(3–4), 297–310.

Tanaka, J. W., Kiefer, M., & Bukach, C. M. (2004). A holistic account of the own-race effect in face recognition: Evidence from a cross-cultural study. *Cognition, 93*(1), B1–B9.

Triandis, H. C. (2004). The many dimensions of culture. *Academy of Management Executive*, *18*(1), 88–93.

Trompenaars, F., & Hampden-Turner, C. (1997). *Riding the waves of culture: Understanding cultural diversity in business*. London: Nicholas Brealey Publishing.

Wurtz, E. (2005). Intercultural communication on web sites: A cross-cultural analysis of web sites from high-context cultures and low-context cultures. *Journal of Computer-Mediated Communication, 11*(1), 274–299.

Yuki, M., Maddux, W. W., & Masuda, T. (2007). Are the windows to the soul the same in the East and West? Cultural differences in using the eyes and mouth as cues to recognize emotions in Japan and the United States. *Journal of Experimental Social Psychology, 43*, 303–311.

Language Considerations in Intercultural Markets

Introduction

Chapter 7 focuses on language considerations in intercultural markets. It investigates the role of language in intercultural marketing, focusing on the interaction between language, communication, and culture. It sheds light on the influence of cultural conditioning on verbal and non-verbal communication preferences. It discusses the components of language, links between language and sensory experiences, an-d layers of language. It sheds light on the classic communications model and the cultural aspect of noise, as well as on the notion of linguistic imperialism. It further discusses linguistic considerations for naming strategies. The case-in-point examples include unique characteristics of a language, brand naming in the car industry, K Pop, and universal principles for brand naming. The mini-case in this chapter discusses brand naming considerations in China.

Chapter Objectives

- Understand the links between language and culture.
- Learn the components of language with relevance for marketing.
- Understand the connection between language and sensory experiences.
- Understand layers of language and their influence on marketing.
- Learn the basic communications model and its challenges in intercultural contexts.
- Critically assess the concept of linguistic imperialism.

Intercultural Language Considerations

- Understand the relevance of language for brand naming strategy.
- Become familiar with the concept of ethnolinguistics.

Warmup question: *How can marketers use their host country language to their advantage?*

Communications Model

The traditional *communications model* involves a *source, encoding, transmission process, decoding process*, and *feedback* (Turow, 2010). The information is transmitted by the sender, or the source, which could be a person or a group. The sender first encodes the message in a way that can be perceived and understood by a desired audience. The message is then transmitted to the receiver via different channels that could be perceived by the five senses; the receiver then engages in the process of decoding, or deciphering and translating the message using their own receiving mechanisms and mental models, in a way that has meaning and makes sense to them; finally, the receiver sends feedback to the transmitter.

This process can be interrupted by noise which can be environmental, mechanical, or semantic, and it can interfere with message delivery. Noise happens when messages are not decoded correctly due to external interference, and it causes communication breakdowns.

In their seminal model of communication, Shannon and Weaver (1963) argued that there are three types of communication problems, or noise: technical, semantic, and problems of effectiveness. Technical problems relate to the level of accuracy with which the message could be transmitted within a given channel, which may cause communication problems. In the contemporary communications context, this may refer to the different communications media, all of which have their limitations as well as their advantages.

The semantic level of noise relates to the precision with which the meaning of the message can be conveyed, while the efficacy level refers to the effectiveness with which the received meaning affects the behavior of the transmitter. For example, semantic noise happens when a speaker and a listener have different interpretations of certain word meanings (Shrivastava, 2012). Syntactical noise refers to grammatical inconsistencies such as wrong

163

uses of verb tenses during a sentence or inaccurate declensions, which often happen due to the fast pace of language exchanges and communication in languages other than one's native language.

Incorrect grammar can cause miscommunication regarding the individual's expression of emotions if words have more than one connotative meaning in different cultures or contexts. Because individuals are likely to use their own interpretations of the word meanings to infer what someone else intended to communicate, the original message can be lost (Alder & Gundersen, 2007).

We can also talk about *cultural noise* that happens when one side disregards and possibly offends the other due to cultural reasons, prejudices, or ethnocentrism. It is very important for international marketers to be aware of cultural noise (Czinkota & Ronkainen, 2007). Perceptual encoding and decoding gaps can originate from the cultural differences between the sender and the receiver, and they can distort communication between people from different cultures.

Language barriers could cause noise through each stage of the communications cycle, although many other factors could cause noise when communicating across cultures. Cultural noise is not directly related to foreign language fluency, but rather to the differences in cultural values, perceptions, and mental frames that influence communication.

In sum, culture affects how people encode messages, the medium they chose to transmit the message, and how the messages are decoded or interpreted by the receiver, and this exerts a strong influence on all aspects of marketing practice.

What are the sources of noise in intercultural communication?

Language and Culture

It is important for marketers to understand the role of language in intercultural marketing and the interaction between language, communication, and culture. *Language* is the medium of culture – it is formed by culture, while culture is also influenced and impacted by language. Language is a symbolic system of meaning shared among people who identify with one another and with a group they belong to. Language is a "collective memory bank" of the cultural cognition of a group, and much of it was formed in earlier human history (wa Thiong'o, 1986).

Like culture, language is learned, shared, and contextual. It consists of verbal and nonverbal aspects, both of which are equally important to understand because they carry strong cultural meanings. Language is used not just as a tool for information exchange, but also as a symbolic system. It has the power to create and shape symbolic realities, such as values, perceptions, and identities through discourse. Understanding a language is closely connected to understanding the culture which it represents (Everett, 2005). The meaning behind the language is closely linked to the customs and values of a culture, and it enables understanding between individuals.

The nature of language also exerts a strong influence on information processing. For example, the visual nature of Asian scripts such as Chinese, Japanese, or Korean, influences information processing styles – Asians pay more attention to visual information. Structural differences between these languages and English affects consumer memory of verbal information. In these languages, information is coded primarily in a visual manner (Schmitt, Pan, & Tavassoli, 1994). Thus, when it comes to brand names, visually distinct fonts or calligraphy may be more important in these Asian languages, whereas jingles and phonetic associations may be more important for English-speaking consumers.

While most languages use alphabetic scripts with symbols representing sounds, Chinese, Japanese, and Korean languages use logograms, or written characters that represent a word or an entire phrase. Thus, memory hinges on phonological clues for consumers using alphabetic scripts, and consumers using logographic scripts rely more on their visual memory. This suggests that advertisements relying on alphabetic scripts in these Asian markets should not use any distracting auditory information. The same applies for advertising catering to consumers using logograms, where complex visual symbols should be avoided (Tavassoli & Han, 2001).

How does the nature of a language affect branding and advertising across cultures?

Layers of Language

We can distinguish between different *layers of language* such as denotative and connotative language aspects presenting two principal methods of describing the meanings of words (Allan, 2007). *Denotative meaning* is the strict meaning of a word and its precise, literal definition found in a dictionary. *Connotative meaning* is the emotional and imaginative association surrounding a word. It implies suggestive meanings which have strong cultural implications. For example, in denotative sense, "chicken" stands for an animal, whereas saying that someone is a chicken to describe personality implies that they are a coward in a denotative sense. In its connotative terms, "Hollywood" calls to mind such things as glitz, glamour, and celebrities. In its denotative meaning, Hollywood is an area of Los Angeles.

Connotative meanings may change over time depending on the broader socio-cultural and political context in a country. We can gain a better understanding of this concept by analyzing how some popular brands change over time. For example, some of the most popular car names in the 1960s in the U.S. included Thunderbird, Falcon, Charger, Comet, Mustang, and Barracuda. In the 1970s, the cars were usually branded as Rabbit, Pinto, Colt, Civic, Starlet, or Gremlin. Names evoke powerful associations with the spirit of the time they represent.

Connotative meanings are also different across geographies, and the same word or expression may imply different things depending on a specific country's context at a given point in time. For example, saying "Good day" in some parts of Europe may imply it is not raining on that day, while the same expression in Africa may mean that it is raining, especially in more dry areas.

Because of how the usage of words changes over time, words that denote approximately the same thing may acquire additional meanings or connotations, and these meanings can be either neutral, positive (ameliorative), or negative (pejorative). For example, referring to the same thing we can say "vagrants" with a negative connotation, "no fixed address" with a more neutral meaning, and "homeless" with a potentially positive connotation that triggers empathy with people who do not have a home. These interpretations are also influenced by personality factors and thus it is risky to rely purely on the assumed cultural standards at a given point in time. These evolving meanings are a result of cultural conditioning, personality factors, as well as the interaction between cultural, political, and economic contexts.

Non-verbal communication conveys meanings without using words. This type of communication can be divided into voluntary non-verbal communication, which includes intentional movements, poses, and gestures. On the other hand, involuntary non-verbal communication refers to unintentional body movements or facial expressions which often reveal ones' true feelings and opinions. Much like verbal language, nonverbal language also differs from country to country. These differences refer to manners and customs, dos and don'ts, glances, gestures, and changes in the voice register or tone to emphasize or alter what is said or what is intended.

It is important to remember that in the low-context cultures, the emphasis of communication is on spoken language – what is said is what is meant. On the other hand, in a high-context culture, verbal communication does not necessarily carry an explicit message, that is, what is said may not be what is meant. Thus, the hidden cultural meaning should be deciphered, and body language and tone of the voice help in this process.

Understanding the subtle nonverbal communication differences between cultures is very important for marketing efforts across cultures. Psychologist Albert Mehrabian suggested the "7%-38%-55%" rule to illustrate that much of what is exchanged hinges on nonverbal clues. He argued that the tone of the voice accounts for 38% of what is communicated, the body language accounts for 55%, while words only account for 7% of communication. One may or may not subscribe to this distribution; nonetheless, it is crucial to remember the importance of nonverbal language, and the differences across cultures.

How can marketers use nonverbal communication successfully across cultures?

Components of Language

We can observe different language components inclusive of semantics, syntactics, phonetics, and pragmatics. *Semantics* is the study of meaning, and how the actual standalone words carry the meanings we intend them to carry. *Syntactics* is the study of grammar, the language structure, and the rules of combining the individual words into sentences that make sense. *Phonetics* studies the sound system in a language, and *pragmatics* focuses on analyzing how a certain language is used in a particular context of a community and culture in a given time and place. Understanding these concepts becomes particularly complex when looking at languages other than our own. For example, some languages are tonal, such as the Chinese (four tones), Vietnamese or Thai (five tones), while Wobé, a Kru language spoken in the Ivory Coast has fourteen tones.

A Case in Point: Unique Language Characteristics

Unique characteristics of a language can present both challenges and opportunities for marketers. These idiosyncratic characteristics of a language need to be taken into consideration when internationalizing brands.

Such is the case of the Chinese language. For example, Chinese is logographic – one character can present a word or an entire sentence. This means that the word meanings are holistic, and that they can only be interpreted in a context – the same word can mean different things depending on the context.

Furthermore, there are no spaces between the individual words in Chinese. Chinese also has many homophones – the same spoken word can be represented by numerous different characters, depending on the intended meaning. Finally, Chinese language is also tonal and the tones used to pronounce a word can change its meaning completely.

Getting the phonetic element, or tone correct is important not only due to general linguistical competence, but also because different tones give words very different meanings. For example, in the Chinese language, the four tones can mean distinctly different things. The neutral syllable "ma" could mean four distinctly different things depending on the four tones. Using the first tone (a level higher pitch), or a "mā" it means mother (妈, in Chinese); with the second tone (rising from a lower to a slightly higher pitch), "má", it means hemp (麻, in Chinese). The third tone (falling-rising), or "mǎ" gives it a meaning of a horse (马, in Chinese), while the fourth tone (falling from a higher to lower), "mà", means to scold (骂, in Chinese).

Are there any unique language components in your host country that could be used to a marketer's advantage?

Language and Sensory Experiences

Beyond the aforementioned considerations, consonants, vowels, and a length of the vowel (long vs. short) can represent a unique *sensory experience* solely on the basis of sound. This is an important consideration for branding across cultures according to branding experts. Moon and Depeux (2019) derive inspiration from the French linguist Claude Hagège who suggested that many languages have ideophones that symbolize a sensory impression beyond its sound.

The authors share Hagège's quote from his book, *Dictionary of Language Lovers* (Dictionnaire amoureux des langues, in French original): "many languages possess . . . ideophones, or words that offer a sound painting of an idea, to symbolize a state, a sensory impression, a way of being or moving, an action that is not necessarily reproducing itself from a noise." Creation of brand names, they suggest, should leverage this power of ideophones to evoke ideas and sensations. Ideophones are words that evoke ideas through sound, and have the power to create vivid sensations or sensory perceptions of sound, shape, or actions.

Some brands are quite successful in using universal principles of language for their naming and brand translation strategies. Brands always seek ways to express universal concepts in a similar fashion across cultures; ideophones offer this possibility across cultures. Some examples in English include zigzag, swish, splish-splash, or tick-tock.

Are there any ideophones in your host country language?

A Case in Point: Car Naming and Sound Meaning

How does this translate to brand naming strategies? For example, Renault's brand Kadjar for an SUV is composed of sharp, swift, repetitive sounds that cause one to open and close the mouth very rapidly. This ideophone contains distinct syllables which in combination project a sense of a "cut," or symbolically, its speed.

The length of the word is also important to the product symbolic meaning. For example, many city cars use mono-syllable names to symbolize both quick and easy cars such as Seat Mii, Up! VW Up! Suzuki Swift, Ford Ka+, Honda Jazz, as shown in Figure 7.1. Subaru BRZ plays on the brevity of three letters, thus also projecting the sound of breeze, a feeling when cruising in a slick sports car (adapted from Moon & Depeux, 2019).

Intercultural Language Considerations

Moon and Depeux (2019) show us that "even when a brand name may seem meaningless, there is a strong likelihood that the seemingly arbitrary name may quietly shape consumers' perceptions – which in turn has the potential to impact the global performance of a name by striking a distinct emotional chord with customers."

Figure 7.1 Car brand naming strategies.
Source: Courtesy of Labbrand Brand Innovations.

Do you know any other brands that used sounds in a similar fashion?

A Case in Point: Universal Approaches to Brand Naming

We can see universal approaches to brand naming strategies in the example of K-pop. The enthusiasm of its fans could be interpreted through the symbolic concept of the ARMY (Adorable Representative M.C. for Youth). Branding experts attribute its success

Intercultural Language Considerations

largely to its naming strategy, and their use of acronyms as shown in Figure 7.2.

While language localizing is a daunting task for many brands, a universal approach to acronyms and numbers has helped the K-pop genre to design a successful brand name that resonates across cultures (Yan & Ju, 2019).

Figure 7.2 Use of acronyms in brand naming.
Source: Courtesy of Labbrand Brand Innovations.

Figure 7.3 shows four common principles brands can use across cultures for universal-focused brand naming principles, regardless of culture and language.

Intercultural Language Considerations

Figure 7.3 Brand naming principles.
Source: Courtesy of Labbrand Brand Innovations.

Can you think of any other brand examples with similar approaches to branding?

Brand Translation

Some brands are poorly localized, and consequently, their brand names can get lost in translation across cultures. Interestingly, some industry segments seem to have traditionally had more blunders than others. Such is the case of car companies. When Mercedes Benz first expanded to China, its "Rush" brand was allegedly translated as "bensi" (奔死, in Chinese). Although it was a close phonetic match, it actually means "rush to die." The company later rebranded to "benchi" (奔驰, in Chinese), which means "running quickly."

General Motors marketed the small car "Nova" to its consumers across different regions with a great deal of success, except for Italy and Spain where

Intercultural Language Considerations

the term is closely related to the words "don't go." Consequently, the company had to change the car name Nova to "Corsa" upon realizing the mistranslation.

Examples of poorly thought-out brand names are found in other industries and cultures. For example, a Middle Eastern washing powder "Barf," in Farsi – the brand's original domestic language – means "snow," to suggest that the clothes are white-clean after using the powder. However, it was a problem for English-speaking audiences!

Some brands had to change their brand names in the local markets because of phonetic differences between languages and difficulties in pronouncing their home brand name in another language. For example, the French food company Danone eventually changed their brand to "Dannon" for American consumers, who repeatedly pronounced the brand as "dan-one." Pepsi, on the other hand, localized its brand to "Pecsi" for the Argentinian Spanish-speaking market because the "ps" sound isn't natural for the Argentinian Spanish-speakers. Because of the linguistic difficulties, the brand was not a very popular choice to order from the restaurant menus at first.

Other elements should also be considered when deciding on the level of linguistic localization and brand translation, such as, for example, the legislative environment of a country. In Canada's Quebec province, the fast food chain KFC – Kentucky Fried Chicken – is known as PFK, or an abbreviation of its French name, "Poulet Frit Kentucky," due to the strict naming law in the Canadian French-speaking province.

How can brands avoid mistranslation of brand names across cultures?

Linguistic Imperialism

Imperialism is a policy of extending a country's power and influence through colonization, use of military force, or other means. Related to this we can talk about *linguistic imperialism* which implies dominance of one language over others. Linguistic imperialism could lead to a stigmatization of local language and literature, disillusionment with the native culture and heritage, and the local languages and dialects dying out. Some researchers see this as "linguistic hierarchization," and they have tried to establish why some languages are used more and others less. There are various factors, structures, and ideologies that facilitated this process throughout history (Phillipson, 1997). Although today the concept of linguistic imperialism is often associated with English, we can find other examples in history such as French

173

dominance over English following the French invasion of England in the 11th century AD, or the dominance of Japanese over Korean in the early 20th century.

Edward Said, a linguistic scholar and the founder of postcolonial studies argued that culture – that is, 19th- and early 20th-century European culture – has had a privileged role in modern history, long after colonialism had actually ended. He suggested that imperialism "lingers where it has always been, in a kind of general cultural sphere as well as in specific political, ideological, economic, and social practices" (Said, 1993, pp. 3–8).

Perspectives differ on what is and what isn't considered linguistic imperialism. Some researchers referred to linguistic imperialism as a form of *linguicism* (Skutnabb-Kangas, 1988), and they draw a parallel between linguistic dominance and social hierarchies based on race, ethnicity, or gender. They point at the fact that English and French speakers, for example, do not see the fast spread of their native languages as problematic, whereas people who do not speak these languages may have a different view.

Language spread is not a natural or an "agent-less" process (Phillipson, 1997). It is a result of political, military, or commercial agendas. Commercial considerations in particular play a strong role in sustaining language dominance. As linguist David Crystal suggested "it may take a military powerful nation to establish a language, but it takes an economically powerful one to maintain and expand it" (1997, p 10).

The practice of using a former colonial language as a medium of education today has been criticized in many former colonial societies, for example Senegal for French language or India for English language. Gandhi was cited saying that "the medium of a foreign language through which higher education has been imparted in India has caused incalculable intellectual and moral injury to the nation" (cited in Panigrahy, 2006, p. 8).

English language is used as *lingua franca* across multiple fields of communication, in teaching as well as in business. It is also increasingly used in non-English-speaking countries to reach niche consumer groups and reflect new identities – for example, it has been used in advertising in China or in Russia to reflect the belonging to the new cosmopolitan community. Nonetheless, there are concerns over linguistic imperialism and the dominance of English over native languages, some of which are at a risk of disappearing.

Is linguistic imperialism relevant today? What do you think of Gandhi's statement?

174

Intercultural Language Considerations

Native Language Influence

Markets where consumers do not have a mastery of English or do not speak it at all currently represent almost 70% of the world, while over 50% of all global consumers prefer to search for information in a local language. Today, over 50% of Google's search results are delivered to people outside of the United States. Google is available in more than 130 languages.

There is a strong link between the language in which the content is written and the consumer's willingness to purchase. Customers respond more favorably to marketing stimuli in their native language. According to Kelly (2012), over 70% of global consumers spend most of their time on websites in their own language, and for 56% of them the ability to obtain information in their own language is more important than the price. Considering that many consumers never purchase products and services in other languages, it is important to translate a website into multiple languages. Also, translating a website into multiple languages could increase traffic by 50%.

European statistics in particular suggest that there is a strong native language preference even in countries where people traditionally speak multiple languages. A Gallup survey suggests that less than half of all the respondents in the European Union would purchase products and services in languages other than their mother tongue. In fact, almost nine out of ten Internet users when given a choice of languages always visit a website in their own language (Euro Barometer, 2011). Many Europeans are multilingual but they still prefer to buy in their own native language!

Against this backdrop, it is important to engage not just in local language translation, but also to strike a balance between translation to local languages and marketing in English for certain product categories. This decision depends on the product type, industry, and the degree of consumer cosmopolitanism.

Customization across culture involves language translation; however, sometimes marketing only in a local language is not ideal. English is the language of business, education, or prestige in certain contexts. People from different cultures can share some cultural elements and language preferences although their native languages may be different – for example, religion, certain professions (higher education, IT), or consumer culture (e.g., geeks).

Ethnolinguistics

Cultural linguistics, also called *ethnolinguistics*, explores the relationship between language and cultural conceptualizations (Sharifian, 2017). Collectively stored cultural knowledge influences lexicon and grammar, or how language is organized. Language has a sociocultural grounding, and different cultures organize and categorize domains of knowledge differently based on their language (Palmer, 2006). Cultural cognition embraces cultural knowledge that emerges from the interactions between members of a cultural group across time and space (Sharifian, 2017). We can distinguish between concepts such as cultural schema, cultural category, and cultural metaphors collectively known as "cultural conceptualizations" (ibid). Palmer (1996, p. 3) suggested that "language is the play of verbal symbols that are based in imagery." In this case, imagery is not just visual but is also conceptual.

Cultural schemas communicate cultural meanings, and these meanings are unique to cultural groups. Sharifian (2017) offers the example of the word "privacy" as a schema of meanings which are only understood by in-group members – privacy means different things to different people. The concept of privacy has different interpretations in philosophical, political, and legal research and there is no single interpretation of the term (Roessler & Mokrosinska, 2015).

Cultural categorizations begin early in life (Mareschal, Powell, & Volein, 2003). They include cultural metaphors which involve conceptualization of one domain in terms of another, and these conceptualizations are different across cultures. For example, in the Indonesian language (Bahasa) the concept of heart is not associated with love, but rather it is "hati" or the liver that stands for the emotion of love (Poppy, 2008). In Chinese, which is a highly contextual language, the same character could stand for either heart or mind (心, xin, in Chinese) depending on the context. Thus, for example, the word "psychology" (心理学, xinlixue in Chinese) literally means the science of the mind and/or the heart.

A Word of Caution

Simply speaking a foreign language does not guarantee successful communication across cultures or intercultural communications competence. Understanding deeper cultural meanings and their conceptualizations is

Intercultural Language Considerations

necessary for achieving a deeper understanding of culture (Polzenhagen & Hans-Georg, 2007). Understanding cultural conceptualizations is paramount for successful intercultural communication because conceptualizations are necessary for constructing cultural meanings. Miscommunication can happen when brands fail to understand how cultures conceptualize their meanings and experiences through their cultural schemas, categories, and metaphors.

Mini-Case: Brand Naming Considerations in China

It is important for international brands to understand the deeper connection between the language and the brand identity in Chinese. Because of the nature of Chinese language, not everyone in China is familiar with Latin characters or the Romanic script. Although Chinese consumers can recognize alphabetic letters, they do not use them to memorize the brands. For example, L'Oréal, a French personal care company, is known as "欧莱雅" (ōu lái yǎ) in China and it is very popular there. When shown the L'Oréal logo in its alphabetic version, consumers read it as "欧莱雅" (ōu lái yǎ) because it is more natural for them to connect to a brand through its Chinese name.

For this reason, some international brands decided not to have an official Chinese name. Such is the case of Lacoste, a French clothing and accessories brand. Since the name "Lacoste" isn't the easiest one for Chinese consumers to read or pronounce, the crocodile icon became the brand's main distinguishing feature. However, because of the decision not to have a Chinese brand name, Lacoste enabled the coexistence of many copycats. Its crocodile shaped logo has been copied by many local brands with a different English and Chinese name like Cartelo or Crocodile (Noyes, 2018).

Some brands have found successful formulas for localizing in the Chinese market. For example, rather than using its "driving machine" positioning that works in most international markets, BMW translated its brand in China as a "precious or treasured horse" or "baoma" (宝马, in Chinese). Horses have a deep symbolic meaning in the Chinese artistic and cultural tradition, and they represent power and resilience. "Bao" (宝, in Chinese) or "precious," is a phonetic compromise for the first letter of the BMW brand name, and it also stands for something highly treasured, while "ma" (马, in Chinese) means "horse."

Intercultural Language Considerations

Coca Cola's brand localization in China is often referred to as one of the most successful transliterations ever. Its Chinese brand name, "Ke Kou Ke Le" – (可口可乐, in Chinese), which literally means: "can-mouth-happy," stands for "happiness to the mouth," "tasty fun," or "let your mouth rejoice." According to urban legend, at first, the company considered phonetic approximation in the original version of its Chinese brand and it sounded something like kēdǒu kěn là (蝌蚪啃蜡, in Chinese), which means something like "bite the wax tadpole."

Most brands found that in China a combination of both phonetics as well as semantics is crucial for a successful brand localization. The companies choose different emotional triggers in order to resonate with the local audiences. For example, Reebok, a U.K. footwear and apparel company, was transliterated as "rui bu" (锐步, in Chinese) which means "quick steps" to stress the quality of its athleticwear. The Reebok original name meaning in Afrikaans, "grey rhebok," or a type of African antelope, is not known to many people.

Nike, on the other hand, managed to find a local brand name in China that resonates with its brand identity while at the same time reflecting the phonetics of its brand. In Chinese it is transliterated as "nai ke" (耐克, in Chinese) and it means "enduring and persevering," two highly regarded qualities in the Chinese culture. Some brands, however, decided on a compromise approach and bypassed the phonetics to emphasize their brand value. Such is the example of Marriott, which was introduced to China as "wan hao" (万豪, in Chinese), or the "10,000 wealthy elites." The number 10,000 stands for an unlimited amount of something, and it is affiliated with abundance in Chinese.

Mini-Case Questions

- What other examples do you know of a language with unique linguistic considerations?
- How can brands turn linguistic challenges into opportunities?
- What is the best approach for localizing Western brands in Western languages that don't use Romanic script, such as the Cyrillic script?
- How about non-Western languages?
- Should Western brands try to localize their names in the non-English-speaking markets at all cost?
- How should English language brands approach this challenge?

Intercultural Language Considerations

Chapter Guiding Questions

Think about *branding* and *messaging considerations* in your host country and how they relate to the use of language. Try answering the following questions:

- Will your brand name have the same meaning in a different language?
- Might there be more than one meaning?
- Are your brand name and brand associations such as a tagline or mantra compatible with and relevant to your target audience?
- Are there are any connotative meanings affiliated with your brand name in your host country? How about associations with your slogan, mission, vision, or positioning?
- Are there any similar-sounding words which might have different connotations? Are these connotations good or bad?
- Are there any existing brands or products with a similar name?
- How does your brand name sound to a native ear?
- What kind of reaction does it produce?
- Against the current political and economic context in your host market and in your industry of choice, what are the benefits/risks of using English?
- What are the pros and cons of bilingual promotional campaigns?

References

Adler, N. J., & Gundersen, A. (2007). *International dimensions of organizational behavior*. Boston, MA: Cengage Learning.

Allan, K. (2007). The pragmatics of connotation. *Journal of Pragmatics, 39*(6), 1047–1057.

Crystal, D. (1997). *English as a global language*. London: Cambridge University Press.

Czinkota, M. R., & Ronkainen, I. A. (2007). *International marketing* (8th ed.). Mason, OH: Thomson Higher Education.

Euro Barometer. (2011). *User language preferences online, analytical report*. Retrieved from https://ec.europa.eu/commfrontoffice/publicopinion/flash/fl_313_en.pdf

Everett, D. L. (2005). Cultural constraints on grammar and cognition in Pirahã: Another look at the design features of human language. *Current Anthropology, 46*(4), 621–646.

Kelly, N. (2012). Speak to global customers in their own language. *Harvard Business Review*. Retrieved from https://hbr.org/2012/08/speak-to-global-customers-in-t

Mareschal, D., Powell, D., & Volein, A. (2003). Basic level category discriminations by 7- and 9-month-olds in an object examination task. *Journal of Experimental Child Psychology, 86*, 87–107.

Moon, S., & Depeux, N. (2019). Art of naming: Making sense of sound – Sound symbolism & naming. *Labbrand Brand Innovations*. Retrieved from www.labbrand.com/brandsource/art-of-naming-making-sense-of-sound-sound-symbolism-naming

Noyes, B. (2018). The six laws of Chinese brand naming. *Labbrand Brand Innovations*. Retrieved from http://www.labbrand.com/brandsource/issue-article/six-laws-chinese-brand-naming

Palmer, G. B. (1996). *Toward a theory of cultural linguistics*. Austin, TX: University of Texas Press.

Palmer, G. B. (2006). Energy through fusion at last: Synergies in cognitive anthropology and cognitive linguistics. In G. Kristiansen & R. Dirven (Eds.), *Cognitive linguistics: Foundations and fields of application*. Berlin and New York: Mouton de Gruyter.

Panigrahy, R. L. (2006). *Consequences of demographic transition in India*. New Delhi: Discovery Publishing House Pvt. Ltd.

Phillipson, R. H. L. (1997). Realities and myths of linguistic imperialism. *Journal of Multilingual and Multicultural Development, 18*(3), 238–248.

Polzenhagen, F., & Wolf, H. G. (2007). Culture-specific conceptualisations of corruption in African English: Linguistic analyses and pragmatic applications. In F. Sharifian & G. B. Palmer (Eds.), *Applied cultural linguistics: Implications for second language learning and intercultural communications* (pp. 125–168). Amsterdam and Philadelphia: John Benjamins.

Poppy, S. (2008). Did he break your heart or your liver? A contrastive study on metaphorical concepts from the source domain organ in English and in Indonesian. In F. Sharifian, R. Dirven, N. Yu, & S. Neiemier (Eds.), *Body, culture, and language: Conceptualizations of internal body organs across cultures and languages* (pp. 45–74). Berlin and New York: Mouton de Gruyter.

Roessler, B., & Mokrosinska, D. (2015). *Social dimensions of privacy: Interdisciplinary perspectives*. Cambridge: Cambridge University Press.

Said, E. (1993). *Culture and imperialism*. London: Chatto & Windus.

Schmitt, B. H., Pan, Y., & Tavassoli, N. T. (1994). Language and consumer memory: The impact of linguistic differences between Chinese and English. *Journal of Consumer Research, 21*(3), 419–431.

Shannon, C. E., & Weaver, W. (1963). *A mathematical theory of communication*. Chicago, IL: University of Illinois Press.

Sharifian, E. (2017). Cultural linguistics: The state of the art. In E. Sharifan (Ed.), *Advances in cultural linguistics* (pp. 1–28). Singapore: Springer.

Shrivastava, S. (2012). Comprehensive modeling of communication barriers: A conceptual framework. *IUP Journal of Soft Skills, 6*(3), 7–19.

Skutnabb-Kangas, T. (1988). Multilingualism and the education of minority children. In T. Skutnabb-Kangas & J. Cummins (Eds.), *Minority education: From shame to struggle* (pp. 9–44). Bristol: Multilingual Matters.

Tavassoli, N. T., & Han, J. K. (2001). Scripted thought: Processing Korean Hancha and Hangul in a multimedia context. *Journal of Consumer Research, 28*(3), 48–93.

Turow, J. (2010). *Media today. An introduction to mass communication* (3rd ed.). New York: Routledge.

wa Thiong'o, N. (1986). *Decolonising the mind: The politics of language in African literature*. London: Heinemann.

Yan, S., & Ju, R. (2019). What's in the Name: K-pop's naming strategy. *Labbrand Brand Innovations*. Retrieved from http://www.labbrand.com/brandsource/whats-in-the-name-k-pops-naming-strategy

Research Considerations in Intercultural Markets

Introduction

Chapter 8 discusses research considerations in culture studies. It encourages students to critically assess the prevalent models for cultural analysis, and it provides insight and guidelines for choosing a research method that is most suited for the selected cultural group. It sheds light on the importance of a cultural fit between the research method and the epistemological framework. The chapter also assesses the ability of various methods to capture the intricacies of culture, such as large-scale surveys which have become the norm in culture study. It expands on etic and emic research approaches, and points at the quantitative-qualitative research dichotomy. It discusses ethnography and netnography as promising methods for analyzing culture. Finally, the chapter also discusses the importance of placing cultural analysis against a backdrop of the broader political and legal context in a host country, and the links between economy and culture. Case-in-point examples include the use of ethnography by Best Buy, netnographic research by Listerine, and the use of cultural metaphors. The mini-case included with Chapter 8 is Nike.

Chapter Objectives

- Understand the main challenges in culture research.
- Learn about cultural factors affecting the choice of research methods.
- Become familiar with qualitative and quantitative research differences.
- Learn about the importance of epistemological frameworks.

- Understand the advantages of ethnographic and netnographic methods for studying culture.
- Learn about etic and emic research approaches for studying culture.
- Understand the links between economics, legal, and cultural systems.

Warmup question: *What is the best research approach for understanding cultures different from ours?*

Challenges in Culture Research

The influence of culture has been actively researched in marketing over the past couple of decades. However, the role and influence of culture on consumers remain rather difficult to assess (Caprar, Devinney, Bradley, & Kirkman, 2015). Notwithstanding the substantial body of research analyzing the influence of culture, there is evidence that a poor performance in international markets could be attributed to culturally based misunderstandings, cultural imperialism, and ethnocentric predispositions (Chaney & Martin, 2011).

Many concerns have been brought up due to our poor understanding of cultural influence. These concerns are attributed to a number of reasons, inclusive of overdependence on a limited number of research methods, and the dichotomy between quantitative and qualitative research methods, as well as between etic and emic approaches to analyzing cultures.

Since the 1970s, the field of culture study in international business and management has been dominated by a bipolar paradigm based on cultural dimensions which has traditionally been used to study the influence of culture in marketing. Most cultural models interpret cultural differences at a national country level, using nation-states as the core unit to measure cultural differences. This approach is based on the idea of national culture differences that can be measured and quantified on a fixed scale.

These classifications are based on the idea of fairly stable, universal cultural dimensions such as individualism vs. collectivism, or masculinity vs. femininity. These approaches also interpret values as objective variables that could be numbered and measured in quantitative terms (Birkinshaw, Brannen, & Tung, 2011). For example, studies using these methods often interpret the Chinese as collectivistic and Americans as individualistic by default (Fang, 2005–2006).

There are numerous concerns over applicability of these traditional methods for exploring cultural influence because they focus on analyzing cultural expressions on a static, binary (either/or) scale. Increasingly, researchers have called for novel approaches that will help us to grasp the dynamic, continuously evolving and multidimensional aspects of culture.

Cultural researchers are also concerned over the long-standing dichotomies between different methodological approaches such as quantitative vs. qualitative and etic vs. emic research methods. In particular, the "onion" metaphor of culture has been criticized as an example of a "deterministic" paradigm. This research approach seeks objectivity, measurement, and prediction (McSweeney, 2002) which is hard to apply in social science. This approach is also based solely on analytical logic – it stipulates that any unity must be divided into its constituent parts in order to understand the "absolute truth," rather than focusing on the whole and the interconnectedness between its constituent parts.

What are some limitations of the traditional models used to understand culture?

Western-Centric Research Methods

Additional concern exists over a universal applicability of traditional methods because they were devised in the West and with Western cultural values in mind. Furthermore, most of them have been designed prior to the era of globalization. Western concepts have dominated management and marketing research despite calls for novel theories and concepts to capture management puzzles or phenomena of the "East" (Barkema, Chen, George, Luo, & Tsui, 2015). There are growing concerns that academic research remains deeply anchored in Western perspectives and contexts, and that it is not internationalizing successfully to accommodate for the dynamic global changes. In other words, is not sufficiently tapping into new, non-Western concepts and theories (Li, 2016).

Herdin, Faust, and Chen (2020) suggest that a historic dominance of Eurocentrism eventually led to the marginalization of non-European research paradigms in academia. Research has been grounded in the Western (namely, traditional European) philosophy and thinking patterns. Arguably, this could be attributed to the expansionist policies of the European countries from the 15th century onwards (ibid).

This situation has traditionally allowed for the growth of the West's sphere of influence at multiple levels. The economic hegemony was followed by scientific dominance, and these Western-centric traditional models were accepted as eternally valid. A call for their re-evaluation has been more prominent since the end of the 20th century and at the turn of the millennium. In social sciences, a body of research focused on this critical reflection on Western models for studying culture and communication has been named "de-Westernization" (Herdin et al., 2020). This is not to say that all Western models should be challenged, but rather that research should also accommodate different approaches for analyzing culture in non-Western countries that today constitute 70% of the planet.

Why is it important to incorporate non-Western models in academic research?

Choosing a Research Approach

Epistemological Framework

At the outset of a research project, it is essential to choose the right *epistemological framework*. Epistemology is the theory of knowledge with regard to its methods, validity, and scope. The epistemological framework presents an underlying approach to any research project and it serves as a set of founding assumptions vis-à-vis the subject (Van de Ven, 2007). The main epistemological frameworks in management research are interpreted as those of positivism and post-positivism, realism, pragmatic constructivism, and interpretivism. Traditionally, there has been a dichotomy in the research between positivism vs. interpretivism (Weber, 2004), or between positivism and post-positivism vs. constructivism (Guba & Lincoln, 1989).

Positivism has been the prevalent method to study culture in marketing, and it has been used primarily in quantitative research. It departs from the assumption that there exists an objective world that can be described and represented directly through empirically observed facts. Methodologically speaking, it is characterized by the use of statistical and quantitative methods for data collection and interpretation. This approach suggests that causality is defined as the empirical conjunction of events, representing knowledge as it objectively is (Gephart, 2013). Thus, the "truth" arises from a correspondence between hypotheses and the empirically observed facts (Boisot & McKelvey, 2010).

Nonetheless, the prevalent positivistic approach based on large-scale quantitative surveys has been criticized by Eastern and Western researchers alike. As Morin (2008, p. 31) suggested, logical positivism "could not avoid playing the role of an epistemological policeman forbidding us to look precisely where we must look today, toward the uncertain, the ambiguous, and the contradictory."

Increasingly, interpretivist and constructivist – the non-essentialist – approaches are seen as more capable of grasping the essence of culture. *Interpretivism* is often seen as an umbrella term encompassing different schools of thought drawing on phenomenology. This research attempts to understand reality through the meanings that people assign to it (Orlikowski & Baroudi, 1991).

Researchers using *constructivism*, sometimes called "social constructivism," seek to develop subjective meanings of their experiences. They look for a complexity of views, and try to negotiate the subjective meanings formed through interactions. Rather than starting with a theory or a hypothesis, researchers in this paradigm inductively develop theories or patterns of meaning (Lincoln & Guba, 2000). Both interpretivism and constructivism are used in qualitative research.

What are the advantages and the disadvantages of the positivistic research epistemology? What about interpretivist and constructivist approaches?

Research Method

Marketers are divided in terms of preferences for qualitative or quantitative research methods. These two research methods differ in their objectives, the nature of questions being posed, the type of data being gathered, and the research instruments used for data collection.

Quantitative research generates numerical data or information that can be converted into numbers. Only measurable data can be collected and analyzed in this type of research. *Qualitative research* on the other hand generates non-numerical, mainly verbal data. The information gathered is analyzed in an interpretative, subjective manner, rather than with statistical methods.

One of the main differences between the two is a degree of flexibility. Quantitative methods use structured questionnaires and ask the questions in

Intercultural Research Considerations

the same, or a very similar order. They also have a fixed range of response categories (for example, multiple choice, Likert scale, or dichotomous questions). On the other hand, questions asked in qualitative research are open-ended and more flexible, and they could be tailored toward each individual or group of respondents.

A lack of methods diversity and an over-reliance on quantitative research methods have been among the main challenges in culture research to date. Although the quantitative method has a distinct advantage because it allows for comparison and generalizability of the data, nonetheless, relying on this approach alone for studying culture is problematic. There are concerns over its adequacy for capturing the complexity and the intricacies of cultural influence. This is especially the case because the large-scale cross-cultural self-administered surveys have become the main instrument in global marketing research. The quantitative approach to studying cultures is based on the notion of cultural dimensions, which are analyzed as fairly static and stable constructs.

However, an over-reliance on this approach is problematic, and it has contributed to some of the challenges that the culture study field is currently facing. These challenges became particularly apparent with the rise of Asian economies, as well as the development of the global service sector that brought about an unprecedented number of interactions between people from different cultural backgrounds. Additional issues arise because the traditional methods used to study culture have been conceived around Western cultural values of openness. This is problematic because many non-Western cultures, in contrast to those in the West, favor more reserved and indirect forms of expression.

In spite of calls for application of more qualitative approaches to analyze culture, there is an increased reliance on quantitative research methods. Quantitative surveys using large samples to study the influence of culture in international business and marketing are seen as the "hard science" (Birkinshaw, Brannen, & Tung, 2011), in comparison to other methods.

Researchers have increasingly expressed concern over this situation. Because of the over-reliance on a small number of quantitative methods, there are concerns over a "widening gap between the accelerating complexity of markets and the capacity of most marketing organizations to comprehend and cope with this complexity" (Day, 2011, p. 183).

Although the quantitative research approach has been prevalent in culture research, it is important to remember that this method too faces both known and unknown sources of bias and selectivity no matter how large the data set is (Boyd & Crawford, 2012). Importantly, researchers have increasingly challenged the capacity of quantitative methods for their inability to stimulate creativity and innovation (Cayla & Arnould, 2013).

How can marketers decide which survey method to select for analyzing culture?

Survey Instrument

Cultural factors should inform research along all steps of the research process, from research design and choice of research methods to data analysis and interpretation. For example, there are distinct differences in how people deal with surveys and how respondents react to questions and survey scales (Harzing, 2006). These differences should be accounted for; otherwise, market research could be flawed. Due to their cultural conditioning, some respondents may have tendencies to answer the survey questionnaires in a certain pattern, regardless of its content.

Traditional *quantitative surveys*, if used blindly, could lead to biased conclusions or misinterpretations (Dolnicar & Grün, 2007). Cultural specificities also present an important source of variation that could affect the reliability of results (Douglas & Craig, 1983). Both the verbiage used in the scales as well as the end points on a scale (e.g., 1 or 5) are interpreted in culture-specific terms. The end points of a scale are particularly prone to different cultural interpretations.

For example, some cultures are more likely to pick either extreme or middle values on a scale. Some cultures, such as Mexican, tend to choose the extreme response categories (Beuthner Friedrich, & Ramme, 2018). This extreme response style (ERS) is a tendency to prefer the extreme response categories or the end points on a scale, rather than the mid-points on a rating scale (Bolt & Newton, 2011). On the other hand, we can also observe a non-extreme response style (NERS). This style is interpreted as a tendency to avoid the extreme responses (Wetzel, Carstensen, & Böhnke, 2013). For example, on a 5-point Likert-type scale this would lead to most results being on a scale of 2–4. A mid-point response style (MRS) is also related to the mental frame that embraces paradoxical thinking and reconciliation between contradictions, often found in East Asian cultures due to the traditional inclination to embrace the "Yin-Yang" thinking.

Intercultural Research Considerations

The Likert scale questions in fact may not be suited for many East Asians who have a tendency to pick the middle answers, and also to show a tendency to agree with questionnaires regardless of their content. Nonetheless, attitude measures such as the Likert scale can be used between different countries with some commonality such as Japan, South Korea, and China (Yu Keown, & Jacobs, 1993). This tendency to agree with questionnaires, called the "acquiescence response style (ARS)" or the "agreement tendency" is also different across cultures (Martin, Engelland, & Collier, 2011), and needs to be taken into consideration.

For example, people in Southern Europe are likely to have higher ARS scores than in the European North-West (van Herk, Poortinga, & Verhallen, 2004). Thus, they may also be more likely to select the "strongly agree" and "agree" answers. The opposite tendency of ARS is a DRS, a "disacquiescence response style" or a "disagreement tendency." DRS suggests a tendency to disagree with questionnaire items regardless of their content, and to pick the "strongly disagree" and "disagree" answers to most questions (Baumgartner & Steenkamp, 2001).

It is challenging to determine suitable survey methods across cultures (Malhotra, 1994). It is important for the researcher to be aware of the sources of cultural biases and not exploit them or misinterpret the survey results. Thus, it is important to use the scales that are free of cultural biases, as well as to understand how cultural wiring affects responses to certain scales. Any research instrument should be adjusted to the unique cultural environment and it should not be biased toward any single culture. Ideally, rather than relying on a single method, intercultural researchers should employ multiple methods of data collection (Triandis & Brislin, 1984).

For example, demographic questions may have to be specified differently for some cultures since a definition of the household size or family structure could be different, given the presence or absence of the extended family.

Regardless of which instrument is selected, it is important to avoid linguistic bias in cultural research. One of the ways to avoid linguistic bias in the questionnaire is by applying a back-translation technique. This implies that a bilingual translator should first translate the questionnaire into the respondent's language; then, the questionnaire should be translated from the base language by a bilingual speaker whose native language is the target language, and this version should then again be translated into the base language.

Nonetheless, even this approach does not guarantee that bias will be completely eliminated. The success of this process hinges on the researcher's continuous re-evaluation along all steps of the research process. It is important to remember that no scales can be implemented in another culture without customization – relying solely on good linguistic translation may lead to what Douglas and Nijssen (2003) called a "pseudo-etic trap," or a false sense of confidence based on linguistic accuracy.

Western countries have been the primary source of research scales and survey instruments used in cross-cultural studies. As such, many of these etic scales are not applicable in other countries. For example, arguably, the consumer ethnocentrism scale (CETSCALE) developed in the West may not be readily applicable in non-Western countries because it assumes that the consumer ethnocentrism concept is universal and measurable the same way across cultures. The scale assumes that morality concepts are universal; however, moral reasoning is different across cultures (Henrich, Heine, & Norenzayan, 2010). Furthermore, concepts such as ethnocentrism may be understood differently across cultures – for example, small countries in absence of domestic manufacturing may rely on imports and have a greater dependence on foreign brands (Douglas & Nijssen, 2003).

How can researchers select the most suitable research method based on cultural considerations?

Qualitative Research

There is an increasing awareness of the importance of *qualitative methods* in marketing research, especially in the domain of culture study. Qualitative methods provide unique insight that is hard to generate through quantitative surveys, and they can also help to reduce the psychological distance between the researcher and the research context. Qualitative research can also help to clarify the often contradictory behaviors, beliefs, opinions, emotions, and relationships of individuals.

Nonetheless, certain conditions should be met for the qualitative research to take place. For example, this type of research requires pre-existing relationships and trust between different parties. It also requires extensive knowledge of cultural clues, and familiarity with the language and patterns of social interactions in a given cultural group.

There exist a multitude of qualitative research approaches available to marketing researchers. For example, these include the *grounded theory* (Glaser & Strauss, 1967), *case study* approach (Wynn & Williams, 2012), *narrative research* (Pinnegar & Daynes, 2006), *phenomenological research* (Stewart & Mickunas, 1990), *action research* (Davison, Martinsons, & Ou, 2012), *design studies* (Pascal, Thomas, & Romme, 2013), or *critical research* (Myers & Klein, 2011). Although this diversity presents a source of richness and expands the possibilities for the researcher, it may also lead to confusion – it is hard to decide which method to select because there are significant overlaps among them (Avison & Malaurent, 2013). Some of the main qualitative research methods are outlined here.

The *narrative study* approach focuses on life stories of a single or a small number of individuals, and their stories are gathered using multiple types of (mostly textual) information (Pinnegar & Daynes, 2006).

Phenomenological research focuses on a larger group and the common phenomena experienced by the group. This research approach has strong philosophical grounding in the works of European philosophers Edmund Husserl and Martin Heidegger (Stewart & Mickunas, 1990).

Case study research is seen as a choice of "what" is to be studied, or a method involving a study of an issue or a problem using the case as an illustration. A case study approach usually involves multiple sources of information inclusive of audiovisual materials, documents, and reports (Denzin & Lincoln, 2005).

The *grounded theory* approach in particular has been recommended as a suitable method for generating new theory about culture. This approach, first developed by Glaser and Strauss (1967), aims to move beyond mere descriptions and generate or discover a theory, a schema, or a process. This theory development is generated or "grounded" from the data emerging in the field, and it is shaped by a large number of participants in order to generate a theory (Strauss & Corbin, 1998).

This perspective is sometimes associated with post-modernism, often driving inspiration from the work of the French philosopher and social theorist Michel Foucault (1972). Foucault was one of the most influential as well as the most controversial philosophical figures in post – World War II Western thought. He criticized the social sciences for failing to answer the fundamental questions of humankind, but also challenged the claim that positivist methods offer an exclusive standard and present an ultimate path to true or legitimate knowledge.

Qualitative research techniques, for the most part, include participant observations, in-depth interviews, and focus groups. *Participant observations* involve data collection through observations in the natural context of the participants, with diaries of their behavior, their responses, and interactions which are not explicitly explored through interviews. Ideally, these should be conducted in their natural environment such as workplace, school, or even home.

In-depth interviews, usually semi-structured, are used for collecting personal perspectives and stories, especially on sensitive topics. They are used successfully to understand cultures, and allow researchers to poke cultural expressions more in-depth. These interviews are usually 45 minutes to 1 hour long, and should ideally be held in the respondent's native language and their natural setting. *Focus groups* are used for exploring the behavior that reflects cultural norms in a group, and for identifying the shared issues within a group or a subgroup. This approach requires a skilled moderator and the willingness of the group to spend a couple of hours together in a controlled environment and share their views in front of others. Focus groups are not ideal for cultures characterized by a more reserved expression or "face "considerations.

A number of considerations should be taken into account when selecting a qualitative research method, inclusive of the research question, the nature of the research problem, as well as characteristics of a specific cultural group. For example, depending on how hesitant or willing the respondents are to discuss their opinions and feelings in a group setting, either focus groups or in-depth interviews should be selected. Any techniques used in the process, such as association (word association), expressive (role playing), completion techniques (sentence or story completion) or non-verbal stimuli, should be based on a strong knowledge of cultural cues.

What factors influence the choice of qualitative research methods?

Ethnography

Ethnography and netnography present promising qualitative research methods for understanding cultural complexity. *Ethnography* brings insight into issues that otherwise cannot be easily understood by doing experiments or through other forms of qualitative study. Consequently, ethnography has gained popularity in both social and consumer research. Ethnography refers to fieldwork and the approach to data collection, as well as to data interpretation and presentation. It relies strongly on the researcher as the main research instrument and his or her skills and interests, and it depends strongly on the researcher's reflection in the process.

Ethnography has the power to reveal hidden realms of culture because it helps to understand what people really do, rather than what they say or even think they do; considering that people are not the best predictors of their own behavior, it is important to study them in-situ, namely in their natural settings, and to approach customers as social beings (Elliott & Jankel-Elliott, 2003). Unlike other research approaches, the ethnographic research method helps us to observe group behavior and interactions, and not just the individuals. This feature of ethnographic research presents its distinct advantage over other qualitative methods. Unlike other research approaches, ethnography requires immersion in a culture and it thus enables the researcher to fully understand human experience in a community (Cunliffe, 2010).

Ethnography is the recommended method for studying complex phenomena that are not easy to quantify (Fraenkel & Wallen, 1990). As a fine-grained approach to understanding details of human experience and the complexity of human behavior, it could help to complement the prevalent "logico-scientific" or the positivistic mode of knowing (Bruner, 1986, p. 13). In the culture study field, a positivistic method may not be able to fully grasp the "particulars of human experience, including the contradictions and dilemmas of people's everyday lives" (Cayla & Arnould, 2013, pp. 1–2).

In social study, field ethnography aims to provide a "thick" description of culture with a great amount of detail (Geertz, 1973), and its goal is to tackle complexity by going for depth and not just breadth, seeking understanding rather than prediction (Alvesson & Skoldberg, 2000). However, ethnography has been adjusted for management research where it has been adapted, focused, and more narrowly defined.

The ethnographic approach generates detailed contextual data, including the seemingly insignificant details which may otherwise be taken for granted. These details could shed a surprising light on culture, enabling the researcher to grasp the complex nuances of cultural influence. As Van Maanen (2011, p. 221) suggests, culture increasingly has a small "c" – this means that ethnography plays a role in demystifying culture, rather than elevating it to a level of religion, or some mysterious force that cannot be deciphered.

As an interpretive craft, ethnography focuses more on "how" and on "why" rather than on "how much" or "how many." Thus, at the core of the ethnographic quest is "not what culture is (and the semantic elasticity surrounding the concept) but – and in keeping with pragmatic principles – what culture does" (Van Maanen, 2011, p. 221).

Ethnography is also seen as a collaborative "sense-making" approach to research. This approach could help to provide the unique means of understanding the complex market realities by helping managers to grasp the complexity of consumer cultures. The "sense-making" approach in ethnography implies discovery and negotiation of meaning, and this approach carries a moment of "surprise" which is a central element of ethnography (Van Maanen, 2011).

Nonetheless, ethnography is often frowned upon by management scholars who are traditionally used to quantitative research methods. The ethnographic approach is at times seen as an overly subjective and interpretative practice, and there are concerns that it almost entirely hinges on the orientations of the ethnographer. Some researchers therefore believe that it cannot achieve the same results as traditional methods.

In response to this, ethnographic researchers suggest that these negative views fail to recognize that interpretative practices are, in fact, central to all sciences that deal with social practices. They also suggest that it is not possible, or even easy, to ask people details about their own culture because culture is a deeply ingrained construct that many people cannot talk about with any degree of separation or objectivity. For this reason, they suggest, "living the culture" or immersing oneself in it through an ethnographic method is a better way of obtaining this insight.

This is contrary to the traditional belief that surveys are the best tools for marketers to use to understand consumers by simply asking them about their needs and preferences. The argument for ethnography is based on the belief that consumer reporting about their behavior is not the best reflection of their actual behavior. Thus, in the era of big data that dominates consumer research, companies are increasingly relying on ethnography and integrating it with other research methods.

In the context of intercultural marketing, ethnography helps companies to gain more insights into the social aspects of consumer behavior, the influence of brands on social relations, and the consumer self-concept. Ethnography allows researchers to immerse themselves in the consumers' lifestyle in order to understand their point of view in detail and depth.

Intercultural Research Considerations

Ethnographic Method

Ethnographers need to decide on the concept of the ethnographic field and what it entails, and how long to spend there. The field can be anywhere in the consumers' natural environment – office, home, car, school, and so on. Although this type of research is very time consuming, researchers are encouraged to spend long hours with the participants, often much of it in the background as observers to see the natural consumer behavior emerge without being intrusive. The length of time spent with the participants is determined based on the type of research and the nature of the research question.

Recruitment of participants in ethnographic research could be done through traditional recruiting methods. Snowball sampling is often used in ethnographic research, where one participant introduces others from the same social network based on similarity or shared usage patterns.

The *data collection process* is increasingly conducted through digital tools, and audio or video recording. Lifelogging, or mobile ethnography, is also a popular tool because it gives a taste of the participant's everyday life. This method implies that smartphone users take videos or photographs of themselves, often through apps that could provide insight into behaviors of thousands of people at the same time. These tools are, however, used in conjunction with traditional field notes and they should not replace these traditional ethnographic methods that involve note-taking.

Digital ethnography differs from traditional ethnography in the toolkit a researcher uses. Digital ethnography implies the use of blogs, social media, and smartphones, while in the traditional ethnography researchers use cameras, notepads, and so on. Digital ethnography uses tools such as social media analytics, eye tracking, Vox Pop videos, online diaries, and similar tools. A lot of consumer interactions are happening on social media, which means that a lot of consumer feedback is readily available for researchers. This feedback is spontaneous, organic, and non-prompted, without directions from the researcher.

Eye tracking is a popular technique increasingly used in ethnographic research. It requires the participants to wear special glasses tracking their eye movements during shopping or Internet browsing, thus reflecting their natural shopping behavior. In *Vox Pop videos*, participants record short video messages with their thoughts, and they share almost instantaneously with the researcher, revealing how participants interact with brands and products. *Online dairies* allow researchers to get instant insight into consumer lives, capturing consumer experiences in their everyday lives and collecting more longitudinal data.

Data analysis in ethnography is usually done through a combination of manual coding, as well as software such as NVivo or Atlas, which help with ordering and visualization of codes identified in the ethnographic data.

Ethnographers usually convert observations and interviews into text, and then code the text and sort the codes into concepts and themes to determine patterns and issues relevant for the topic. This process usually starts with open coding, identifying the "in-vivo" codes, that is, the literal terms used by the respondent. These are then converted into categories which emerge as the research unfolds through axial coding that seeks relationships between different concepts (Strauss & Corbin, 1998).

What are the main ethnographic method advantages for studying culture?

A Case in Point: Ethnography at Best Buy

Insights from Consumer Research Associates (2020) suggest how ethnography can be used in retail in the example of Best Buy, a large U.S. consumer electronics retail chain. Best Buy were interested in expanding their product portfolio to include health and fitness products. In particular, they wanted to find out whether this product extension would be accepted by customers and whether they would be open to the health and fitness shopping experience in addition to what they are used to at Best Buy. More specifically, they wanted to attract more female shoppers.

To collect this data, Best Buy conducted ethnographic research. They recruited participants for in-home interviews in order to understand their decision-making process and consumer triggers for buying home fitness equipment. They also conducted shop-alongs both to Best Buy as well as to other competing centers for observations and for collecting additional data points. Furthermore, they observed female shoppers who had recently purchased fitness equipment in their homes.

This allowed them to understand consumer expectations and helped to integrate fitness equipment with the traditional home electronics product portfolio. Today, Best Buy incorporates a wide range of home gym equipment at affordable prices, and it also offers opportunities to stream virtual workouts at home (adapted from Consumer Research Associates, 2020).

How can ethnographic research be used to understand consumer behavior across cultures?

Netnography

Undoubtedly, the Internet has created unparalleled opportunities to gather customer insight. This is particularly the case in the service industry, where interactions are now easier to capture and observe over time. Owing to the rapid advancements of information technology, the service delivery context is constantly changing, as well as the idea of service experience across cultures. Service customers are now active online before, during, and after interactions with service providers, and this creates a wealth of information about their activities and experiences (Ostrom, Parasuraman, Bowen, Patrício, & Voss, 2015).

Netnography is an online research method that has its origins in ethnography, and it is applied in the digital communications context. Like ethnography, it belongs to the qualitative, interpretive research methodology, and it has been adjusted to the needs of the digital space. Much like ethnography, it is also a process of systematic recording of human culture. Netnography uses tools such as targeted forums, focus chat rooms, or blogs.

Netnography is used to gain access to a widespread consumer base via cyberspace. It presents a cost-effective, unobtrusive, and accurate way of obtaining consumer data. People spend a considerable amount of time online, and a large amount of data is available to researchers. Online communities have a strong influence on culture and on its manifestations, and they direct and guide the behavior of cultural groups (Kozinets, 2010). Most people also tend to be more open about their feelings and opinions online than in real life. With that in mind, netnography could provide valuable insight into individual behavior as well as the ecosystems that individuals are connected to. This insight is rather hard to obtain through other types of research.

Netnography has a number of benefits compared with other research methods. Data collected with the netnographic method are naturalistic and rich in insight, often reflecting the fine nuances of the customers' lived realities (Rokka, 2010). Netnography is particularly useful for sensitive research topics in order to elicit relevant data on issues that cannot be tackled easily (Keeling, Khan, & Newholm, 2013). It also has a distinct advantage of being cheaper than the traditional ethnography because it requires less time in the field (Kozinets, 2006).

Netnography differs from ethnography in that it is based primarily on the observation of textual content, namely the textual discourse between the participants, and it does not include participatory observational inferences as in ethnographic research.

Although netnography can be interpreted as "ethnography online," it is less intrusive – ethnography requires immersion and a high level of contact with the participants (Giesler & Pohlmann, 2003). Netnographic data is sometimes also considered to be more accurate considering that respondents are in their remote, private setting. Generally, people are also more likely to provide unbiased responses when they are anonymous. This can be illustrated with the famous Oscar Wilde quote: "Man is least himself when he talks in his own person. Give him a mask, and he will tell you the truth."

Companies increasingly rely on netnographic data. For example, Toys"R"Us observed its 860+ Instagram accounts using Brandwatch Analytics. In 2016, Toys"R"Us launched a new program, allowing each of its 860+ stores to launch its own Instagram account, and empowering each store to own the creation of its content and to manage the online community to best suit its own customers (Brand Watch, 2020).

What are the advantages of netnographic research?

A Case in Point: Netnography at Listerine

Companies are increasingly using netnography to obtain deeper insight into consumer behavior. For example, netnographic research helped Listerine to obtain insights about consumer perceptions of their brand. They used social media content generated through Internet forums and blogs focusing on discussions about Listerine.

Netnographic data analysis suggested that consumers' positive perceptions focused around Listerine's germ-killing action, while the most prevalent complaint from the consumers was that Listerine is too harsh on their gums. The analysis helped them to discover new opportunities for introducing a Soothing Power flavor and a non-alcohol-based formula.

Furthermore, insights from this research also helped them to discover new ways to promote the product: this knowledge helped Listerine to also promote the product as a toenail fungus treatment and a mosquito repellent, considering that many consumers use it for personal and home care (Netbase, 2010).

How can marketers make the best use of netnographic methods in intercultural campaigns?

Netnographic Research Challenges

Because netnography happens in the virtual space, some traditional research approaches had to be adjusted for this type of research, and they have been a subject of research debate. For example, the definition of research ethics becomes somewhat different in netnographic research because questions arise as to whether online communities are in fact public or private. Although there are a number of ongoing debates regarding the ethical codes of conduct for netnographic research, there is no single consensus among researchers about this issue (Rokka, 2010).

There is a real possibility for netnography to do harm if the data is not properly handled and presented. Therefore, it is important that netnographic researchers fully disclose their presence and intention of the research and ensure anonymity of all respondents. Furthermore, the question of what cultural communities entail in the virtual space also arises, as the rules of behavior are different than those in offline communities.

Some other limitations of netnography include concerns over authenticity and quality of data. Often, it is difficult to establish the demographics of people posting online, and therefore this type of research may not be fruitful for topics that are closely related to demographic factors. Due to this difficulty in establishing the demographics of the participants, the netnographic approach might be unsuitable for research that is sensitive to factors such as age, ethnicity, or gender. Moreover, as with ethnography, netnography faces limitations in regard to possibly generalizing implications to customer groups outside of the online platforms or online communities being studied.

Can netnography be used in a similar fashion across different cultures? What are some unique considerations when conducting netnographic research across cultures?

Etic and Emic Research Approaches

The distinction between "etic" and "emic" approaches was initially proposed by linguist Kenneth Pike (1967). These two terms made it into business research through social psychology and they became common words in the English language (Headland, Pike, & Harris, 1990). The terms were derived from linguistic concepts of phonetics (the universal laws of language and the function of sounds in a language, regardless of their meanings) and phonemics (the meaning and context of words, acoustics, and external properties). By dropping the root ("phon"), the two suffixes (emics, etics) became stand-alone terms to distinguish between "local" vs. "universal" in any discipline.

The difference between these two approaches has thus been defined as a difference between the universal and the particular. Linguistically speaking, an emic approach reflects the sounds specific to a particular language, while an etic approach refers to sounds which are similar in all languages (Adler, 1983).

Etic and emic approaches in the culture study present two general research approaches used to operationalize the concept of culture: "emics" apply only in a particular culture while "etics" present universal aspects of a culture (Berry, 1989). Etic researchers seek to identify and segregate common components and universal aspects of a culture through hypotheses testing, and they assume that all cultures could be generalized, analyzed, and compared in a uniform fashion. Conversely, emic researchers seek to understand culture from the perspective of the locals.

Comparative studies using the *etic approach* present the most common approach in culture studies. However, numerous tensions exist between universal and indigenous approaches in academic research (DeJordy, 2005), especially in regard to the validity of assumptions from the original (Western) culture in a new setting (Niblo & Jackson, 2004). Notably, Hofstede's

Intercultural Research Considerations

dimensional approach is the main example of culture studies using etic approaches.

This has led to concerns over the imposed etic approach from a dominant culture, and the tension between etic and emic approaches is increasingly becoming an important topic in management and marketing research (Rohlfer & Zhang, 2016). This tension is closely linked to the discussions around measuring and understanding the effects of culture, which remains a fundamental challenge for researchers – the inability to properly assess cultural roles and influences is seen as a hindrance to the development of the international business field as a whole (Sinkovics, Penz, & Ghauri, 2008).

The *emic approach* requires extensive presence at a point of data collection and an in-depth understanding of the contexts (Morris, Leung, Ames, & Lickel, 1999). Arguably, possibilities to achieve this on a large scale are reduced due to language and cultural barriers, and the limited availability and willingness of many cultural groups to participate in such immersive research. Tsui, Xin, and Wang (2006, p. 4) call this immersion approach "plunging into the sea" (tiao jin da hai, 逃进大海, in Chinese) as the best way to truly understand culture. However, an issue of validity arises when applying emic measures from one nation to another, a challenge which is yet to be resolved in academic research (Tsui, Nifadkar, & Ou, 2007).

Traditionally, it was the anthropologists who were interested in understanding culture from the emic perspective (Smith & Bond, 1993). Today, the importance of this approach is understood in management too. There is a great overlap between etic and emic approaches and business literature suggests the importance of their integration (Berry, 1999). However, it is difficult to integrate these two approaches and obtain results that are both culturally adequate as well as comparable across cultures. Thus the "combined etic-emic" approach has been suggested as a solution which would involve identifying an etic construct with universal status, using emic ways of measuring this construct, and making cross-cultural comparisons through this construct.

These are important considerations because emerging economies are no longer merely consumer markets, and it is increasingly important to understand emic perspectives. Increasingly, they are expanding their business and also investing in the developed economies. Nonetheless, an over-emphasis on emic approaches could lead to an emic bias. This presents a concern, much like concerns over the dominance of etic approaches. Thus, although there are notable tensions between these two approaches, both perspectives are seen as valuable, and they are deemed inseparable in order to fully understand the social phenomena.

Research also suggests that differences between the two perspectives are in fact inevitable: because the researcher's value system always guides the design, data collection, and reporting of the study, selectivity may occur, whether intentionally or not, due to the preconceived categories (Yin, 2010). In ethnographic research, the goal is to produce a holistic cultural portrait that incorporates both the views of the participants (emic) as well as the views of the researcher (etic) (Creswell, 2007).

What are the advantages of using an emic approach to culture? How about the risks?

Alternative Approaches to Studying Culture

Asian scholars in particular have raised concerns over the prevalent positivistic epistemology and the dominance of quantitative, etic research methods to study culture, which have led to over-simplification of cultures (Li, 2016). Faure and Fang (2008) suggested that the prevalent approach used to investigate culture is based on bipolarization of national cultures, assuming a linear rationality and the "non-contradiction" principle. For example, national cultures are described as either individualistic or collectivistic in the majority of studies (Fang, 2012).

Eight Paradoxical Value Pairs

Cultures are not characterized with stable and fixed orientations. Rather, all cultures possess paradoxical propensities and thus they could also be understood through a paradox lens. One such operationalization of a paradox approach to culture study is found in the framework of "eight contradictory value pairs" that embraces contradictory values within any culture. Rather than analyzing value orientations on a static scale, this framework suggests that a situation renders certain values more salient over their opposites in a given group and a given context (Faure & Fang, 2008). This framework provides an alternative to marketers for analyzing cultural values not just as a fixed construct, but also through the tensions between opposing considerations.

The framework of "eight contradictory value pairs" proposed by Faure and Fang (2008) is inspired by the Chinese "Yin-Yang" thinking, and it presents an operationalization of this thinking approach to cultural analysis. Although it was inspired by the Chinese culture, nonetheless it can inform analysis of any culture. All cultures have paradoxical orientations, and cultures change in the process of interaction with other cultures.

This framework appears similar to the traditional cultural dimensions because it deals with pairs of opposite values; however, it is distinctly different. Rather than characterizing a national culture on a fixed scale of either (one value)/or (another) at a nation-state level, this framework suggests that the same cultural or subcultural group can be characterized with both of these opposing considerations.

Thus, for example, a culture can be characterized with preferences for *both* family and group orientations, *as well as* individuation. These opposing values become more or less dominant based on a specific context or a situation, allowing for contextual segmentation of cultures. For example, certain purchasing decisions, such as those involving high involvement products – a house, or private education for children – may be more influenced by broader family considerations (parents, grandparents), whereby the opinions of a broader family may be detrimental for this decision. Other purchasing decisions, even within the same high-involvement category – such as a car – may be more influenced by individual or peer group considerations. Also, some groups may value their "connections" vs. an individual's "professionalism" differently depending on the stages of the purchasing journal, or a type of service.

Thus, unlike the traditional methods for studying cultures that classify cultures on a fixed scale of either one or the other, this approach helps researchers to understand cultural complexity: members of the same culture can hold mutually contradictory value orientations, which may become more or less dominant in a given situation. Thus, these value characteristics are not treated as fixed points on a national culture scale, but are rather seen as potential in a culture. Table 8.1 shows "eight contradictory value pairs" (Faure & Fang, 2008).

According to the French philosopher François Jullien (2017), we can reveal the hidden realms of culture if we embrace paradoxes in culture and observe the tensions embodied in the process of culture change. Jullien suggests that we should approach cultures as dynamic concepts, and through the lens of tensions that exist in the process of change that all cultures inevitably undergo, rather than through its stable characteristics that represent fixed points on a measurement scale.

Intercultural Research Considerations

Table 8.1: Eight contradictory values approach to studying cultures

Eight Value Pairs	Explanation
Guanxi vs. professionalism (G vs. P)	Guanxi, a web of connections and favors based on reciprocity as a form of social investment, vs. qualifications, legacy, and performance
Face vs. self-expression and directness (F vs. SED)	Face, moral character, and prestige, indirect communications style to preserve one's own/ give face to others, vs. direct, open expression
Thrift vs. materialism and ostentatious consumption (T vs. MOC)	Thrift and frugality, as traditional expressions of modesty/self-restraint, vs. consumption lifestyle and ability to afford new products and services
Aversion to law vs. respect for legal practices (AL vs. RL)	Self-regulating moral mechanisms and a tendency to favor relationships over legal contracts, the rule of men vs. the rule of law
Family and group orientation vs. individuation (FGO vs. I)	Family as the basic unit with utmost authority and society as extended family, vs. individualism, pleasure seeking and pursuing personal goals
Respect for etiquette, age, and hierarchy vs. respect for simplicity, creativity, and competence (EAH vs. SCC)	Respect for hierarchy and ancestors in a ritualistic, structured society, copying role models, vs. individual creativity and innovation
Long-term orientation vs. short-term orientation (LTO vs. STO)	Time orientation influenced by the agricultural past, time seen as circular and unlimited, vs. short time units influenced by economic interests
Traditional creeds vs. modern approaches (TC vs. MA)	Rites, rituals, ancestor cult, religion, and superstition, vs. scientific development, modernization, innovation, and economic growth

Source: Faure and Fang (2008).

Deriving inspiration from both Asian as well as European philosophical heritage, Jullien argues that the applicability of the "universal" (seen in the literature as "etic") in regard to culture should be re-visited and challenged in today's globalized world. Furthermore, in the Western tradition, research traditionally used the concepts derived from natural science, and subsequently applied them in the complex social world, which became a problem when analyzing cultures.

Arguably, the process of globalization has also imposed uniformization, which suggests that we seek absolute similarities (and differences) to deal with new phenomena and thus we reduce cultures to "common" and "universalism" traits. In today's world, Jullien suggests, the idea of universal values seen as the "European culture" is largely outdated, especially in Europe, which is trapped between its own ideal of the European culture and the contemporary global reality.

Acknowledging that cultures have paradoxical propensities implies that we acknowledge that cultures are characterized with traits which are both opposing as well as complementary. Certain traits in a culture can become more or less salient depending on a specific context and a situation, and they should not be approached as fixed constructs. Therefore, it is important to understand the interaction between situation and culture, and the conditions under which consumers are likely to align their thinking with sociocultural norms (Hong & Mallorie, 2004). Embracing paradoxes that exist within cultures can also help researchers to understand the influence of context on consumer decisions, which traditional dimensional models are unable to capture due to their context-free nature (Birkinshaw et al., 2011).

How can a paradox lens inform cultural analysis? Could eight paradoxical value pairs be customized to other cultures? If so, what other pairs of opposing yet complementary values could you identify in your home culture?

A Case in Point: Cultural Metaphors

In an attempt to move past the dominant, dimensional approach to cultures, Gannon (2011) proposed the concept of *cultural metaphors* as an additional set of lenses for analyzing cultures. Gannon suggested that a metaphor is "any distinctive or unique activity, phenomenon, or institution with which all or most members of a given culture emotionally and/or cognitively identify" (p. 4). These metaphors include, for example, French wine as a symbol of the French culture, or the Chinese family altar as a unique metaphor for the Chinese culture.

Gannon suggested that we could categorize cultures based on the metaphors that cultures use. Using this perspective, we can relate to cultures as, for example, "authority ranking cultures," using the symbolism such as "India's Dance of Shiva," or the "Thai Kingdom"; "market pricing cultures," using a metaphor such as American football, or a traditional British house; "equality matching cultures," using a symbol of German symphony, or a Swedish stuga (a cabin or a cottage); or "cleft national cultures," using symbols such as Italian opera or a Nigerian marketplace (Gannon, 2003).

Gannon suggests that we can use a cultural metaphor of the Japanese garden to understand the Japanese culture, for example. The Japanese garden includes the following key features: Wa, or group harmony; Shikata, or the accuracy with which one conducts an activity, pointing at a seemingly excessive, large number of rules governing behavior, such as not crossing the street at a red light at 2 a.m. although there is no one in the area; Seishin, or spirit training designed to make the mind control the body through the use of techniques such as meditation, judo, and kendo or sword fighting (ibid, p. 6). "Wa" could be explained from the perspective of the traditional Japanese garden setting where different elements such as water, sunlight, and soil interact in harmony to enable the plants to grow. This harmony between the garden elements is used as a metaphor to describe harmony in interpersonal interactions as well as harmony between humans and nature.

Gannon's concept of cultural metaphors presents an emic approach to understanding cultures. Unlike cultural dimensions that seek unifying characteristics across cultures for the sake of their comparison, and thus generalization, the idea of cultural metaphors focuses on the unique characteristics in a culture that may not be found in other cultures.

Are there any cultural metaphors in your host culture that could be used in your project?

Economics and Culture

Culture cannot be separated from the economic context. Equally, understanding cultural context helps to explain the economic development patterns of a country. Culture, institutions, and economic forces interact with each other and influence each other.

Cultural attitudes are pervasive, and they exert a strong influence on economic developmental patterns. Even when people move around to distinctly different countries, cultural attitudes can continue to shape economic outcomes for a long period (Hyde, 2015). For example, immigration studies have shown that second-generation immigrants seem to retain cultural beliefs and values of their parents' home country.

Cultural Economics

An economic system is a system of production, resource allocation, and distribution of goods and services within a society. It includes a combination of various institutions, agencies, decision- making processes, and patterns of consumption that comprise the economic structure. Traditional economics, however, does not incorporate a cultural context. Economists usually treat cultural identity as an external factor. The influence of culture on economy has traditionally been downplayed by economists, who tend to interpret factors of production and technical progress as the main determinants of economic performance (DiTella & MacCulloch, 2014). On the other hand, other social sciences, such as anthropology, sociology, and psychology assume that culture is a central factor in economics (Hutter, 1996).

When a country opens its doors to international trade, the goods designed for a "global consumer" arrive, raising the welfare of people responsive to these types of products. These situations lead to an economic shock such as opening of a market that can bring about some permanent changes in values, cultures, and preferences. This process is not easily reversible. This could also result in lower incentives for the parent to transmit their culture to their offspring, and in value conflicts between the generations, as younger people adopt new cultural attributes different from those of their parents.

Culture and economics have engaged in a dialogue for a relatively short time, over the past few decades. The economists started exploring the relationship between cultural values and the economy, acknowledging that culture provides context for the economy, and economy changes the context of culture. *Cultural economics*, a branch of behavioral economics, analyzes how culture affects economic outcomes. It focuses on how needs and tastes are formed in society from the perspective of cultural value systems (Guiso, Sapienza, & Zingales, 2006).

Cultural economics acknowledges that cultures evolve with economic and political practices. Culture affects economic activity through the choices that people make about how to allocate scarce resources and manage assets. These choices influence adoption of technology, savings, or labor market participation decisions.

One of the main differences that separates cultural economics from traditional economics is an assumed difference in how individuals arrive at their decisions. The traditional economic science interprets consumer decision making as mostly rational and individual. Cultural economics, on the other hand, acknowledges that individuals will also arrive at their decisions based on the trajectories of thinking, and on the values and norms that guide individuals and groups in their decision-making processes.

Differences in cultural beliefs and value systems have also been used to explain the differences in economic organization models across countries. Economists are increasingly trying to understand a two-way relationship between culture and the institutions that govern the operation of markets. For example, French economist Thomas Piketty (1995) suggests that economic beliefs can be divided into two factors: the first emphasizes beliefs regarding poverty and the role of individual needs when determining income, and the second stresses the role of merit in determining income and attitudes about the desirability of private property ownership. Cultures relate to these issues differently.

The origin of cultural differences could also be explained by looking at economic and other factors. Oftentimes, economic conditions may in fact be the root cause for deeply held cultural beliefs and values. For example, a high disease concentration in a region may be correlated with measures of collectivist attitudes and xenophobia – a collective fear of outsiders could be a rational response to an increased risk of disease.

There are also differences in attitudes toward female participation in the labor force. For example, some differences are seen between regions that historically grew crops and lent themselves to plow use (including wheat and barley) compared with other regions that grew crops lending themselves

Intercultural Research Considerations

to hand tillage (like millet and sorghum). Modern-day female labor force participation is higher in the latter, and attitudes lean more toward gender equality (Hyde, 2015).

Family structures can give clues about underlying cultural attitudes, such as whether children leave home after marrying, and how inheritances are distributed across children. For example, a strong emphasis on family ties in a country is often correlated with a proliferation of family businesses.

Cultural beliefs have also been linked to ecology. Cultures are interpreted as the "systems (of socially transmitted behavior patterns) that serve to relate human communities to their ecological settings" (Keesing, 1974, p. 75). For example, researchers studied two groups of fishermen living in the Brazilian state of Bahia but in very different circumstances. One group lived near a lake, where fishermen found it most efficient to work alone in small boats, and accepted direct competition with each other for the best fishing territory. The other group lived on the sea coast and, in response to the different conditions there, they fished on larger boats in groups, making cooperation and teamwork keys for success (Hyde, 2015).

Research has also established that there are cultural differences in experiments using economic concepts such as the ultimatum game or the prisoner's dilemma where subjects face decisions about how much money they are willing to give to others, or whether they should rely on other participants, and there are cultural variations (Henrich et al., 2005).

Nonetheless, the link between economy and culture remains relatively unexplored. Thus far, studies have focused on the so-called "high" culture such as theatre arts, painting, and sculpture. Everything not covered by this definition, namely the "popular culture" remained in the hands of the market and was a matter of the industrial economic analysis.

Can you detect any links between the economic and cultural systems in your host culture?

Culture and Financial Behavior

Cultural influence has also been demonstrated in the domain of financial behavior. There are differences between cultures in how people manage and value their assets and cash, and how they relate to money management in general. Investment behaviors can be interpreted through the lens of culture. For example, the influence of culture can be seen through the factors predicting stock valuations. In countries like Jordan, 84% of variability in stock returns are accounted for through money supply, interest rate, and industry growth (Ramadan, 2012).

In Zimbabwe, on the other hand, the main factors include money supply and oil prices (Jecheche, 2012), while in India most importance is placed on the exchange rate, wholesale price index, and the price of gold (Basu & Chawla, 2012).

A Word of Caution

Before embarking on cultural research, it is important to be aware of the references we have to our own cultural values because they could influence our perception of others. Our own cultural assumptions influence decisions and how we interpret others (Lee, 1966). These perceptions, called the *self-reference criterion* (SRC), could prevent us from becoming fully aware of cultural differences and they could hinder objectivity when approaching different cultures. It is important to be aware of this, and to critically assess any possible biases or even prejudices we may hold in relation to other cultures as a result of our own SRC.

Researchers aim at establishing models that are replicable across cultures in order to draw universally generalizable implications. However, achieving this universality appears to be more of an ideal rather than a realistic research goal. While etic models may lead to over-simplification of culture, on the other hand, emic bias can also result in misleading conclusions.

One possible solution is to develop a so-called "derived etic model" that implies the development of multiple emic models in different cultural settings and then establishing the common items across these different scales. Even so, researchers should be careful, and avoid generalizations by eliminating the outliers in a scale. Namely, eliminating all outliers may make the model reductionistic and too general, reducing its ability to grasp the subtlety and the nuances of a culture.

A dialogue between differing approaches is necessary in order to achieve a balanced view. This is particularly important when it comes to expanding the Western-centric portfolio of methods traditionally used to research culture. By incorporating critical views from the Global South, the West could get additional perspectives to enable self-reflection and to expand the boundaries of research (Herdin et al., 2020).

Mini-Case: Nike

Nike is one of the world's most recognizable footwear and athletic apparel brands in the world. Their international brand recognition could be attributed to a number of tactics that have helped Nike to capture the attention of diverse audiences across cultures.

Nike's advertising seeks to appeal to emotional triggers in each culture. Rather than focusing on selling its products, Nike has directed its efforts toward building up customer emotions toward the brand. This is seen in their slogan "Just do it," which has remained relevant since 1988 when it was first introduced. This is also reflected in their advertising catchphrases such as "Your only limit is you." Although this means different things to different cultures, it appeals to positive emotions of activity and success, which are universal across cultures. Nike's brand symbolism appeals to similar universal emotions and it is also reflected in their name – the Greek goddess of victory.

Another intercultural marketing tactic used by Nike is the concept of Nike ID. It allows customers to customize products according to their own cultural preferences including colors, visual patterns, or logos of their regional sport clubs. Nike launched a number of culture-specific products in collaboration with local companies. For example, it collaborates with CLOT, a Hong-Kong based company, to introduce a Silk Royale pattern with a Chinese theme on its sneakers.

Nike has also tapped into street fashion trends across cultures by incorporating various local lifestyles and cultural habits in its marketing campaigns. The company recognized the importance of streetwear that has become one of the most disruptive forces in fashion across the world.

Successful use of sponsorships and the world's leading athletes further helped to create legacy and legitimacy for Nike in different cultures. For example, partnership with Manchester United helped not only in the European markets but it also appealed to numerous football fans who support the club around the world. The use of technology through iPhones, iPods, or sports watches has helped to connect millions across the world into a community of active or aspiring athletes, regardless of their culture. Forums like NikeTalk, which started off to discuss sneakers and sneaker collecting, became forums to discuss sports, music, and popular culture.

Nike has also become known for sponsoring diverse athletes. One such athlete is Amna Al Haddad, a young sportswoman and Olympic weightlifter from Dubai, United Arab Emirates. This sponsorship inspired Nike to launch Pro Hijab, or a hijab for female athletes and sportswomen from Islamic cultures. Amna suggested that Nike were studying her "from the neck down, not from the neck up" when assessing her sporting needs, and at first, they overlooked the importance of her head (Fast Company, 2017).

Amna inspired them to solve one of the biggest sportswear challenges for Muslim female athletes: engaging in sporting activities freely while remaining true to their culture. This has helped Nike to become a company that offered cultural innovation, which has helped them to target a much larger audience for its products.

Mini-Case Questions

- What was the main driver of Nike's success in international markets?
- How did Nike approach emotional branding, or the pathos element of persuasion?
- How successful was Nike's social engagement in different markets?

Chapter Guiding Questions

Think about the best ways to research culture in your selected host country. Also, access the broader legal and economic contexts in your host country.

- Are there any prominent cultural traits that may drive the choice of research methods?
- What opposing or paradoxical cultural considerations might exist in your target group?
- How do these paradoxical traits interact and how are they expressed in different situations?
- Which of the "eight contradictory value pairs" apply to your target group? Are there additional similar pairs of opposing value orientations in your group?
- How is the dominance of cultural values influenced by a context of consumption? What are the factors that render certain values more dominant?
- For example, would the same values be predominant across different stages of the purchasing journey? If so, how would that affect promotional efforts? Or, how would this affect different types of purchasing decisions, such as high vs. low involvement?

- What is the legislative environment like in relation to promotional channels, especially advertising? Are there any specific laws governing advertising that could affect your campaign?
- Other than purchasing power, what economic factors may exert influence on culture in your host country?

References

Adler, N. J. (1983). A typology of management studies involving culture. *Journal of International Business Studies, 14*(2), 29–47.

Alvesson, M., & Skoldberg, K. (2000). *Reflexive methodologies: Interpretation and research*. London: Sage Publications.

Avison, D., & Malaurent, J. (2013). Qualitative research in three ISjournals: Unequal emphasis but common rigour, depth and richness. *Systèmes d'Information et Management, 18*(4), 75–123.

Barkema, H. G., Chen, X., George, G., Luo, Y., & Tsui, A. S. (2015). West meets East: New concepts and theories. *Academy of Management Journal, 58*(2), 460–479.

Basu, D., & Chawla, D. (2012). An empirical test of the arbitrage pricing theory—The case of Indian stock market. *Global Business Review, 13*(3), 421–432.

Baumgartner, H., & Steenkamp, J-B. (2001). Response styles in marketing research: A cross-national investigation. *Journal of Marketing Research, 38*(2), 143–156.

Beuthner, C., Friedrich, M., & Ramme, I. (2018). Examining survey response styles in cross-cultural marketing research: A comparison between Mexican and South Korean respondents. *International Journal of Market Research, 60*(3), 257–267.

Berry, J. W. (1989). Imposed Etics – Emics-derived Etics: The operationalization of a compelling idea. *International Journal of Psychology, 24*(6), 721–735.

Berry, J. W. (1999). Emics and Etics: A symbiotic conception. *Culture & Psychology, 5*(2), 165–171.

Birkinshaw, J., Brannen, M. Y., & Tung, R. L. (2011). From a distance and generalizable to up close and grounded: Reclaiming a place for qualitative methods in international business research. *Journal of International Business Studies, 42*(5), 573–581.

Boisot, M., & McKelvey, B. (2010). Integrating modernist and postmodernist perspectives on organizations: A complexity science bridge. *Academy of Management Review, 35*(3), 415–433.

Bolt, D. M., & Newton, J. R. (2011). Multiscale measurement of extreme response style. *Educational and Psychological Measurement, 71*(5), 814–833.

Boyd, D., & Crawford, K. (2012). Critical questions for big data provocations for a cultural, technological, and scholarly phenomenon. *Information, Communication, & Society, 15*, 662–679.

Brand Watch. (2020). *How Toys"R"Us scaled its image analysis to enhance its customers' experience.* Toys"R"Us Customer Story. Retrieved from www.brandwatch.com/case-studies/toysrus-customer-story/

Bruner, J. S. (1986). *Actual minds, possible worlds.* Cambridge, MA: Harvard University Press.

Caprar, D. V., Devinney, T. M., Bradley, L., & Kirkman, P. C. (2015). Conceptualizing and measuring culture in international business and management: From challenges to potential solutions. *Journal of International Business Studies, 46*(9), 1011–1027.

Cayla, J., & Arnould, E. (2013). Ethnographic stories for market learning. *Journal of Marketing, 77*(4), 1–16.

Chaney, L. H., & Martin, J. S. (2011). *Intercultural business communication* (4th ed.). Upper Saddle River, NJ: Pearson Prentice Hall.

Consumer Research Associates. (2020). *Best Buy.* Retrieved from https://consumer-research-associates.com/case-study-best-buy/

Creswell, J. W. (2007). *Qualitative inquiry and research design: Choosing among five approaches* (2nd ed.). Thousand Oaks, CA: Sage Publications.

Cunliffe, A. (2010). Retelling tales of the field: In search of organizational ethnography 20 years on. *Organizational Research Methods, 13*(2), 224–239.

Davison, R. M., Martinsons, M. G., & Ou, C. X. J. (2012). The roles of theory in canonical action research. *MIS Quarterly, 36*(3), 763–786.

Day, G. (2011). Closing the marketing capabilities gap. *Journal of Marketing, 75*(4), 183–195.

DeJordy, R. (2005). *A vision for overcoming challenges in cross-national management research and practice.* Best Paper Proceedings of the Academy of Management Annual Meeting (V1–V6).

Denzin, N. K., & Lincoln, Y. S. (2005). Introduction: The discipline and practice of qualitative research. In N. K. Denzin & Y. S. Lincoln (Eds.), *The Sage handbook of qualitative research* (2nd ed.). Thousand Oaks, CA: Sage Publications.

DiTella, R., & MacCulloch, R. (2014). *Motu working paper 14–06,* Motu Economic and Public Policy Research, May 2014.

Dolnicar, S., &. Grün, B. (2007). Cross-cultural differences in survey response patterns. *International Marketing Review, 24*(2), 127–143.

Douglas, S. P., & Craig, S. C. (1983). *International marketing research.* Englewood Cliffs, NJ: Prentice-Hall.

Douglas, S. P., & Nijssen, E. J. (2003). On the use of "borrowed" scales in cross-national research: A cautionary note. *International Marketing Review, 20*(6), 621–642.

Elliott, R., & Jankel-Elliott, N. (2003). Using ethnography in strategic consumer research. *Qualitative Market Research: An International Journal, 6*(4), 215–223.

Fang, T. (2005–2006). From "onion" to "ocean": Paradox and change in national cultures. *International Studies of Management & Organization, 35*(4), 71–90.

Fang, T. (2012). Yin Yang: A new perspective on culture. *Management and Organization Review, 8*(1), 25–50.

Fast Company. (2017). Meet the Muslim woman who inspired Nike to enter the Hijab business. *Fast Company*. Retrieved from www.fastcompany.com/40407096/meet-the-muslim-woman-who-inspired-nike-to-enter-the-hijab-business?partner=bof

Faure, G. O., & Fang, T. (2008). Changing Chinese values: Keeping up with paradoxes. *International Business Review, 17*(2), 194–207.

Foucault, M. (1972). *The archaeology of knowledge*. New York: Pantheon Books.

Fraenkel, J. R., & Wallen, N. E. (1990). *How to design and evaluate research in education*. New York: McGraw-Hill.

Gannon, M. J. (2003). *Understanding global cultures: Metaphorical journeys through 28 nations, clusters of nations, and continents* (3rd ed.). Thousand Oaks, CA: Sage Publications.

Gannon, M. J. (2011). Cultural metaphors: Their use in management practice as a method for understanding cultures. *Online Readings in Psychology and Culture, 7*(1). Retrieved from https://scholarworks.gvsu.edu/orpc/vol7/iss1/4

Geertz, C. (1973). *The interpretation of culture: Selected essays*. New York: Basic Books.

Gephart, R. P. (2013). Doing research with words: Qualitative methodologies and I/O psychology. In R. Landis & J. Cortina (Eds.), *Modern research methods for the study of behaviour in organizations* (pp. 265–318). New York: Taylor & Francis Psychology Press.

Giesler, M., & Pohlmann, M. (2003). The anthropology of file sharing: Consuming Napster as gift. *Advances in Consumer Research, 30*, 273–279.

Glaser, B., & Strauss, A. (1967). *The discovery of grounded theory: Strategies for qualitative research*. New York: Aldine Publishing Company.

Guba, E. G., & Lincoln, Y. S. (1989). *Fourth generation evaluation*. London: Sage.

Guiso, L., Sapienza, P., & Zingales, L. (2006). Does culture affect economic outcomes? *Journal of Economic Perspectives, 20*(2), 23–48.

Harzing, A. W. (2006). Response styles in cross-national survey research: A 26-country study. *International Journal of Cross Cultural Management, 6*(2), 243–266.

Headland, T. N., Pike, K. L., & Harris, M. (Eds.). (1990). *Emics and Etics: the insider/outsider debate*. Newbury Park, CA: Sage Publications.

Henrich, J., Boyd, R., Bowles, S., Camerer, C., Fehr, E., Gintis, H. . . . Tracer, D. (2005). Economic man in cross-cultural perspective: Behavioral experiments in 15 small-scale societies. *Behavioral and Brain Sciences, 28*(6), 795–815.

Henrich, J., Heine, S., & Norenzayan, A. (2010). The weirdest people in the world? *Behavioral and Brain Sciences, 33*, 61–135.

Herdin, T., Faust, M., & Chen, G. M. (Eds.). (2020). *De-westernizing visual cultures: Perspectives from the global south*. Baden-Baden: NOMOS Publishing.

Hong, Y., & Mallorie, L. M. (2004). A dynamic constructivist approach to culture: Lessons learned from personality psychology. *Journal of Research in Personality, 38*, 59–67.

Hutter, M. (1996). The impact of cultural economics on economic theory. *Journal of Cultural Economics, 20*(4), 263–268.

Hyde, T. (2015). What have economists learned about culture? Understanding the interplay between culture and institutions. *American Economic Association*. Retrieved from www.aeaweb.org/research/what-have-economists-learned-about-culture

Jecheche, P. (2012). An empirical investigation of Arbitrage pricing theory: A case Zimbabwe. *Research in Business & Economics Journal*, 6(1), 1–11.

Jullien, F. (2017). Le commun plutôt que la communautarisme. In Y. Barou (Ed.), *Les cultures d'entreprise européennes* (pp. 17–40). Paris: Des îlots de résistance.

Keeling, D., Khan, A., & Newholm, T. (2013). Internet forums and negotiation of healthcare knowledge cultures. *Journal of Services Marketing*, 27(1), 59–75.

Keesing, R. (1974). Theories of culture. *Annual Review of Anthropology, 3*. Palo Alto, CA: Annual Reviews, Inc.

Kozinets, R. V. (2006). Click to connect: Netnography and tribal advertising. *Journal of Advertising Research*, 46(3), 279–288.

Kozinets, R. V. (2010). *Netnography. Doing ethnographic research online*. Thousand Oaks, CA: Sage Publications.

Lee, J. A. (1966). Cultural analysis in overseas operations. *Harvard Business Review*, 44(3), 115–122.

Li, P. P. (2016). Global implications of the indigenous epistemological system from the East: How to apply Yin-Yang balancing to paradox management. *Cross Cultural & Strategic Management*, 23(1), 42–77.

Lincoln, Y. S., & Guba, E. G. (2000). Paradigmatic controversies, contradictions, and emerging confluences. In N. K. Denzin & Y. S. Lincoln (Eds.), *The handbook of qualitative research* (2nd ed., pp. 163–188). Beverly Hills, CA: Sage Publications.

Malhotra, N. K. (1994). Survey methods of data collection for domestic and international marketing research. In S. J. Levy, G. R. Frerichs, & H. L. Gordon (Eds.), *The Dartnell marketing manager's handbook* (3rd ed., pp. 300–327). Chicago, IL: The Dartnell Corporation.

Martin, W. C., Engelland, B. T., & Collier, J. E. (2011). Assessing the impact of acquiescence response bias on marketing data. *Marketing Management, 21*(1), 31–46.

McSweeney, B. (2002). Hofstede's model of national cultural differences and their consequences: A triumph of faith – A failure of analysis. *Human Relations, 55*(1), 89–118.

Morin, E. (2008). *On complexity*. Cresskill, NJ: Hampton Press.

Morris, M., Leung, K., Ames, D., & Lickel, B. (1999). Views from inside and outside: Integrating emic and etic insights about culture and justice judgment. *Academy of Management Review*, 24(4), 781–796.

Myers, M. D., & Klein, H. K. (2011). A set of principles for conducting critical research in information systems. *MIS Quarterly*, 35(1), 17–36.

Netbase. (2010). *Example Netnography on Listerine*. Retrieved from www.netbase.com/blog/example-netnography-on-listerine/

Niblo, D., & Jackson, M. S. (2004). Model for combining the qualitative emic approach with the quantitative derived etic approach. *Australian Psychologist, 39*(2), 127–133.

Orlikowski, W. J., & Baroundi, J. J. (1991). Studying information technology in organizations: Research approaches and assumptions. *Information Systems Research, 2*(1), 1–28.

Ostrom, A. L., Parasuraman, A., Bowen, D. E., Patrício, L., & Voss, C. A. (2015). Service research priorities in a rapidly changing context. *Journal of Service Research, 18*(2), 127–159.

Pascal, A., Thomas, C., & Romme, G. L. (2013). Developing a human-centred and science-based approach to design: The knowledge management platform project. *British Journal of Management, 24*(2), 264–280.

Pike, K. L. (1967). *Language in relation to a unified theory of the structure of human behavior*. The Hague: Mouton.

Piketty, T. (1995). Social mobility and redistributive politics. *Quarterly Journal of Economics, 110*, (3), 551–584.

Pinnegar, S., & Daynes, J. G. (2006). Locating narrative inquiry historically: Thematics in the turn to narrative. In D. J. Clandinin (Ed.), *Handbook of narrative inquiry*. Thousand Oaks, CA: Sage Publications.

Ramadan, Z. (2012). The validity of the arbitrage pricing theory in the Jordanian stock market. *International Journal of Economics and Finance, 4*(5), 177.

Rohlfer, S., & Zhang, Y. (2016). Culture studies in international business: Paradigmatic shifts. *European Business Review, 28*(1), 39–62.

Rokka, J. (2010). Netnographic inquiry and new translocal sites of the social. *International Journal of Consumer Studies, 34*(4), 381–387.

Sinkovics, R. R., Penz, E., & Ghauri, P. N. (2008). Enhancing the trustworthiness of qualitative research in international business. *Management International Review, 48*(6), 689–713.

Smith, P., & Bond, M. (1993). *Social psychology across cultures: Analysis and perspectives*. New York: Harvester Wheatsheaf.

Stewart, D., & Mickunas, A. (1990). *Exploring phenomenology: A guide to the field and its literature* (2nd ed.). Athens, OH: Ohio University Press.

Strauss, A., & Corbin, J. (1998). *Basics of qualitative research: Techniques and procedures for developing grounded theory* (2nd ed.). Thousand Oaks, CA: Sage Publications.

Triandis, H. C., & Brislin, R. W. (1984). Cross-cultural psychology. *American Psychologist, 39*(9), 1006–1016.

Tsui, A. S., Nifadkar, S. S., & Ou, A. Y. (2007). Cross-national, cross-cultural organizational behavior research: Advances, gaps and recommendations. *Journal of Management, 33*(3), 426–478.

Tsui, A. S., Xin, R., & Wang, H. (2006). Organizational culture in China: An analysis of culture dimensions and culture types. *Management and Organization Review, 2*(3), 345–376.

Van de Ven, A. H. (2007). *Engaged scholarship: A guide for organizational and social research*. Oxford: Oxford University Press.

van Herk, H., Poortinga, Y. H., & Verhallen, T. M. M. (2004). Response styles in rating scales: Evidence of method bias in data from six EU countries. *Journal of Cross-Cultural Psychology, 35*(3), 346–360.

Van Maanen, J. (2011). Ethnography as work: Some rules of engagement. *Journal of Management Studies, 48*(1), 218–234.

Weber, R. (2004). The rhetoric of positivism versus interpretivism: A personal view. *MIS Quarterly, 28*(1), 3–13.

Wetzel, E., Carstensen, C. H., & Böhnke, J. R. (2013). Consistency of extreme response style and non-extreme response style across traits. *Journal of Research in Personality, 47*(2), 178–189.

Wynn, D., & Williams, C. K. (2012). Principles for conducting critical realist case study research in information systems. *MIS Quarterly, 36*(3), 787–810.

Yin, R. K. (2010). *Qualitative research from start to finish*. New York: The Guilford Press.

Yu, J. H., Keown, C. F., & Jacobs, L. W. (1993). Attitude scale methodology: Cross-cultural implications. *Journal of International Consumer Marketing, 6*(2), 45–64.

9 | **Conclusion**

Intercultural Promotional Plan: A Recommended Structure

Use guiding questions at the end of each chapter to help you analyze your host country's culture. You needn't answer all the questions – refer to the ones that help to guide your thought process. Integrate cultural factors and culture analysis with strategic marketing considerations in each section.

Promotional plan structure

1. Executive Summary
2. Rationale
3. Country Snapshot
4. Industry Overview and Opportunity Assessment
5. Segmentation
6. Product
7. Strategies and Tactics
8. Conclusions

1. Executive Summary

Executive summary is a short introductory paragraph summarizing the project, written at the end. Keep in mind the main goal of your project: a plan for promoting a brand in a distinctly different country of choice with focus on cultural factors.

219

2. Rationale

In this short section, briefly discuss why you selected the specific brand and host country. You will get an opportunity to elaborate later on. Identify the main opportunities and challenges and justify your choice in one or two paragraphs.

3. Country Snapshot

Describe your host country. Avoid presenting too many facts and figures, and focus on the insight which is directly relevant for your project. What is the most important country data that could affect your marketing efforts? In this section, you can use the themes discussed in Chapter 1.

4. Industry overview & opportunity assessment

Analyze the industry landscape in your host country. Discuss the main competitors and stakeholders that could influence your marketing decisions. What other foreign brands succeeded or failed in your host country and in that industry, and why? What is the regulatory landscape like?

5. Segmentation

Describe your target customers, their likely preferences and their purchasing patterns. Focus on the influence of culture on their consumption patterns. Refer to Chapters 2 through 6 for the main concepts.

6. Product

Based on your analysis of macro, micro and customer factors, discuss how you will localize elements of your marketing mix including product, price and placement. Discuss promotional factors in the next section. Justify your choice to standardize or localize the specific elements of the mix.

7. Promotional strategies

Discuss promotional strategies. Suggest how you will customize them towards your host culture. Assess how you'd use different IMC tactics, referring also to advertising regulatory landscape. Refer primarily to Chapters 1, 2 and 7 for main concepts.

8. Conclusions

This is a brief section summarizing the plan. Assess any research challenges, referring to Chapters 1 and 8 for main concepts.

Glossary of Key Terms

Advertising
Aristotle's triangle
Asia-centric communication paradigm
Aspirational relation to brands
Aspirational values

Branding blunders
Boycotts
Brand engagement
Brand ignorance
Brand involvement
Brand promise
Brand social impact
Brand tolerance
Brand translation
Buycotts

Circular-traditional time
Communications model
Connotative meaning
Constructivism
Consumer behavior
Consumer Culture Theory (CCT)
Colors
Cosmopolitan consumers
Cross-cultural research
Culture
Cultural categorizations
Cultural economics
Cultural icons
Cultural imperatives

Cultural metaphors
Cultural noise
Cultural norms
Cultural schemas
Cultural symbols
Cultural values
Cultural value orientations
Cultures of achievement
Cultures of honor
Cultures of joy

Denotative meaning

Economic nationalism
Economics of simplicity
Eight paradoxical values
Emic approach to culture
Epistemological framework
Essentialist approach to culture
Ethnic marketing
Etic approach to culture
Ethnocentrism
Ethnography
Ethnolinguistics
Ethos
Etic approach to culture

Focus groups

Global core
Globalization
Glocal consumers
Glocalization
Grounded theory

Harmony
Heroes
High context cultures
Hofstede's dimensions of culture
Homogenization ("McDonaldization") of culture

222

Horizontal cultural orientation
Hybridization of culture

In-depth interviews
Information-oriented cultures
Integrated marketing communications (IMC)
Intercultural Affinity Segmentation Framework
Intercultural communication competence
Intercultural research
Interpretivism

Language
Language components
Layers of language
Linear-separable time
Linguistic imperialism
Local consumers
Logos
Low context cultures

Market segmentation
Modernization
Monochronic time
Moral reasoning
Multicultural research

National culture
Nethnography
Nonconforming
Non-essentialist approach to culture
Nonverbal communication

Onion metaphor of culture

Paradoxical thinking
Participant observations
Pathos
Perceived Brand Globalness (PBG)
Periphery
Personal selling
Philosophical traditions

Polarization of culture
Polychronic time
Positivism
Procedural-traditional time
Processing of stimuli
Psychological processes
Public relations (PR)

Qualitative methods
Quantitative research
Quantitative surveys

Relationship-oriented cultures
Religious value systems
Religiosity
Rituals

Sales promotion
Self-construal
Self-reference criterion
Semiotics
Semi-periphery
Sensory experience
Soft power
Space orientations
Standardization/adaptation variables

Targeting
Thinking style
Trompenaars' & Hampden-Turners' dimensions of culture
Trust

Universal human values
Utilitarian relation to brands

Vertical cultural orientation

World's religions

Xenocentrism

Index

Page numbers in *italic* indicate a figure and page numbers in **bold** indicate a table on the corresponding page.

achievement vs. ascription 153
acquiescence response style (ARS) 189
advertising 38–44, 107
Airbnb 61, 88–89
Al Haddad, A. 211–212
Al Rayan Bank 135
Alibaba 113, 124
Amazon 113
Aniston, J. 60
Apple 155
archetypes 20
Aristotle's triangle 83–85
Asia-centric communication paradigm 120–121, 122–125
aspirational values 41

Baidu 113
Barbie 73–75
Barf 173
Barneys, E. 42
Belt and Road Initiative (BRI) 3, 4–5
Benetton 129
Best Buy 196–197
Big Hit Entertainment (BTS) 15, *171*
blockchain 87
BMW 84, 177
Bouba and Kiki experiment 61–62, *62*
boycott 11–12

brand ignorance 35–36
brand involvement 35–36
brand naming principles *172*
brand promise 21–36
brand social impact 25–26
brand tolerance 36
brand translation 172–173
branding blunders 1, 30–33, 172–173
branding engagement 36
Breninger, B. 55
British Vogue 128
BRZ (Subaru) 169–170, *170*
BTS *see* Big Hit Entertainment (BTS)
Buddhism 129–133, **132**
buycott 12

Carrotmob 12
Chik-fil-A 128
China 4–5, 11, 16–17, 29–30, 32–33, 34, 36, 59, 71, 73–75, 91, 177–178
Chinese language 168
Chomsky, N. 40
Christianity 129–133, **132**
circular-traditional time 146
Club Med 29–30
Coca Cola 5, 27, 178
colors 59–60
combined etic-emic approach 201–202

225

Index

communication competence (CC) *see* intercultural communication competence (ICC)
communications model 163–164
connotative meaning 165–167
constructivism 186
consumer behavior 54
Consumer Culture Theory (CCT) 53–54
consumer ethnocentrism scale (CETSCALE) 190
convenience cost 18
cosmopolitan consumers 13
cross-cultural research 64, 183–185
Crunch 63, *63*
cultural categorizations 176–177
cultural economics 207–210
cultural electives 71
cultural exclusives 71
cultural icons 56
cultural imperatives 70
cultural metaphors 66, 177, 205–206
cultural noise x, 164
cultural norms ix, 5, 30, 69–75
cultural schemas 176–177
cultural symbols 55–56, 57–58
cultural value orientations 69, 149–152
cultural values 5, 40, 67–69
culture vi, ix, 13–15, 39–43, 51–75, 110–111, 141–157, 193, 202–206
cultures of achievement 91–92
cultures of honor 91–92
cultures of joy 91–92

Dannon 173
Dao 102–103
denotative meaning 165–167
Depeux, N. 61, 63, 170
Disneyland Paris 157–158
DKNY 128

ecological globalization 2
ecology 209
economic nationalism 11; *see also* ethnocentrism

economics of simplicity 5–6
eight paradoxical values 202–205, **204**
Electrolux 30
emic approach to culture ix, 65, 200–202
emojis 55
Epimenides paradox 108
epistemological framework 185–186
essentialist approach to culture 65
Esso *see* ExxonMobil
ethnic marketing 65
EthniFacts 92–93
Ethnocentrism viii, 1, 10–13, 135
ethnographic method 195–197
ethnography 192–197
ethnolinguistics 176–179
ethos 84
etic approach to culture ix, 65, 200–202, 210
Euro Disney *see* Disneyland Paris
ExxonMobil 7
eye contact 146–147

Facebook 113
facial expression 147
family structures 209
Feather 63, *63*
feng-shui 158
Fenty Beauty 94–96, *96*
Fiat 36
financial behavior 209–210
Firestone Tire and Rubber Company 42
focus groups 192
Foucault, M. 191
France 43–44

Gandhi 174
Ganges River 71
Gannon, M.J. 205–206
Gap 32
Geico 85
General Motors 172–173
global core countries 14
globalization viii, 1–46
glocal consumers 13

Index

glocalization viii, 5–6, 33
Google 8, 113, 175
Greece 40
grounded theory 186
guanxi 106–107

H&M 31, 128
Häagen-Dazs 71, 74–75
Hagège, C. 169
Hall, E. 52, 141, 148
Hampden-Turner, C. 55, 83, 152–154
hamsa 57–58, *58*
harmony 122–125, *124*
Heidegger, M. 191
heroes 60
high-context cultures 52, 141–145
Hinduism 129–133, **132**
Hofstede, G. 83, 148–152, 154–156,
    200–201
Hofstede's dimensions of culture
    148–152, 154–156
homogenization of culture 13–14
Hong Kong Disneyland 158
horizontal cultural orientation 154–155
humor 40–41
Husserl, E. 191
hybridization of culture 13–14

ideophones 169
Ikea 128–129, 143–145, *144*
in-depth interviews 192
India 15, 59, 71
individualism vs. collectivism (IDV)
    149–150
individualism vs. communitarianism 152
indulgence vs. restraint (IND) 151–152
information-oriented cultures 154
integrated marketing communications
    (IMC) 36–39
Interbrand 36
Intercultural Affinity Segmentation
    framework *93*, 93–94
intercultural communication
    competence (ICC) 121–122

intercultural research 64
internal vs. outer 153–154
interpretivism 186
Iran *134*
Islam 57–58, 129–136, **132**, *134*,
    135–136
Islamic art 133–134, *134*
Islamic finance 135–136

Japan 59, 206
Japanese gardens 206
Jazz (Honda) 169–170, *170*
Jordan 210
Jordan, M. 60
Joyview *see* Club Med
Judaism 57–58, 129–133, **132**
Jullien, F. 203–205

K-pop 15, 170–171, *171*
Kadjar (Renault) 169
KFC 173
kissing pope campaign 129

L'Oréal 177
Lacoste 35–36, 177
language x, 164–179
language components 167–168
Latin America 17
layers of language 165–167
liar's paradox *see* Epimenides paradox
Liberia 59
Likert scale 188–189
Lime *63*, 64
linear-separable time 145–146
linguistic imperialism 173–176
Lisbon Sardine Festival 60
local consumers 13
locavorism 11
logos 84–85
long-term orientation vs. short-term
    orientation (LTO) 151
loose cultures 69
low-context cultures 52, 141–145
Lucky Strike 42

227

Index

Lux soap 128
luxury brands 19–21

macro-boycotts 12
Malaysia 125
Mardi Gras 60
marketing segmentation 85–87
Marriott 178
masculinity vs. femininity (MAS) 150–151
McDonaldization of culture *see* homogenization of culture
McDonalds 28
mega infrastructure projects *see* Belt and Road Initiative (BRI)
Mehrabian, A. 167
melamine 34
Mercedes Benz 172
middle classes 15–17
milk 31
Milk Makeup *63*, 64
modernization 1, 42–43
modest fashion 127–128
monochronic time 145
Moon, S. 170
moral reasoning 106–107
multicultural research 64

national culture 66–67
nazars 57
Nestlé 5
Netflix 113
netnography 192, 197–200
neutral vs. emotional 153
Nike 42, 60, 178, 211–212
Nivea 31
non-essentialist approach to culture 65–66
non-verbal communication 166–167
nonconforming 72
nutritional information 155–156

Oatly 89–91, *90*
onion metaphor of culture 55, 184
Orange *63*, *63*

Paco Rabanne *22*, 22–23
Pampers 32
paradoxical thinking 107–112
Parker, S.J. 128
participant observations 192
pathos 84
Pepsi 32–33, 173
perceived brand globalness (PBG) 33–35
perfume 22–23
periphery countries 14
personal selling 37
philosophical traditions 102–103
phonetics 167
Piketty, T. 208
polarization of culture 13–14
polychronic time 145
positivism 185–186
power distance index (PDI) 149
pragmatics 167
pricing 18
procedural-traditional time 146
processing of stimuli 107
psychological cost 18
psychological processes 101
public relations (PR) 38, 42, 143

qualitative methods 190–192
qualitative research 186–188, 190–192
quantitative research 186–188
quantitative surveys 186–190
Quorn 23–25, *24*, *25*

Reebok 178
relationship-oriented cultures 154
religiosity 125–127
religious values systems 125–129
Rihanna 94–96, *96*
rituals 60–61
Ritzer, G. 14
Rosatti, C. 63

Safran *63*, *63*
Said, E. 174

Index

sales promotion 37
Saussure, F. 61
Schwartz, S. 82, *82*
self-construal 105–106
self-reference criterion (SRC) 210
semantics 167
semi-periphery countries 14
semiotics 61–64
sensory experience 63–64, 168–170
sequential vs. synchronous 153
services 17–19
shariah finance *see* Islamic finance
Smart Water 60
Sofitel Hotels & Resorts 43–44, *44*
soft power 3–4
South Korea 15, 125–126
space orientations 146–147
specific vs. diffuse 152–153
Standard Oil *see* ExxonMobil
standardization/adaptation variables
 6–10
Starbucks 11, 71
Stelling, O. 123–124
Sulwhasoo *124*
Superbowl 27
superstitions 25, 91
Surva 60
sustainability 89–91
Sweden 42
Swift (Suzuki) 169–170, *170*
syntactics 167

Target 12
targeting 86
Tencent 113
thinking style 103–105
Tibet 36
tight cultures 69
time cost 18

Tokyo Disneyland 157
Toyota 30
Toys"R"Us 198
Trompenaars, F. 55, 83, 152–154
Trompenaars' and Hampden-Turners'
 dimensions of culture 152–154
trust 86–87

Uber 12, 28–29
uncertainty avoidance (UA) 150
Unhate campaign 129
United Kingdom (UK) 40
universal human values *82*, 82–85
universalism vs. particularism 152
Unstereotype Alliance 26
Up! (VW) 169–170, *170*
urbanization 16–17, 43
utilitarian relation to brands 34–35

Vakil Mosque *134*
Van Maanen, J. 193
vertical cultural orientation 154–155
Vodafone 34

Walmart 6
Western-centric research methods
 184–185
Whirlpool 6
Wilde, O. 198
world's religions 129–136, **132**

xenocentrism viii, 1, 10, 12–13
xenophobia 208

yin-yang symbolism 110–111, *111*,
 120, 188, 203
yoga 15

Zimbabwe 210

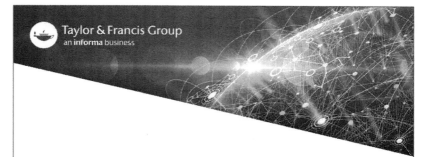